ILLU
MIN

ILLU
MIN

A HISTORY OF MEDIEVAL BRITAIN IN TWELVE ILLUMINATED MANUSCRIPTS

MICHELLE P. BROWN

REAKTION BOOKS

IN MEMORY OF MY FRIEND, WILL NOEL

Published by Reaktion Books Ltd
Unit 32, Waterside
44–48 Wharf Road
London N1 7UX, UK
www.reaktionbooks.co.uk

First published 2025

EU GPSR Authorised Representative
LOGOS EUROPE, 9 rue Nicolas Poussin, 17000, LA ROCHELLE, France
email: contact@logoseurope.eu

Printed and bound in India by Replika Press Pvt. Ltd

A catalogue record for this book is available from the British Library

ISBN 978 1 83639 037 4

CONTENTS

PREFACE

Illumino – illuminate, light; from the Latin *illuminare*, to light up, to adorn, to illuminate, to enlighten.

This book seeks to relate the history of medieval Britain by means of the biographies of twelve outstanding illuminated manuscripts, ranging from about 700 to 1550. Each book serves as a portal into the lives of those who made them and those who caused them to be made. These, in turn, serve as springboards into a consideration of the era in which each book came into being, the intriguing specific circumstances of their production and the fascinating human interest stories and project-management challenges surrounding them.

Illuminated manuscripts are among the most complex and fascinating forms of evidence for the Middle Ages. They bring together the world of ideas, literature, science, faith, politics and most areas of human thought expressed in written text and visual illustration and symbolism. This is coupled with the materiality of the way in which they were produced, the techniques and materials, the social context and economic implications and the exchange of culture, ideas and goods through trade and other means of interaction across time and space. Like people, they have biographies, known as their provenance, and through sensitive investigation these can reveal when and where the manuscripts were born, who gave birth to them, where they have been, whom they have met over the succeeding centuries of their lifespans and why we should seek to understand more about them in the present.

The manuscript projects that I have chosen to focus on will begin with people fired by their faith and ethos to compose or copy works intended to change their world, sometimes as solitary feats of heroic patience undertaken in challenging physical conditions, producing books that served as places of public assembly as cult-books or travelled as ambassadors for their nations. Moving through time, following the evolution of manuscript production, we examine the benches of the communal monastic scriptorium at which monks and nuns took their turns as part of their *opus Dei* ('work for God'), if they had the aptitude for such work, and to court schools with scholars recruited by reforming rulers such as Charlemagne and Alfred the Great. Books made in these circumstances were for recipients ranging from monarchs to anchoresses – and for saints. From around 1200 book production shifted in its main focus to the urban and university landscape, with mendicants, clerks in minor orders and numerous craft-specialists – both male and female – working in family units in neighbouring streets. They catered for the needs of a wide variety of patrons and 'off the peg' sales, all coordinated by entrepreneurs known as stationers who negotiated sales and subcontracted out the work. The ateliers of fashionable leading artists were also involved in some of the manuscripts. Unusual projects also occurred, with patrons taking the work in-house to control it and with authors or artists occasionally making books primarily for themselves or as a form of desktop publishing. Populating these projects with the actual people involved in their creation will allow the manuscripts to serve as windows into the mindsets of their age, as will the range of subject-matter that these diverse books cover.

And so, the reader passes through the portals of the painted pages of the key manuscripts and their relatives, to meet those who commissioned, made and used them and to venture out into the world they inhabited. In so doing, the subjects and methodologies of history, art history, book history and even a little archaeology are encountered and together form a picture, from a rather different angle than usual, of the long Middle Ages in Britain, from the post-Roman period to the Reformation.

Rather than impede the progress and enjoyment of the reader with hefty footnotes, which almost every sentence of the text warrants, I have included specific bibliographies for each chapter at the end of the book, as well as a general and subject bibliographies, to enable detailed further reading on aspects of their contents.

1

THE EIGHTH CENTURY: BISHOP EADFRITH'S DESERT OF THE BOOK

THE LINDISFARNE GOSPELS (BRITISH LIBRARY, COTTON MS NERO D IV)

The British Isles have a long history of visual communication, stretching back well into prehistory. The practice of writing, per se, and of decorating written matter began, however, through their contact with Rome. Julius Caesar and other classical commentators refer to the 'Keltoi' (Celts). This was a term that Greeks and Romans used to refer to 'the others/strangers', in the same way that the Germanic Anglo-Saxon settlers who occupied a large part of what had become the Imperial Roman province of Britannia during the fifth and sixth centuries would come to refer to the Romano-British inhabitants as 'Wealas' (Welsh), which had the same meaning. Caesar also wrote in his *Commentary on the Gallic War*, his account of the Roman Republic's wars against the Gaulish tribes in the 50s BC, that the Celts had a distinctive social structure, as well as sharing an Indo-European language that bifurcated into two branches in Britain: Goedelic or Q Celtic (found in Ireland, the Isle of Man and what would become Scotland) and Brythonic or P Celtic (found in Wales, Cornwall and Brittany). Part of this social hierarchy of aristocratic warriors (*equites*), freemen and slaves included a professional meritocracy of bards, jurists and priests known collectively as druids (*druides*), in which men and women alike could participate. They also possessed distinctive Iron Age artistic styles, known as Hallstatt (from around 800 BC) and La Tène (from around 400 BC), named after distinctive archaeological find spots in Austria and Switzerland (with Iberia emerging as an important and early focus). The Celts (whose very existence is questioned by some current archaeologists and historians, as they share many features in common with the Germanic peoples) were not a unified people but a plethora of different tribes that shared cultural and structural features and who spread to the western coast of Ireland and eastwards, even reaching Greece and what is now Turkey.

The druids, who were formally trained over many years in mnemonic retention of large bodies of information, favoured oral transmission over written records, since the former enabled them to preserve their elitist social status as the guardians of knowledge, and because, like Plato and Pliny, they were concerned that reliance upon writing weakened the memory. However, there is evidence that trading contact and travel had made them familiar with the writing systems of Rome and by at least the first century AD they had developed their own proto-writing system called ogam/ogham (after their god of learning, Ogmios), which grouped the vowels and the consonants into groups of five strokes, arranged around a base line such as the edge of a standing stone or a stick (in the Irish Iron Age epic the *Táin Bó Cúailnge*, or 'Cattle Raid of Cooley', the hero Cú Chulainn can halt an entire army at a river by writing an ogam taboo on a stick). This written language was not suitable for lengthy texts but served commemorative or talismanic functions. Similarly, the Germanic peoples also developed an early form of writing known as runes, which originated as sticks being placed to form symbols resembling Graeco-Latin letter-forms, which were each named after a tree. Reading the runes became a popular form of divination. Both groups of peoples had highly decorative visual cultures, with their art showing the influences introduced by contact with the cultures of the Mediterranean.

When the Romans began their conquest in AD 43 (following on from Caesar's exploratory expeditions of 55 and 54 BC) the British Isles were occupied by Iron Age Celtic tribes, who had assimilated into earlier Bronze Age society (which incorporated some descended from earlier Neolithic peoples who had first settled the land to farm). Literacy, as we understand it, was introduced by Rome for administrative, military and commercial use and was taught in schoolrooms and army barracks, as elsewhere in the empire, with Latin being the international lingua franca, facilitating international communications.

There are many inscriptions, on different surfaces, from Roman Britain and also handwriting on papyrus scrolls and wax tablets, although such organic substances do not survive well archaeologically, owing to the environmental conditions created by the British climate. Only one illustrated manuscript, though, is thought perhaps to survive: the Vergilius Romanus (Vatican City, Biblioteca Apostolica, Cod. Vat. lat. 3867), or Roman Virgil, a fifth-century illustrated manuscript of the *Aeneid* and *Bucolics* by the Roman poet Virgil. Its nineteen coloured illustrations are in a flattened, linear provincial style that is very different to the painterly illusionistic naturalism of a similar volume, the Vergilius Vaticanus or 'Vatican Virgil' (Vatican City, Biblioteca Apostolica, Cod. Vat. lat. 3225), made in Rome around 400. The more two-dimensional, simplified style of the former finds some parallel in the narrative mosaics of Roman Britain, such as the Low Ham mosaic depicting Dido and Aeneas from the *Aeneid* (now in Somerset County Museum, Taunton) and one recently unearthed to the west of Peterborough, the Rutland Mosaic, depicting the Trojan War from the *Iliad*, both thought to date from the fourth century. These demonstrate familiarity with the classic epics among wealthy Romano-Britons and the craftsmen who made them, which might suggest that they were read in Roman Britannia. Stylistic similarities to the Vergilius Romanus manuscript have led the

British archaeologists Ken Dark and Martin Henig to suggest that it may even have been made in Roman Britain.

The gradual collapse of the Roman Empire under its own weight and under pressure both from those trying to enter it and from those who were ideologically opposed to it led Emperor Honorius, head of the western half of the empire, to issue a letter in 410 known as the 'Honorian Rescript', cutting Britannia loose in a curious reverse Brexit. The empire, as it still stood, could no longer afford to maintain the defences and infrastructure of such a peripheral land. The province was no more.

From 380 Christianity had been the state religion of the empire, and Britain after Roman rule continued to have a relationship with the Church in Gaul, thus maintaining what is increasingly thought to be a measure of post-Roman continuity. In Britain, the administration, church and military had long been staffed by locals or those imported from other provinces in continental Europe, and even by federal auxiliaries and others from beyond the empire's *limes*. They and their descendants limped on, keeping things afloat, in areas such as Cumbria, towns around Hadrian's Wall and parts of Wales. The inscribed stones of Cornwall and South Wales indicate some continuity in Roman-style literacy, lettering and local infrastructure, and some monastic centres of learning, such as Llantwit Major in South Wales, survived but patchily. Other areas, especially along the east and south coast, saw an influx of Germanic raiders and settlers, while the west coast and the northern border were subject to attacks from those to the north of the Clyde–Forth line and from Ireland. The writings of fifth- and sixth-century clerics such as St Patrick – a patrician from northwest Britain or Strathclyde, who was taken as a slave by the Irish, escaped to Gaul to train as a religious and returned to convert his captors on behalf of the churches of Britain and Gaul as the 'Apostle of Ireland' – and the Welsh monk Gildas indicate how close relations were between the churches of Britain, Brittany and Ireland (to which, as early as 431, the bishop Palladius had been sent from Gaul by the pope). Some other British kingdoms, such as Strathclyde, Rheged and Catterick, survived the Germanic tide and also maintained a literate Christian tradition. Elsewhere apostasy and paganism increasingly prevailed. This period of resistance is the historical core of the phenomenon of the Age of Arthur, who in many ways symbolizes the retention of the status quo in the face of a reversion to a tribal patchwork presided over by warlords, the behaviour of whom – like big fish eating up little fish – led to the survival of the fittest, whose territories became kingdoms.

Ireland played an important part in the reconversion of Britain. With the zeal of the newly converted (Ireland having escaped conquest and absorption into the Roman Empire), men and women stepped willingly aboard what was known as 'the boat with no oars' to go wherever the new God had work for them to do – in an age of plague, famine and warfare – bringing healing, education and a message of hope. Missionaries travelled across Britain and to the Continent, founding strings of monastic houses to form supra-territorial federations united by a common founder-figure. One such was that of St Columba, a prince of the powerful Irish Uí Néill dynasty who became a bishop and, following a conflict involving the first known case of intellectual property rights infringement, which he lost, left Ireland in 563 and founded the monastery of Iona on a small Inner Hebridean island off the west coast of Scotland, to minister to the Irish expat community of the kingdom of Dál Riada and to launch a mission to the Picts (the 'painted/tattooed ones', as Caesar called the early inhabitants of northern and central Scotland). His followers would eventually extend his monastic federation (*paruchia*) into southern Scotland, northern England, the Midlands and as far south as Essex. One of these foundations was Lindisfarne, founded in 635 by Aidan of Iona and his companions as a spiritual powerhouse for the conversion of Northumbria and for its rulers, based at nearby Bamburgh in Bernicia (the northern part of the kingdom, with York being the focus for the southern part, Deira).

Columba is said to have died on Iona in 597, the year that St Augustine of Canterbury arrived in Kent from Rome, having been sent by the great missionary pope Gregory the Great. He is thought to have brought with him the St Augustine Gospels (Cambridge, Corpus Christi College, MS 286), which are still used for incoming archbishops of Canterbury to swear their oath upon. The illuminated manuscript features an image of St Luke as a seated classical author, in toga and sandals. He is identified by his half-length symbol, the bull, and flanked by doors bearing narrative scenes from the Life of Christ, recalling the early carved wooden doors of the great basilica of Santa Sabina in Rome. The Germanic peoples at the time of the manuscript's creation were being introduced to the uses of classical figurative art; in circa 600 Pope Gregory would write to Bishop Serenus of Marseille asking him to stop his iconoclastic destruction of such depictions, cautioning that in images the illiterate read. Gregory thereby opened the door to the history of Western art, rather than taking the aniconic route favoured by Jewish and Islamic art, for fears of idolatry.

Gregory also recognized the value of working with existing tradition. In 604 one of Augustine's followers, Bishop Mellitus of London, wrote to the wise pope, seeking guidance on the approach to existing places of worship. He was told, essentially, that if there was a party going on he should join in and that places where folk had brought their hopes and fears for generations should be embraced – unless evil were taking hold there – and made the focus of the new faith. Thus, holy wells used since prehistory and Roman nymphaea became the sites of hermits' cells and pilgrimages or were used as baptistries. Many a church has an earlier standing stone watching over it: Rudston in East Yorkshire has one of the largest phallic-looking prehistoric menhirs towering over it still. Christian feasts were timed to coincide with the traditional celebrations of the passing of the agricultural year and Easter was named for the Germanic goddess Eostre.

Burial practices chart the gradual process of conversion. The assemblages of goods needed to sustain the dead in the afterlife were not part of the Christian philosophy, where the soul was freed from its earthly needs and desires. Nonetheless, as kings and their people teetered on the verge of conversion, or as those who buried them clung to the old rites of passage, burial barrows such as the imposing Sutton Hoo ship mound in Suffolk and that of the Prittlewell Prince near Southend in Essex contained chambers full of the deceased, their personal ornaments and weaponry, the trappings and feasting ware of the mead-hall, trade goods and tribute from near and as far as Byzantium and Coptic Egypt, symbolizing the extent of the imperium and networks of the dead leader and his people. Sutton Hoo and Prittlewell both also contain Christian artefacts, such as the silver Byzantine spoons engraved with the names Saul and Paul, perhaps an example of the origins of silver baptism spoons as gifts. Bede relates that King Redwald of East Anglia, who may have been the occupant of the Sutton Hoo mound, was forced to accept baptism in Canterbury by his overlord, the newly converted King Ethelbert of Kent, and took his baptism gifts back to his manor of Rendlesham, placing them in the temple. Sometime between 637 and the early 640s King Sigebert of East Anglia, who had resigned his throne to become a monk, was forced by his people to lead them into battle against the ferocious King Penda the Pagan of Mercia. He did so carrying a wooden cross, not a sword, and although he was the first to fall and lost the battle, he won the war: East Anglia did not apostatize and remained Christian henceforth.

Christian burials were generally aligned on an east–west axis, so that the deceased might arise at Christ's Second Coming and face Judgement from the east. The earlier of these might contain some dress items, such as the recently excavated grave of a young German bride at Trumpington in Cambridge, which contains her veil pins, her key chatelaine (for wives were often the household or estate managers) and a fine gold and garnet cross. A similar cross formed part of the assembly of contact relics placed in St Cuthbert's coffin when his remains were translated to the high altar at Lindisfarne in 698. Another of the treasures therein is thought to have been the St Cuthbert Gospel (British Library, Add. MS 89000), a little copy of the Gospel of St John, written at the twin monastery of Monkwearmouth–Jarrow in Northumbria in the late seventh century. This small book contains the same number of gatherings as that which Bede says were in the copy that St Cuthbert studied with his master, Boisil, at Melrose (perhaps intentionally representing that book mentioned in Cuthbert's *Life*) and bears the earliest surviving English binding. This is executed entirely in distinctive Coptic (Christian Egyptian) fashion, with unsupported sewing,

The St Cuthbert Gospel (British Library (BL), Add. MS 89000), a pocket Gospel of St John in the earliest English binding, executed in Coptic Egyptian fashion, made at Monkwearmouth–Jarrow in the late 7th century and later found in the coffin of St Cuthbert.

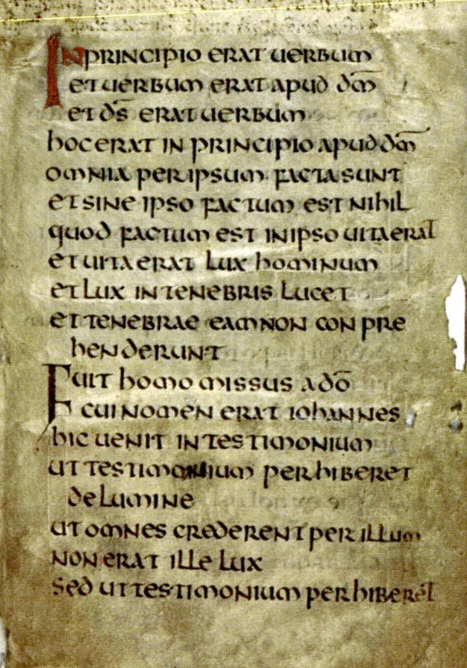

inprincipio erat uerbum
et uerbum erat apud dm
et ds erat uerbum
hoc erat in principio apud dm
omnia per ipsum facta sunt
et sine ipso factum est nihil
quod factum est in ipso uita erat
et uita erat lux hominum
et lux in tenebris lucet
et tenebrae eam non con pre
henderunt
Fuit homo missus a do
cui nomen erat iohannes
hic uenit in testimonium
ut testimonium perhiberet
de lumine
ut omnes crederent per illum
non erat ille lux
sed ut testimonium perhiberet

rather than what soon came to be the Western practice of supported sewing of the gatherings onto cords; it also has a tree of life modelled over raised card beneath its red leather binding, which is tooled with interlace and step patterns filled with blue and yellow pigment. This is a truly remarkable survival and one that attests to the influences from eastern Christianity that travelled along the ancient trade routes from the Mediterranean to the Atlantic seaboard of Europe until the age of the Vikings. I have suggested that St Cuthbert's early shrine may have been modelled upon contemporary Coptic Egyptian bishops' shrines and that the St Cuthbert Gospel, like the Coptic pillow-books supporting the heads of the dead, represented the Book of Life, replacing the ancient Egyptian Book of the Dead. It was written at the end of the seventh century in the fine, rounded script known as uncial, which consciously echoes that found in manuscripts from Gregory's Rome around 600, harking back to the beginnings of the conversion of England.

The uncial of Gregory's manuscripts contained enlarged initials decorated with Christian symbols such as the fish and cross. Their parallels, accompanied by a script derived from a lower-grade hand of the sort used for writing notes by the educated late Roman/early Christian reader, are found in some of the few earliest surviving Irish manuscripts from the late sixth to early seventh century. These exhibit some influence from Late Antique North Africa in their use of colophon decoration – that is, dots, dashes, commas and ivy leaves used to decorate and draw attention to the colophon labels giving the contents on the outside of papyrus scrolls – and dotted surrounds and backgrounds to notable letters. Most of these are now in the Biblioteca Nazionale in Naples and were associated with Bobbio, a foundation of the Irish missionary St Columbanus, who, in his early fifties, left the monastery of Bangor in the north of Ireland to travel the continent, establishing monasteries at Luxeuil in Gaul and St Gall in Switzerland before settling at Bobbio.

Another, the Cathach of Columcille (or 'Battler of St Columba', Dublin, Royal Irish Academy, MS 12 R 33), is thought by some to be the very copy of the Psalms written in Columba's own hand and containing a Latin edition of the text first composed by St Jerome in Bethlehem in the late fourth century that he was accused of plagiarizing. It may post-date his death, however, and might have been made in the early seventh century as a replacement of that famous book associated with him. It may have been made in one of his Irish foundations, such as Derry or Durrow (named after the ancient druidic oak groves), or on Iona. Its enlarged calligraphic initials combine the fish and cross

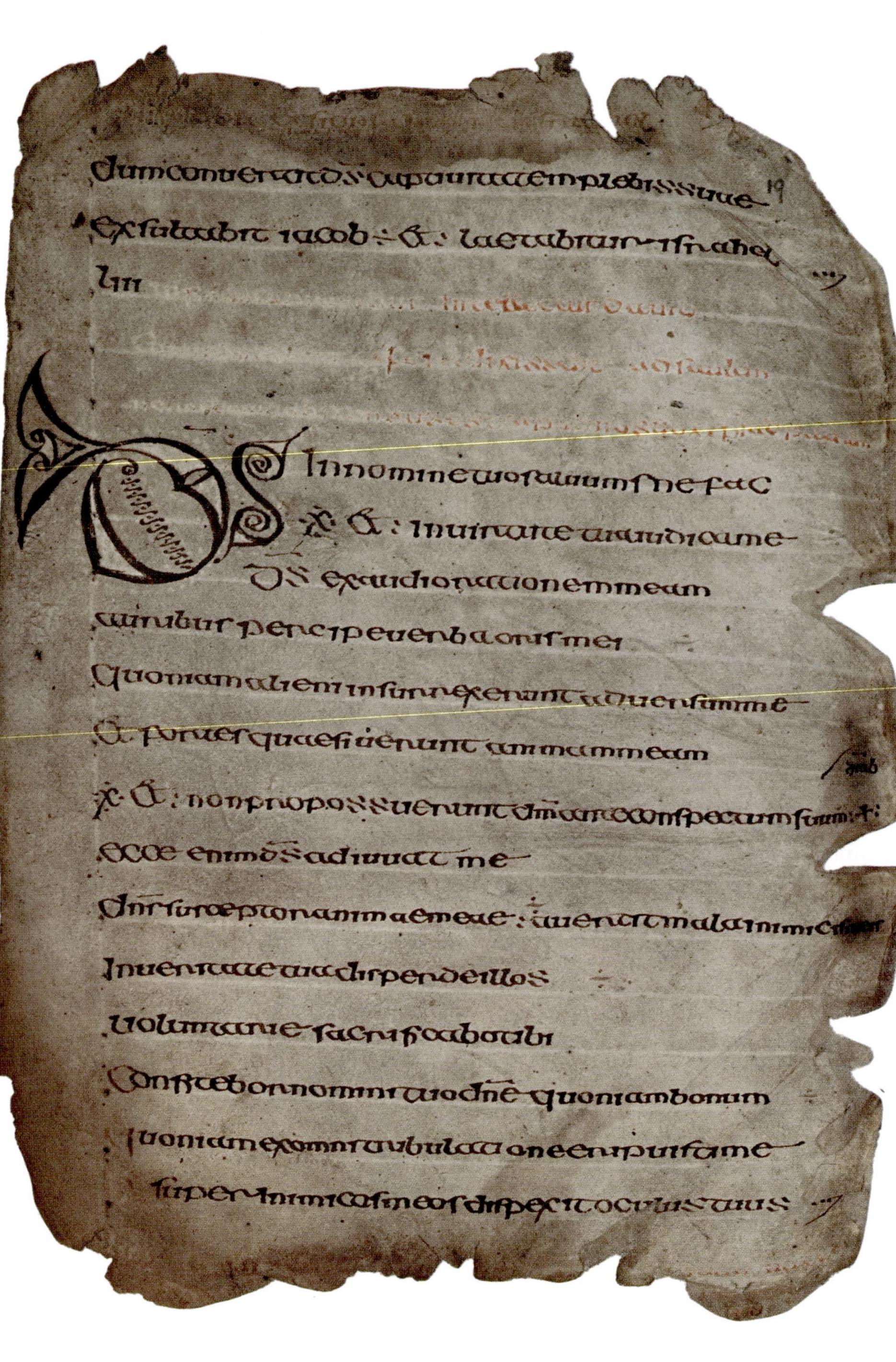

dum conuerterit ds captiuitatem plebis suae 19
Exultabit iacob ÷ et laetabitur israhel
liii

DS in nomine tuo saluum me fac
et in uirtute tua iudica me
DS exaudi orationem meam
auribus percipe uerba oris mei ÷
Quoniam alieni insurrexerunt aduersum me
et fortes quaesierunt animam meam
et non proposuerunt dm ante conspectum suum ÷
Ecce enim ds adiuuat me
dns susceptor animae meae ÷ auertet mala inimicis meis
in ueritate tua disperde illos ÷
Voluntarie sacrificabo tibi
Confitebor nomini tuo dne quoniam bonum
quoniam ex omni tribulatione eripuisti me
et super inimicos meos dispexit oculus tuus

symbols with the curvilinear ornament derived from La Tène art (now termed 'Ultimate La Tène'). The letters following the enlarged initials, which serve to clearly mark the major text breaks, engage in an elegant diminuendo in scale, until they reach the size of the main text script. If it was made on Iona, the main focal point of the posthumous cult of St Columba, the Cathach may well be the earliest decorated manuscript to survive from Britain; it remains, nonetheless, an important early treasure of Ireland.

Faced with mastering Latin as a foreign language and learning to read and write, the Irish developed graphic devices to help understand the text and navigate their way around it. Decorated initials and display scripts were part of this, as were word separation (the Roman practice being to write in *scriptura continua*, without spaces between words, the decipherment of which can feel like untangling a plate of spaghetti) and systematic punctuation. All major contributions to literacy and to book production and reception, these features were also taken up in Britain during the seventh century.

The next great landmark in the decorated/illuminated manuscripts of St Columba's cult is the Book of Durrow (Trinity College Dublin (TCD) MS 57), which probably dates to the second half of the seventh century. It takes these trends further: it contains enlarged major decorated initials and added evangelist symbols and carpet pages of semi-abstract decoration, some with crosses embedded in their patterns, in Coptic fashion. It adroitly fuses elements from 'Celtic' La Tène art, Germanic/Antique interlace and Pictish artistic features and stabilizes its script into an early Insular version of half-uncial, as impressive as Roman uncial but a little quicker to write and which incorporated some lower-case letter-forms, ultimately derived from Roman cursive scripts. But was it made in Ireland, for which it still serves as a national treasure, or on Iona, and if the latter is it still an Irish manuscript, made in a territory they had colonized in Britain, or rather Pictland? The borders of today do not neatly correspond with the political boundaries of the past, let alone its fluctuating cultural areas. Such dilemmas gave rise to the term 'Insular', meaning the culture 'of the islands of Britain and Ireland' from the mid-fifth century to the mid-ninth.

It is, perhaps, worth drawing attention to the fact that the name 'Scotland' actually derives from the *Scotti*, which means Irish. This is because

The Cathach of Columcille ('the Battler of St Columba'), one of the earliest Insular illuminated books (Royal Irish Academy, Dublin, MS 12 R 33, f. 19r). This Psalter has traditionally been thought to be by St Columba's own hand but may have been made a little later, in the late 6th or early 7th century, at his monastery of Iona (now in Scotland) or in Ireland.

the rulers of the Irish kingdom of Dál Riada eventually supplanted the Pictish dynasty, having both conflicted and intermarried with them. In 843 a king who could claim descent from both, Kenneth MacAlpin, became ruler of the new united kingdom of Alba. The only illuminated manuscript from this early period that is known to have been made in Scotland, other than the aforesaid Columban manuscripts probably made on Iona, is the Book of Deer (Cambridge University Library, MS Ii.6.32), a tenth-century Latin Gospel Book with early twelfth-century additions in Latin, Old Irish and Scottish Gaelic. It contains the earliest surviving Gaelic writing from Scotland and is thought probably to have been made at the monastery of Deer in Aberdeenshire, which was founded by saints Columba and Drostan and where the marginal notes were certainly added. It is related to Irish manuscripts stylistically and falls within the Irish pocket-Gospel book tradition. The four evangelists, very simply drawn in a highly stylized fashion, are depicted with strips forming X-shaped crosses on their chests, which resemble the St Andrew's cross of the later Scottish flag but which probably represent straps from the relic boxes worn to carry portable Gospel books, as in early Armenian artistic tradition.

The conversion of the Germanic settlers and the myriad kingdoms that they carved out, which by 700 had crystallized into the major players of Kent, East Anglia, Northumbria, Mercia and Wessex (in order of their political ascendancy from the sixth to the ninth centuries), was a lengthy process undertaken by religious from Ireland, Scotland, Rome and Gaul. The British Church may also have participated in some areas, although the enmity between invader and invaded (reinforced by laws forbidding collaboration) would have largely discouraged this.

In 664 a major synod was convened at Whitby, on the North Yorkshire coast, under the aegis of Abbess Hild, to determine the future affiliation and religious practices (including, crucially, the method of calculating the moveable feast of Easter) of the English Church. This has been presented as a contest between the 'Celtic Church', for which Bishop Colman of Lindisfarne acted as spokesman, and the Church of Rome, represented by Wilfrid, Abbot of Ripon, who was rewarded with the bishopric of York. In fact, it was a struggle for the authority and survival of the Columban federation (which had its own traditions, whereas many other foundations in Ireland already followed those observed in Rome) against the international orthodoxy of Chalcedon, focused upon the patriarchates (of which the papacy in Rome was the westernmost) led by Constantinople. Would the Anglo-Saxon Church be a local church or part of the international ecumenical mainstream? Oswiu, King of Northumbria, decided in favour of the latter.

It may be that the Book of Durrow was made after Whitby. Nonetheless, its symbol of St Matthew (which is a man) prefacing that Gospel, seems to be wearing the Columban tonsure (in which the hair was shaved back from the brow, rather than the corona patch on the pate of the head, commemorating Christ's crown of thorns), but that would have been the case for monks of Iona as well as those of Columba's Irish foundations, as Iona did not conform to the Roman tonsure and other practices until 715. In other respects, the Matthew symbol looks like an Anglo-Saxon or Frankish gold and garnet belt-buckle on legs. The eagle likewise resembles a Migration Period (*c.* AD 300–600) eagle fibula. The symbol of the calf/bull and the lion, however, feature the distinctive hip spirals of Pictish art. During this period, and from perhaps as early as the Roman period, the Picts produced fine silverwork and carved stones featuring both decorative and narrative elements and an enigmatic vocabulary of symbols (including Z-rods, V-rods, mirrors, combs, serpents, bulls, deer, notched rectangles perhaps representing their broch towers and swimming elephants (Pictish beasts based upon classical dolphins)), which have yet to be convincingly decoded but which may have signified status, gender, profession and tribal affiliation. The combination of different cultural styles in the Book of Durrow would certainly fit Iona, or one of Columba's other houses, be it in Scotland, Northumbria or Ireland, with their wide cultural reach.

The post-Whitby period witnessed an ordering of the Church in England by the new Archbishop of Canterbury, who arrived in 669, the erudite Theodore of Tarsus (St Paul's home town in Asia Minor) and latterly Rome, who, with the assistance of his colleague Abbot Hadrian of St Augustine's Abbey, Canterbury (thought to have been a Berber from North Africa, and latterly from the area of Naples), established a remarkable school at Canterbury. There they taught the classical programme of liberal arts including Latin and some Greek (grammar, rhetoric, poetic composition), theology, exegesis, computistics, astronomy, medicine and Gregorian chant; the West Saxon bishop-poet Aldhelm (*c.* 639–709) adds that he studied Roman Law there too. Instruction by structured question and answer and by testing and proofs would have joined the traditional learning by rote and memory-training exercises of the late Roman Empire.

A Northumbrian nobleman turned monk, Benedict Biscop, was charged with accompanying them to England from Rome and stayed to help them teach for a couple of years. He then returned home and founded the remarkable twin monastery of Monkwearmouth–Jarrow ('two places with but one will', as Bede put it, drawing a parallel with the unity of the divine and human wills of Christ) on the rivers Tyne and Wear in 674 and 681–2 respectively. Some of their original masonry and stained glass, made by workmen that Biscop brought from Gaul, as well as sculptures and other artefacts, survive there still. Biscop made five trips to Rome, some accompanied by Abbot Ceolfrith, and they brought back cartloads of icons, panel paintings (which adorned and instructed from the interior walls of his twin foundation) and books, trundling across the Alps. The library that they assembled there salvaged a significant part of the wreckage of Late Antique and Early Christian book culture and enabled the creation of its own school and scriptorium for the copying and creation of books and of scholars – including the Venerable Bede, the only learned Doctor of the Church to hail from these islands and who might be considered an English 'father of the Church'.

Bede (*c.* 673–735) was presented to Biscop's new monastery of Monkwearmouth by his kinsmen at the age of seven and remained there until his death, aged 62, in its twin monastery of Jarrow, having become one of their monks and also a priest. He is only known to have travelled some 100 or so kilometres (65 mi.) from home, to Lindisfarne and perhaps York, but his forty known works (which some scholars would extend to sixty) include 'On the Holy Places', which was still being used as a travel guide to the Near East around 1900, treatises on the nature of things, the nature of time and on the calculation of time, on orthography and grammar, poetry, epigrams and hymns, on biblical exegesis (commenting upon numerous books of the Bible) and on hagiography, to which he added his own verse and prose Lives of St Cuthbert and his Lives of the Abbots of Monkwearmouth–Jarrow. He also wrote the first history of his people, the *Historia ecclesiastica gentis Anglorum* (The History of the English Church and People), completed in 731, in which he invented the concept of 'English', taking the name from his own Anglian people, integrating them into the wider history of Christendom (expressed earlier in the universal *Christian History* of Eusebius of Caesarea, composed in the fourth century). He also showcased therein the system of unified dating from the birth of Christ (BC, AD; BCE, CE), to achieve which, building on some earlier scholars' work, he had to engage in a tremendous amount of computistical analysis and observation of phases of the Moon, becoming in effect a human computer. In the course of this he worked out the gravitational pull of the Moon on the tides and wrote the first tide timetables. His astronomical observations were also informed by the work of the ancient cosmographers. A copy of these observations were given by the monastery to the learned King Aldfrith of Northumbria as a gift. Bede's *Historia ecclesiastica* even gives us our earliest example of Old English poetry, 'Caedmon's Hymn', and on his deathbed he was working on the earliest translation of any part of the Bible into English, St John's Gospel ('the little Gospel that speaks of the things that work of love'), to share with his people. The assistant taking down his words in this last poignant period recorded Bede's own Death Song:

Fore ðæm nedfere nænig wiorðe
ðonc snottora ðon him ðearf siæ
to ymbhycgenne ær his hinionge
hwæt his gastæ godes oððe yfles
æfter deað dæge doemed wiorðe.

Facing Death, that inescapable journey,
who can be wiser than he
who reflects, while breath yet remains,
on whether his life brought others happiness, or pains,
since his soul may yet win delight's or night's way
after his death-day.

(Cuthbert's Letter on the Death of Bede,
Epistola Cuthberti de obitu Bedae, composed in 735).

Bede wrote in his autobiographical note, with which he concluded the *Historia ecclesiastica*, that 'My chief delight has always been in study, teaching and writing,' and that 'in this, as in all things of monastic humility, I was both author, notary and scribe.' This indicates that, unlike most authors in classical antiquity and the Middle Ages, Bede wrote down his own thoughts, rather than dictating. But he goes on to say that he was a scribe, by which he meant the Old Testament scribe (*sofer*), a priestly calling. Bede was not only the greatest teacher and academic of Monkwearmouth–Jarrow (and one of the greatest scholars of the early medieval world), but surely one of the scribes who wrote the works of Scripture for which it was famed, including the Ceolfrith Bibles – three massive single-volume Bibles, which are more like symbolic library buildings than books, containing the best possible editions of the various biblical texts. These were commissioned by Abbot Ceolfrith from the Monkwearmouth–Jarrow scriptorium, one copy being intended for each of the two branches of the twin monastery to serve as reliable exemplars from which further copies could be made of all or part of their texts. The third copy was to accompany the abbot to Rome as a gift for the pope when he set off there on retirement in 716. That book survives still, the Codex Amiatinus (Florence, Biblioteca Medicea Laurenziana, MS Amiatino 1), which is written in uncials by seven scribes, of which I have proposed one hand as Bede's, and which has a prefatory gathering of illuminated diagrams of the relationships between the books of the Bible and the Old and New Testaments, a plan of the Temple and Tabernacle in Jerusalem, a complex image of Ezra the Scribe and a splendid 'Christ in Majesty' at the Second Coming. More building (*biblios*, from which the term 'Bible' comes, meant a library of scrolls) than book, this immense and beautiful tome makes an authoritative, superbly researched statement concerning which books, and which editions of their texts, belong on the shelves of the library of Scripture.

Ceolfrith died en route, in Burgundy, leaving his companions to convey the gift to Rome. The resulting papal letter to his successor as abbot of Monkwearmouth–Jarrow, Hwaetberht, shows that the book-gift worked – the Northumbrian twin monastery was accepted as 'one of us', with all the diplomatic and other benefits that this entailed. When the Abbazia di San Salvatore was founded on Monte Amiata by the Lombard king Ratchis in 743, Ceolfrith's Bible may have been given to it as a papal diplomatic gift, or during the early ninth century when the Carolingian rulers were also having dealings with it, for it was certainly there during the ninth century and remained so until 1786, when it passed to the Medici Library in Florence. While at Monte Amiata, which lay close to the Via Francigena pilgrimage route that led from northwestern Europe to Rome and was traversed by many Anglo-Saxons, Ceolfrith's dedication inscription was erased and the name of a local saint added in place of his. It was not until the 1880s that it was recognized as English work, rather than that of Italo-Byzantine scholars, scribes and illuminators. The book was in disguise, appearing more Roman than the Romans and more Byzantine than the Byzantines, and served as an ambassador for the Church in England, which was now the only place capable of undertaking such work. When St Jerome's reliable Latin edition of the Bible, the Vulgate, was printed in the sixteenth century, scholars assessing various manuscript models determined that the Codex Amiatinus was the best witness to his work, which had been painstakingly reconstructed through the scholarship, editing and expert book production of Bede and his brethren. In so doing, they were perpetuating a mode of publication established by Cassiodorus, a sixth-century Roman senator turned monastic founder, who left the heretical and dangerous Arian court of the invader Ostrogoths to go and found the Vivarium (the 'living things' or 'fishponds') monastery on his estate in southern Italy. This was devoted to the accurate study, editing, copying and dissemination of Scripture. Biscop and Ceolfrith brought some of h is books home with them and Monkwearmouth–Jarrow transmitted its concept of a publishing programme to the Middle Ages. The Ezra image in the Codex Amiatinus was indebted to a Cassiodoran original, but it may have been adapted at Monkwearmouth–Jarrow. The way in which it sits in its programme shows it to have functioned as a complex multivalent image that can be read literally as an illustration of Ezra the priestly Scribe (who wrote down the Hebrew Scriptures from memory after their destruction by the Babylonians)and allegorically as a depiction of Cassiodorus with the Novem Codices, a nine-volume edition of the Bible – one of three editions that he oversaw at the Vivarium – in the book closet (*armarium*) behind him. The spines of those books bear the names of other early editors and translators of the Christian Scriptures, however, and the image also serves to depict them and also Bede, Ceolfrith and all those who take part in the ongoing transmission of the Bible. It is a complex sacred *figura* (symbolic diagram) with many layers of meaning, of a sort that Insular artists and thinkers excelled in.

Bede's own works were extremely popular in his own age, causing the Monkwearmouth–Jarrow scriptorium to produce multiple copies. Three copies of the *Historia ecclesiastica* made there within fifteen years of his death remain intact, an incredibly high rate of survival for the period. The oldest of these, the Moore Bede of about 737 (Cambridge University Library, Kk.5.16), may have been owned by Charlemagne at the end of the century, or by one of the leading scholars he had recruited, Alcuin of York (*c.* 735–804), who is known to have seen one of the great Ceolfrith Bibles and who, as abbot of Tours, started a publication programme inspired by them. The Tours scriptorium produced as many as three of the equally massive Tours Bibles per year there during the first half of the ninth century, which were circulated

CODICIBUS SACRIS HOSTILI CLADE PERUSTIS
ESDRA · DŌ FERVENS HOC REPARAVIT OPUS

as models to other scriptoria around the Carolingian Empire, ensuring some cohesion, textually and stylistically, written in the newly devised multi-purpose Caroline minuscule script, which would largely displace the Anglo-Saxon multi-tiered system of scripts from the late tenth century and which is familiar to us still from our keyboards.

Alcuin's edition of the Vulgate would go on to form the basis of theological studies in the universities of the West from around 1200 onwards. His publication programme was indebted to and perpetuated that of Monkwearmouth–Jarrow, Cassiodorus and Jerome, providing an invaluable line of transmission from the fourth century to the high Middle Ages and beyond, for the Bible and for book culture and learning. Bede the priestly Scribe of Scripture played his own major part in this and his handwriting may survive in the pages of the Codex Amiatinus.

Bede respected the contribution that Lindisfarne and its daughter-houses had made to the conversion of Northumbria, their ascetic tradition and service of God and community. He assisted Bishop Eadfrith of Lindisfarne in shaping the cult of St Cuthbert, to serve as an inspiration for such values, composing new versions of his Life and, I have suggested, helping to shape the bishop's thinking behind his making of the Lindisfarne Gospels as a focal point of the shrine and supplying the Vulgate textual model for the Gospels from Monkwearmouth–Jarrow. Together they serve as two

Opposite: *Codex Amiatinus (Biblioteca Medicea Laurenziana, Florence,* MS *Amiatino 1, f. 5r), Monkwearmouth–Jarrow, early 8th century (pre-716), a complex multivalent image depicting Ezra the Scribe committing the Hebrew Scriptures to writing from memory but also representing the ongoing transmission of Christian Scripture.* Below: *This may be the uncial handwriting of the Venerable Bede, showing some of his distinctive marginal apparatus, in the Codex Amiatinus (Biblioteca Medicea Laurenziana, Florence,* MS *Amiatino 1, f. 67v).*

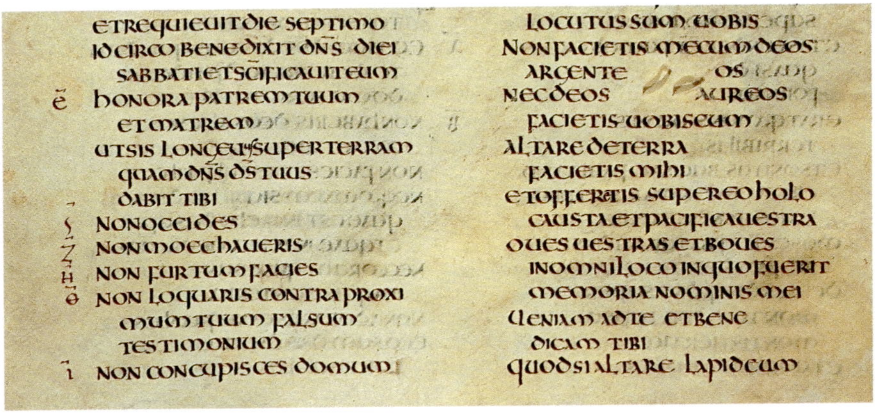

pillars of the Northumbrian renaissance, one of the finest expressions of which is the Lindisfarne Gospels.

Some other great Gospel books were made before this, notably the Echternach Gospels (Paris, Bibliothèque nationale de France, MS lat. 9389) and the Durham Gospels (Durham Cathedral Library, MS A.II.17). These were once thought, by the scholars responsible for writing the commentary to the 1956–60 facsimile of the Lindisfarne Gospels, to have been the work of the same artist-scribe who may have taught the maker of the Lindisfarne Gospels, but who was working later (as the Lindisfarne Gospels was dated by them to 698, when St Cuthbert's relics were translated to the high altar on Lindisfarne). However, I have advanced historical, stylistic and textual evidence that shows both that they cannot pre-date circa 715 and they formed part of the development of the cult by Bishop Eadfrith, assisted by Bede.

The Echternach Gospels is thought to have been made to commemorate the foundation of the monastery that was founded there by St Willibrord, who led a mission of Irish and Northumbrian personnel to the Netherlands who were joined by locals and Merovingians. It is likely that it was made in the Echternach scriptorium, which by the mid-eighth century had incorporated influences from Antique art to produce the Trier Gospels (Trier Cathedral Treasury), conflating the different cultural traditions of those represented there, as well as the Insular legacy of its foundation Gospels, which contains fine Insular decorated initials and evangelist symbol pages, including a vigorous prancing lion with a strong linear design.

The Durham Gospels may have been made at Lindisfarne or Melrose a decade or two before the Lindisfarne Gospels and both were subsequently corrected in part by the same hand, indicating a link in their provenances. Its initials have grown larger, they and their accompanying display script now occupying the entire page, and it contains a stylized Crucifixion miniature in Eastern fashion, depicting Christ in a tunic, accompanied by angels and Stephaton and Longinus, the sponge and spear bearers. Like the Book of Durrow, these books employ a limited palette of red (toasted lead), yellow (orpiment, a trisulphide of arsenic, a by-product of tin mining) and green (verdigris from copper) – the last was also used in Coptic and Merovingian illumination of the period, despite the chemical interaction of the pigments that can cause the verdigris to corrode through the page.

The Lindisfarne Gospels (British Library, Cotton MS Nero D IV) is one of the cornerstones of British identity. Its intricate images are a fusion of stylistic ingredients representative of the variety of peoples and cultures who inhabited the islands of Britain in the aftermath of the Roman Empire and of others stretching as far as the Near East, combining with the elements and the flora and fauna of Creation to form a visualization of eternal harmony, in which all things are one in the divine. This Neoplatonic vision of beauty and the good was created around 715–22 by an Anglo-Saxon bishop of a Celtic monastery: Lindisfarne, a tidal island set in the North Sea near what became the border between England and Scotland. His name was Eadfrith and during his time as bishop (698–722) he worked, along with his friend Bede, to create a sense of identity and cohesion among competing peoples and to further their conversion to Christianity and their contribution on the international stage. Their creation of the cult of St Cuthbert (*c.* 634–687), for which the Lindisfarne Gospels served as a visible focal point at one of the most popular pilgrim shrines of the West, presented a Christian hero to rival those of the pagan past.

Eadfrith made the book over a period of some five to ten years, carving out time from his contemplative life of prayer and study and his active schedule caring for the vast diocese of Islandshire, which stretched from Bernicia (the northern half of the Anglo-Saxon kingdom of Northumbria) up to the Firth of Forth, to do so. He oversaw the provision of pastoral and sacramental care, charitable works, health and education services of the diocese, and was able to meanwhile create the Gospels not by taking turns with others in the scriptorium of a communal-style monastery, but in the manner of the desert fathers of the East, retreating during the penitential seasons of Lent and Advent to a rocky islet, Cuddy's Isle, a splinter from the shore of the main island, as a spiritual survivalist – doing battle with the forces of evil with his pen in the desert of the book. This was a distinctive Columban approach to making important copies of Scripture, one which St Columba himself is said to have practised.

It is possible to glimpse something of the motivation for this when considering some of the comments made upon such scribal feats of heroism by writers likely to have been known to Eadfrith, such as Cassiodorus and Cummian the Sage of Iona, who wrote statements such as, 'The scribe preaches with the pen and unleashes tongues with the fingers' and 'Every word written is a wound on Satan's body.' These writers advocated that, when copying Scripture, the scribe should fill the shelves of his (or her) inner library with things needful to know. They also wrote that, when writing, the scribe of Scripture should engage in a threefold process of *ruminatio* (digesting the meaning of the text), *meditatio* (meditating on its meaning) and *revelatio* (by which they gained a true understanding of God's purpose).

This was a solitary endeavour, a prayerful offering to the Cosmic Logos by one of the most spiritually and actively ethical, experienced members of society on behalf of the whole. Surrounded by the beauty, challenges and curiosity of the natural world and immersed in deep meditative prayer, he deployed his skills as an experimental scientist to create a range of colours to rival those of Byzantium and the Silk Road, using only half a dozen locally available minerals and plants as pigments (from the lichen that grew on the rocks at his feet he fashioned forty shades of purple, varying acid and alkaline additives, referencing Bede's contemporary commentary on the Temple and Tabernacle, which told of the crimson shades of the temple curtains that symbolized the journey of the soul). He also invented the precursor of the lead pencil as a flexible graphic design tool and an early version of the lightbox to enable the drawings for his intricate designs, underpinned by classical Euclidean and Pythagorean geometry, rabbinic number symbolism and Christian theology, to be visible through the vellum skins as he painted them on the other side of the page. In these designs he emphasized the contribution made by different peoples, different languages and different traditions to an emerging Christian culture that extended from the eastern deserts and cities of its birth to the wild coastlines of the North Sea and the Atlantic.

The Lindisfarne Gospels' shelfmark, Cotton MS Nero D IV, is the one it was given in the library of Sir Robert Cotton, who had busts of the Roman emperors and ladies surmounting his shelves, making this the fourth book on the fourth shelf under Emperor Nero. Around 1600 Cotton identified it as the great book of St Cuthbert, which once adorned his shrine in Durham Cathedral and before that at Chester-le-Street and Holy Island (Lindisfarne), where it was made in the generation following the saint's death in 687. 'St Cuddy' is still fondly celebrated in the former Anglo-Saxon

Lead-point backdrawings establishing the design of the St Mark carpet page on the other side of the leaf in the Lindisfarne Gospels (BL, Cotton MS Nero D IV, f. 94r). The compass and divider marks can be clearly seen and the design is underpinned by Euclidean and Pythagorean geometry and the Golden Section to produce an image of perfect harmony and beauty (along Neoplatonic lines, but with the Cross at its centre). This is an erudite, aesthetically and theologically inspired vision. To achieve such sophisticated designs and layout, Bishop Eadfrith invented the precursor of the lead pencil and the lightbox, allowing him to plan every detail of the artistic programme on the backs of the leaves and do the painting on the other sides, through a transparent glass or horn writing slope with backlighting.

kingdom of Northumbria. The manuscript left Durham in the late sixteenth century and became an icon of regional identity when, in the 1850s, Bishop Maltby of Durham condemned Catholic emancipation, icons and relics, causing such uproar that he immediately sought to regain popularity by commissioning a treasure binding as a gift for this key relic of St Cuthbert, to replace the lost original. Maltby's treasure binding, based upon one of the book's cross-carpet pages, still protects the volume, which remains an icon of faith and identity of northeastern England.

The book still fulfils the mission for which Bishop Eadfrith laboured on it, from around 715 until his death in 722, to enshrine a remarkable vision of Creation at a crucial period of Western history. It was made to honour God and St Cuthbert and, as part of his cult, would have been the most seen book, then and now. Most people could not read, so the Esperanto of art was essential. Today display panels and audio-guides help us to understand; then there were informed people with an ability to decode symbols who fulfilled these functions. For over 3,000 years people had conveyed status, ethnic, cultural and faith identities by the metalwork they wore and the ink on their skins, alongside features from other cultures, stretching from the watery western wilderness of the Atlantic to the eastern deserts of Judaea. The painted pages in the Lindisfarne Gospels display a similarly eclectic range of styles and motifs. It is like reading a menu in the latest Anglo-Italian-Franco-Irish/Scots-North African-Middle Eastern fusion restaurant, where the vocabulary would summon up in our imaginations a vast cultural smorgasbord; the individual influences are celebrated, but as part of an enriched multi-cultural feast.

Seeing features redolent of your own traditions interwoven with those of neighbours, for whom you might harbour enmity, would test your Christian resolve, while others spoke of far-off lands, known only from stories. Thus, each of the four Gospels opens with a carpet page of ornament, in which is embedded a cross representing different church traditions – Matthew the Latin cross, Mark the Celtic ring-headed cross, Luke the Greek cross and John the Coptic/Ethiopic tau cross – speaking of different contributions, united in common purpose and harmony, like the Gospels. Art historians termed them 'carpet pages' because they resemble oriental rugs, but prayer mats were used on Good Friday in Europe about 700, including in Northumbria. Eastern Christian practices were influencing the West, as well as Islam.

On the facing decorated incipit pages, the opening words of each Gospel explode across the page, becoming icons of the divine – recalling the beginning of John's Gospel: 'In the beginning was the Word and the Word was with God and the Word was God.' This is a similar solution to unease concerning idolatry and the depiction of God in human form to that adopted later by Islamic and Jewish artist-scribes, who accorded honour by illuminating the very Word of God, rather than illustrating it with figural narrative. The West avoided this when Pope Gregory the Great wrote to Bishop Serenus of Marseilles about 600, telling him to stop defacing effigies, for 'in images the illiterate read.' The didactic value of story-telling art and iconographies was thereby established, paving the way for the history of Western art. But by the time the Lindisfarne Gospels was made, Byzantium was about to launch into a century of iconoclasm, destroying much of its own legacy. The Anglo-Saxons were aware of such Eastern controversies, hosting at least one related summit meeting in Hatfield in 679, in preparation for the Sixth Ecumenical Council in Constantinople in 681. Eadfrith may be showing sensitivity to the debate, as part of the international orthodoxy of which the Anglo-Saxon church, and many of those in Ireland, were part.

Instead, the cosmic Logos is celebrated, with the flora and fauna of Creation sustained by the Word. Inserted into the Roman capital display script are occasional Greek letters and forms reminiscent of Germanic runes and Irish ogham, symbolizing four cultures participating together in transmitting the faith. The text is written in elegant half-uncial script (an Insular adaptation of a Roman hand) and is one of the best surviving copies of the Vulgate, an edition of the Bible produced in Bethlehem by St Jerome around 380 in the vulgar (*vulgata*) language of the empire: Latin. The best surviving versions of this were made in early eighth-century Northumbria, at Monkwearmouth–Jarrow and Lindisfarne. Between the lines are tiny words in Old English – the oldest surviving version of the Gospels in English, added in the 950s by Aldred, a monk who had joined the Community of St Cuthbert after it had moved to Chester-le-Street. Aldred's work helped re-establish English identity in northern England, after its seizure by Vikings, aiding unification. Bede, however, was the first person known to write any biblical text in English, translating John, the 'little Gospel that speaks of the things that work of love', during the final weeks of his life in 735. I have recently demonstrated that Bede's work survives as part of Aldred's gloss to the Gospel of St John in the Lindisfarne Gospels, signalled by the use

Overleaf: *The Lindisfarne Gospels (BL, Cotton MS Nero D IV), Holy Island,* c. *715–22: openings of St Matthew's Gospel (ff. 26v–27r), St Mark's Gospel (ff. 94v–95r), St Luke's Gospel (ff. 138v–139r) and St John's Gospel (ff. 210v–211r).*

dixit ei ihs sic eum
volo manere donec
veniam quid ad te
tu me sequere
exivit ergo sermo iste
in fratres quia
discipulus ille
non moritur
Et non dixit ei ihs
non moritur
sed sic eum volo manere
donec venio
quid ad te
hic est discipulus
qui testimonium
perhibet de his
et scribsit haec
et scimus quia verum
est testimonium eius
sunt autem et alia
multa que fecit ihs
quae si scribantur
per singula
nec ipsum arbitror
mundum capere eos
qui scribendi sunt
libros · amen :—

EXPLICIT LIBER

SECUNDUM

IOHANNEN

+ Litteras me pandat
sermonis fabri
ministra.
Omnes alme
meos fratres
voce saluta :,

+ Trinus et unus deus evangelium hoc ante saecula constituit
+ Matheus ex ore xpi scripsit
+ Marcus ex ore petri scripsit
+ Lucas de ore pauli apostoli scripsit
+ Ioh in prochemio deinde eructavit
verbum deo donante et spiritu sancto scripsit

+ Eadfrið biscop lindisfearnensis aeclesiae
he dis boc avrat æt frymða gode 7 sancte
cuðberhte 7 allum ðæm halgum. ða ðe
in eolonde sint. 7 Ediluald lindisfearneolondinga
biscop hit uta giðryde 7 gibelde sua he uel cuðe.
7 billfrið se oncre he gismioðade ða
gihrino ðaðe utan on sint 7 hit gi
hrinade mið golde 7 mið gimmum æc
mið sulfre ofgylded faconleasfeh :,
7 ic aldred prb indignus 7 misserrimus
mið godes fultummæ 7 sancti cuðberhtes
hit of gloesade on englisc 7 hine gihamadi
mið ðæm ðrim dælum. Matheus dæl
gode 7 sancte cuðberhti. Marc dæl
ðæm biscope. 7 lucas dæl ðæm hiorode
7 ehtoora seolfres mið to inlade.
7 sancti ioh dæl f hine seolfne 7 feover ora
seolfres mið gode 7 sancti cuðberti. þte he
hæbbe ondfong ðerh godes milsæ on heofnum.
Sel 7 sibb on eorðo forðgeong 7 giðyngo
visdom 7 snyttro ðerh sancti cuðberhtes earnunga :,
+ Eadfrið . oeðilvald . billfrið . aldred .
hoc evangelium deo 7 cuðberhto construxerunt :,

Alfredi natus aldredus vocor bonae mulieris filius eximius loquor of a higher-grade red ink, thereby pushing the date of the earliest extant translation of any part of the Bible into English back to 735.

Also introducing each Gospel are evangelist miniatures, each author accompanied by his symbol: Matthew the man, because he wrote of the birth of Christ; Mark, the lion of Judah, symbol of the Resurrection; Luke, the sacrificial calf/bull of the Passion of Christ; John, the eagle who flies to the throne of God to receive the Word, symbolizing the Second Coming. Two are 'beardies', mortal and ageing; two are youthful and clean-shaven. Art historians asserted that the former copied Byzantine models and the latter Roman ones. But the meaning is deeper: the mortal ones are Matthew and Luke, symbolizing Christ's incarnation and death, while the immortals Mark and John represent his Resurrection and Second Coming – a neat visual diptych resolving the centuries-old debate on how Christ could be simultaneously human and divine, by demonstrating that in accepting birth and death, the human will of Christ was obedient to the divine will. These erudite images are stylized and sit framed, like Eastern icons, obliquely embodying the many facets of God.

So how was this complex book made and by whom? Aldred's colophon names Bishop Eadfrith of Lindisfarne as its maker; his successor, Bishop Æthilwald, as its binder; Billfrith the anchorite/hermit as maker of its treasure binding and Aldred as its translator. But he is paralleling the four makers with the four evangelists, casting himself as St John, and is writing over two hundred years later, so cannot be relied upon alone. Lindisfarne had been founded in 635 by St Aidan from Iona, the famous Scottish foundation of the Irish St Columba. Its traditions were influenced by Irish and Eastern desert fathers, as well as by Rome, and it espoused devout worship, asceticism and service in the world. Its cult book was made to grace the shrine of Bishop Cuthbert, who represented reconciliation between traditions and Christian ethical values, which it sought to enshrine in its appearance and in the way it was made. In the Columban tradition only

Opposite: *Aldred's Colophon and Old English Gloss (BL, Cotton MS Nero D IV, f. 259r), the earliest physically extant translation of the Gospels into the English language, added* c. 950s *to the Latin text of the Lindisfarne Gospels – one of the purest witnesses to St Jerome's Vulgate – made on Holy Island,* c. *715–22, by Bishop Eadfrith of Lindisfarne. Aldred may also have incorporated a copy of Bede's translation into English of part of the Gospel of St John, signalled and honoured by being written in red ink, rather than the brown/black of the rest of the gloss, pushing the date of the earliest English version back to Bede's deathbed in 735.* Overleaf: *The Lindisfarne Gospels (BL, Cotton MS Nero D IV), Holy Island,* c. *715–22: miniatures of St Matthew (f. 25v), St Mark (f. 93v), St Luke (f. 137v) and St John (f. 209v).*

imago homi nis
O AGIOS
MATT
HEUS

imago leonis

imago ui tuli
O AGIOS
LUCAS

imago aequilae

seniores, the most tried and tested senior members, often bishops, abbots or anchorites (or their female equivalents), were worthy of the prayerful sacrifice needed to make a copy of the Gospels or Psalms single-handedly, in the manner of the Eastern desert fathers. The maker of the Lindisfarne Gospels was therefore most likely the bishop, Eadfrith, who worked closely with Bede in establishing the cult of St Cuthbert.

At a time when several scribes and artists (male or female, depending on the institution) might take turns at the scriptorium benches to produce an unilluminated library book, this gem was entirely the work of one gifted artist-scribe: the hermit scribe preaching with the pen in the desert of the book, each word an act of prayer transforming the world.

What must it have meant for the busy bishop of a diocese extending from Yorkshire to Edinburgh, responsible for the pastoral, educational, medical and spiritual well-being of his flock, who sang psalms and prayed the Divine Office eight times each day and night, who daily had to prove humility by hard manual labour and engage in sacred study, to carve out time to undertake the migraine-inducing, back-breaking work of making a whole Gospel book? During the forty days of Lent and Advent even the bishop was permitted spiritual retreat. Eadfrith seems to have used his, as had Columba, to make a special copy of sacred text. If the labour was an individual offering, then the resources represent communal buy-in. Some three hundred of the best one-year-old calf-skins were needed for the vellum pages. When you stretch skins, blemishes open up as holes: all medieval manuscripts have them but Lindisfarne contains only a few, hidden in the book's spine. And, unusually, all the skins' spine ridges align. To have obtained so many large, near-perfect skins aligned, in order to reduce the inevitable distortions accompanying fluctuations in temperature and humidity and to prevent flaking of the jewel-like colours (only held onto the pages by beaten egg-white, known as glair), must mean that thousands of skins were available to select from, doubtless donated by many secular and religious estates.

This book also enshrines technical innovations. Its maker invented the lead pencil some three centuries before it became widely used: the pointed metal stylus used to rule the writing lines contained lead in its alloy and left a graphic line; seeing this, he started using it as a design tool, planning each element, down to the one-line initials that form part of the hierarchy of decoration he devised.

Every design element is drawn in lead-point on the back of the pages, using compasses and dividers, Euclidean and Pythagorean geometry and rabbinic number symbolism to lay out the complex pages. This suggests Eadfrith also invented the lightbox. If you use a transparent writing slope of horn or glass and have many candles in front of it and a small candle behind you, or a large window in front and small one behind, you have a lightbox, enabling you to follow your designs by backlighting once you have laid down the first thick layers of pigment. You can flip the leaf over to consult fine detail, rather than designing on offcuts of stone, slate, wood or wax-covered tablets of wood or bone.

Photoshop indicates that some ninety colours were used, but a non-destructive Raman laser analysis shows that this range, comparable to that enabled by the Silk Route, was achieved using six local planta and minerals: toasted red lead, copper verdigris, orpiment yellow, purples from orchil, a lichen that grows on seashore rocks, white from ground-up shells and carbon black from soot, with ink made from oak galls and carbon, with ferrous salts. The maker was evidently an experimental chemist and could obtain forty shades of purple by varying acidity or alkalinity (stale urine producing red). This range was not only aesthetic: Bede had composed a tract on the Tabernacle in which he compared the forty shades of purple used to dye the curtains of the Temple in Jerusalem to stages on the journey of the just soul. Eadfrith also faked lapis lazuli from the Himalayas by boiling the local woad plant. Not content with the colour, however, he suspended particles of hoof and horn gum to emulate ground lapis, which fooled scientists until 2003, for it was not enough to have lapis, you needed the recipe to grind it to the right particle size to get the intense blue.

If Bishop Eadfrith made the book, where and when might he have done so? He was allowed to go on retreat to Cuddy's Isle, a hermitage rock in the bay below Lindisfarne monastery. Here, much of the solitary work could have been undertaken, its North Sea wilderness emulating the deserts of Eastern hermits. But when? The text contains certain clues. The small one-line initials serve to mark different things, signalled by the use of different colours and positioning of red dots: some mark early chapter divisions; some mark the Gospel passages, numbered and listed at the front of the volume within arcaded canon tables in a sort of a proto-computer showing agreement between each of the Gospels. This system was devised by Eusebius of Caesarea in the late fourth century; his letter explaining them, along with others by St Jerome accounting for his Latin edition, also preface the book. Each Gospel also has its own prefaces, including lists of readings (lections) for key feast days – the saints celebrated indicate that the textual model originated in Naples. Other small one-line initials mark lections from three traditions: Naples, St Columba's churches and Rome's new liturgy for the stations of the Cross on Good Friday, which found its way into Roman liturgical manuscripts around 715.

The text of the canon tables relates to that of Aquileia at the head of the Adriatic. This is another symbolic enshrinement of four different traditions and the year 715 figures in them all: Naples was regained from Islam and Arian heresy; Aquileia was healed of a centuries-old schism during which it had two simultaneous archbishops; the Roman stational liturgy was enshrined in liturgical books from about that year, celebrating the unity of reconciliation represented by the Cross; Iona, final bastion of Columban separatism, relinquished its own traditions for dating Easter and the tonsure and conformed to the international orthodoxy of Chalcedon. The next year, Abbot Ceolfrith of Monkwearmouth–Jarrow set off for Rome to retire, taking with him one of three massive single-volume Bibles, the result of painstaking scholarship by Bede and his brethren to reconstruct Jerome's Vulgate. This, the Codex Amiatinus, survives in the Medici library in Florence and served as an ambassador to Rome, showing that in these islands at the edge of the world, the apostolic mission had reached completion. The Lindisfarne Gospels is every bit as sophisticated and international but adopts its own visual solutions to complex issues and situates its maker and his world within a spiritual eternity in which sublime harmony is envisioned – if not now, then in the eternal kingdom to come.

Like other iconic and much-visited landmarks, such as Michelangelo's dome of St Peter's in Rome, the Lindisfarne Gospels carried on being quoted visually in other great Insular Gospel books made later in the century, such as the St Chad Gospels (Lichfield Cathedral, MS 1), whose artist was permitted to study Lindisfarne's main painted pages to design simpler versions of his own in the mid-eighth century. This was probably made at Lindisfarne or, more likely, its daughter-house founded in Mercia at Lichfield by St Chad of Lindisfarne in 669. The manuscript was in Wales by the mid-ninth century, where it served as a focus of St Teilo's shrine at Llandeilo Fawr. There the earliest post-Roman documents freeing slaves were added in its margins, these manumissions representing Christian ethics in action. The Bodmin Gospels soon followed suit and probably also the Lindisfarne Gospels.

During the second half of the eighth century the political and cultural focus shifted to the kingdom of Mercia in the English Midlands, which is discussed in the next chapter. There different styles, emphases and affiliations were expressed in its illuminated manuscripts, many of which fall into what is known as the 'Tiberius Group', named after a distinctive member of the group in the British Library, Cotton MS Tiberius C II, the fourth oldest surviving example of Bede's *Historia ecclesiastica*.

The 'Hiberno-Saxon' tradition continued elsewhere, however, and the Lindisfarne Gospels and related works continued to be referred to visually at the end of the century when a magnificent new shrine book of St Columba was made, the Book of Kells. To borrow an architectural analogy, Kells is the baroque to Lindisfarne's Palladianism, incorporating full-page miniatures of the Temptation, the Arrest and the Virgin and Child and building a vast cast of narrative and symbolic figures and animals, which form part of initials and line-fillers, extending the multivalent reading and rabbinic numerology even further. This breathtaking book was probably begun on Iona, but by 806 the intensity of the Viking raids, which had first targeted Holy Island in 793, caused the monks to move to Kells in Ireland, where it is likely that work on the book continued. Scholars have debated how many artists and scribes were involved; the most recent study by Donncha MacGabhann has argued that it was the work of two people, one of whom was left to continue the work. This would accord with my contention that the spirituality of the Columban federation favoured such major copies of Scripture being the work of a single, spiritually experienced scribe, as Columba himself had laboured single-handedly on his Psalter, in the manner of the desert fathers, and as Eadfrith had on the Lindisfarne Gospels. If that scribe were not also a gifted artist, it may have been considered acceptable to collaborate.

In 1006 the Book of Kells was stolen and found a few months later discarded in a ditch, its treasure binding having been torn off. The spiritual values enshrined in such sublime masterworks of faith, respected in a former age, were not enough to save them in the troubled times to come. They still inspire awe, however, and when the Normano-Welshman Gerald of Wales saw a similar volume at the shrine of St Brigid in the late twelfth century he would still write that it was so intricate and exquisite in its workmanship that you would think it the work not of man, but of angels. This has occasioned speculation as to whether it was the Book of Kells that Gerald saw in Kildare, but there is no evidence for this and a measure of competition between the major monastic federations makes it unlikely that a cult book of St Columba would be at St Brigid's shrine. Rather, Kildare would have had its own magnificent manuscript, its 'book of the high altar'.

2

THE NINTH CENTURY:
BISHOP ÆTHELWALD'S PRAYERBOOK

THE BOOK OF CERNE (CAMBRIDGE UNIVERSITY LIBRARY, MS LL.I.10)

Mercia, named for the Anglian people of the marches or borderlands (now the English Midlands and the Welsh Borders), is the Anglo-Saxon kingdom that emerged supreme from the maelstrom of competing territories in the eighth century, in what was Migration Period Britain. The formidable King Penda the Pagan of Mercia (*c.* 606–655, rose to power from 628) had fought hard to stem the advancing tide of Christianity and of Northumbrian expansion, defeating and killing both Edwin and Oswald before meeting his own death in battle against Oswald's brother, King Oswiu, in 655. The conversion of Penda's son, King Wulfhere of Mercia (r. 658–75), did not prevent him, however, from supplanting Oswiu of Northumbria's overlordship of southern England. Under three particularly strong rulers – Æthelbald (r. 716–57), Offa (r. 757–96) and Cenwulf (r. 796–821) – a powerful Mercian hegemony was formed in which the Anglo-Saxon territories lying south of the River Humber were brought together under the overlordship of the Mercian king. We have all heard of Offa's Dyke, but less known is that Offa established a third archbishopric at Lichfield when Canterbury refused to anoint his son as co-ruler in his lifetime, that he was the first English king to have his queen crowned alongside him at his coronation, that he assassinated most of his relatives to secure the succession, that he had imperial ambitions and embarked upon a trade war with his 'cousin' Charlemagne (who complained of the shorter-than-usual length of English-exported cloaks, to which Offa retorted about the length of Carolingian whetstones for sharpening blades) and that he had minted at Tamworth, his capital, a gold coin (mancus) modelled on Abbasid dinars minted in Baghdad that same year (773), with his own name next to that of Allah.

A mere half century ago there was little known of the book culture of what had become the lost kingdom of Mercia, the study of which having been overshadowed by Sutton Hoo and the golden age of Northumbria. Few manuscripts had been convincingly localized to this most enigmatic area of early Anglo-Saxon England and other limited pieces of evidence of its material culture had received scant attention, despite imposing structures such as the crypt at Repton and sculptures such as those at Breedon on the Hill and Sandbach being readily visible. The historical perception of these 'johnny come lately' people of the marches was one of belligerent opposition to Christian conversion and to the establishment of authority by other fledgling Anglo-Saxon states, notably Northumbria. Much of this, of course, was coloured by the perception of our principal rapporteur of the Insular age – Bede. The leaves of the *Historia ecclesiastica* are metaphorically stained with the blood spilled by wicked Penda the Pagan, the Mercian ruler who allied with the perfidious Christian king of the Welsh, Cadwallon, to oppose the civilizing influence of Northumbria's kings and their missionaries. What, however, might a Mercian have said of the attempts by the rulers of Northumbria, Kent and East Anglia to carve up the map of post-Roman Britain, leaving them to push forward the frontiers against the strangers/Welsh while threatening their flanks with encroachments of their own? This, rather than trenchant paganism, in turn engendered the Mercian alliance with the Christian Welsh whose churchmanship placed them beyond the pale in the eyes of Bede and those who, with Rome, embraced international orthodox practices and structures. The post-Bedan period did not fare much better at the pens of historians seduced by the rise of Wessex and the forging of a nation-state by Alfred and his heirs.

Alfred, of course, became 'the Great', the saviour of learning and religion and defender of the English against the Viking scourge, while the best known of his Mercian precursors, Offa, is remembered mainly for his Dyke and, by some, for his successful attempts to wipe out his own family to neutralize the threat of a takeover. To add ignominy to intrigue, when the Vikings struck, England's immediate fate was ceded to the Danes by Mercia's leaders, while its salvation was left to the scions of Wessex's royal house, the last of whom, Alfred, conducted a courageous guerrilla campaign from the Athelney marshes. This overshadowing of Mercia's achievements in favour of those of the West Saxons is long-lived, probably commencing with the editing out of much of the former's contribution by Alfred's biographer and the compilers of the *Anglo-Saxon Chronicle*. Traces of the Mercian annals linger therein, but they are faint. The victor writes history – in more ways than one. Fortunately, our view now is more balanced, fleshed out by the painstaking work of historians, diplomatists, numismatists and researchers of place names and landscape. Most spectacularly, the body of material evidence has been augmented beyond recognition by a series of major archaeological finds in what has been termed 'l'archéologie du livre': the excavation of evidence from a close study of the materiality of the manuscript book.

Book of Cerne, the Lorica of Laidcenn/Loding, *a protective Irish prayer, with planned Old English gloss (Cambridge University Library,* MS *Ll.1.10, f. 43r), made in Lichfield in the 820s for its bishop, Æthelwald, as his personal prayerbook. The script is Insular cursive minuscule, enlivened by Mercian 'Tiberius Group' whimsical beasties. The initial itself is in the 'Trewhiddle Style' emulating contemporary silver-niello metalwork.*

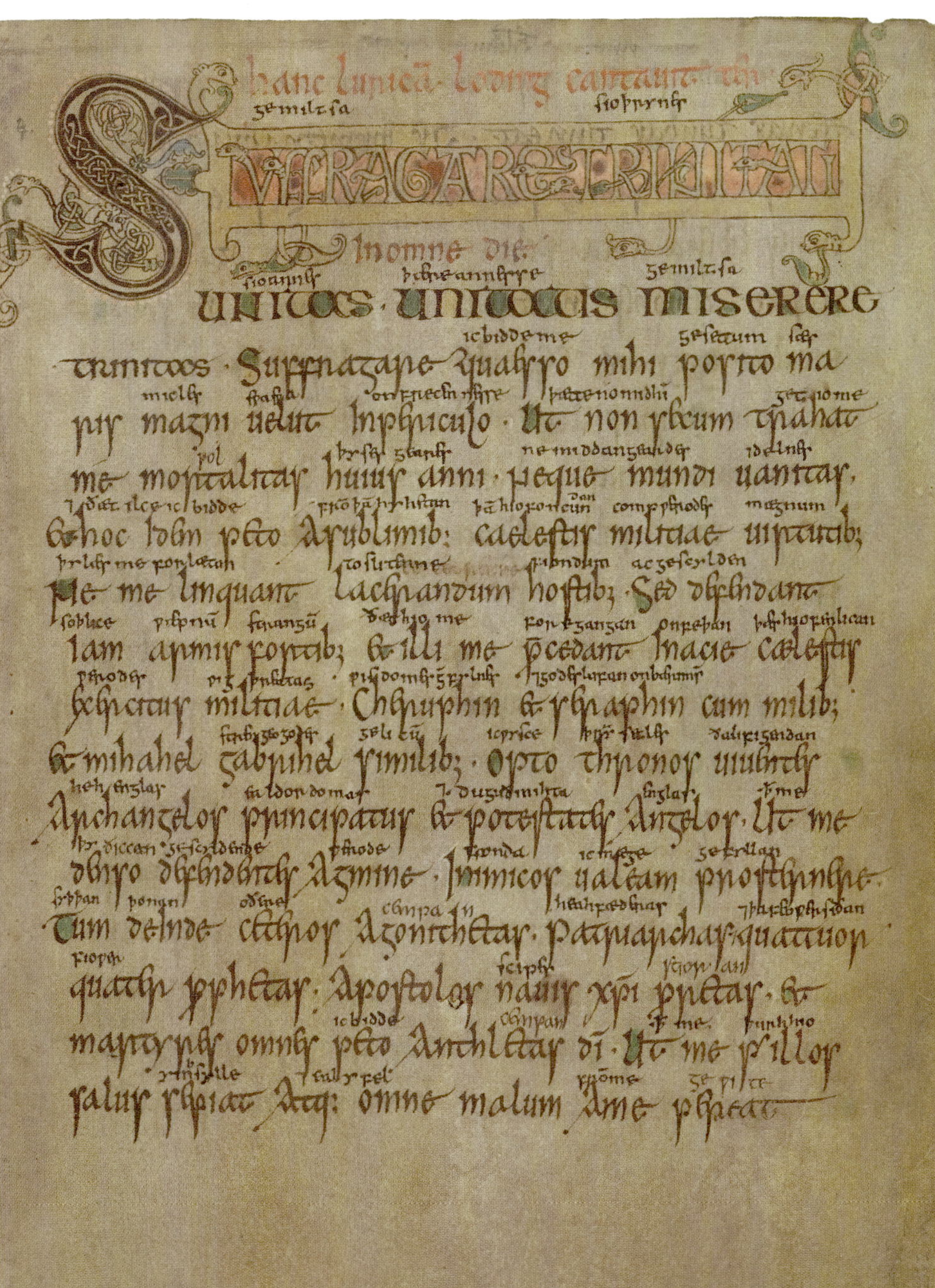
hanc luricam lodgen cantauit ter in omne die.

SUFRAGARE TRINITAS UNITAS UNITATIS MISERERE trinitas. Suffragare quaeso mihi posito maris magni uelut in periculo. Ut non secum trahat me mortalitas huius anni neque mundi uanitas. Et hoc idem peto a sublimibus caelestis militiae uirtutibus; Ne me linquant lacerandum hostibus; Sed defendant iam armis fortibus; & illi me praecedant in acie caelestis exercitus militiae. Cherubin & seraphin cum milibus; & mihahel & gabrihel similibus; Opto thronos uirtutes archangelos principatus & potestates angelorum. Ut me denso defendentes agmine inimicos ualeam prosternere. Tum deinde ceteros agonithetas. Patriarchas quattuor quater prophetas. Apostolos nauis christi proretas. & martyres omnes peto anthletas dei. Ut me per illos salus sepiat atque omne malum a me pereat

At the beginning of the Viking raids, with the sacking of Lindisfarne in 793 and the invasion of Kent from 835, Mercia led the English resistance until it was eventually overwhelmed and King Burgred (r. 852–74) fled to Rome in the face of a concerted Danish invasion. His successor, Ceolwulf (*fl.* 874–9), was the last king of the Mercians, but is dismissed in the *Anglo-Saxon Chronicle* (composed in Wessex during Alfred's reign) as 'a foolish king's thegn' who was a puppet of the Vikings. However, the key role played by Mercia prior to this time was strategically downplayed in West Saxon records in order to showcase their own contribution.

By 878 East Anglia and Northumbria had fallen to the Danes and Mercia was partitioned between the English and the Vikings, with eastern Mercia being absorbed into the Danelaw. In 878 King Alfred of Wessex won a crucial victory at the Battle of Edington and soon afterwards the English-controlled western half of Mercia came under the rule of Æthelred II, Lord of the Mercians (r. *c.* 883–911), who accepted Alfred's overlordship. Alfred adopted the title King of the Anglo-Saxons, claiming to rule all of the free English. In the mid-880s Alfred sealed a strategic alliance between the surviving English kingdoms by marrying his daughter (by his Mercian queen, Ealhswith) Æthelflæd to Æthelred. Æthelflæd, Lady of the Mercians (*c.*870–918), proved a wise and valiant leader and was instrumental in implementing her father's plan to reconquer the Danelaw, alongside her brother, King Edward the Elder.

This turbulent period of violent raiding, rapine and desecration, until the Vikings had carved out a territory of their own (after which many soon began converting to Christianity and settling down to trading and farming), led to the destruction of many of Mercia's cultural assets, including its libraries. A meagre percentage of the books and documents made there still survive, but a number of the illuminated manuscripts that do – many of them evacuated out at the time – form part of what is known as the 'Tiberius Group', named after a typical stylistic member known by its British Library shelf mark, Cotton MS Tiberius C II, an early ninth-century Canterbury copy of Bede's *Historia ecclesiastica*. Another important member of the group is the Book of Cerne (Cambridge University Library, MS Ll.1.10).

The Book of Cerne, also known as the Prayerbook of Bishop Æthelwald of Lichfield (d. 830), was Æthelwald's personal devotional manual, one of four that survive from the Anglo-Saxon kingdom of Mercia. The other three are rare in having been made for, and probably by, women – they present some of the best surviving evidence for female literacy and book production and consumption in this period. These will also be discussed. Together, this little group of books represent the earliest attempt to structure personal prayer around a central theme. In Æthelwald's case this was the Communion of Saints. An original Old English preface instructed him on how to perform his devotions, first prostrating himself before the altar and the whole company of the faithful, past, present and future. A further use of Old English in this remarkable book is the inclusion of a gloss to the Latin *Lorica of Laidcenn/Loding* (composed in Ireland), which is by the main text hand and which was planned, as the generous spacing between the lines indicates.

Mercian scribes also played their part in helping to spread the Word, not only in the most recent of the sacred languages of Scripture, Latin, but also in their own tongue. Alfred is, again, credited with stimulating the use of written Old English to facilitate spiritual and educational revival, although Bede also expressed an interest in the use of the vernacular. The latter, on his deathbed in 735, was translating St John's Gospel to share it with all, free from the persecution that would beset Wycliffe and Tyndale during less tolerant later times.

Fragments of poetry and inscriptions survive from the pre-Alfredian period, but it is the Book of Cerne that contains the earliest continuous prose text to have survived. This is its preface (or 'exhortation to prayer', f. 2r), which I have shown was the work of the original scribe and which asserted the user's inclusion in the communal body of Christ, and the English gloss to the Irish *Lorica of Laidcenn/Loding*, which its rubric says was to be recited thrice each day for protection. The particular benefits of reciting these texts daily may have led to them being in the Old English vernacular, which was the everyday language of the book's owner. Sometime during the next twenty years or so, the Vespasian Psalter also received an interlinear gloss, making it the oldest example of a biblical text in the English language to have physically survived (although, as I have recently sought to demonstrate, Bede's translation of part of St John's Gospel, composed in 735, is preserved in the mid-tenth-century gloss to the Lindisfarne Gospels). Mercian manuscripts therefore provide another prominent landmark in the history of book production and linguistic development in Britain.

The main text opens with the four Passion narratives, one from each Gospel, prefaced by complex images of the evangelists in their human and apocalyptic symbolic guise, with unusual inscriptions that allow the viewer to mentally 'click on' keywords from Scripture in order to interpret the way in which each image is a visual commentary upon aspects of the nature of Christ. For example, in the St Luke miniature on f. 21v the full-length bull symbol, which usually identifies the accompanying human symbol, here occupies most of the page and stands beneath an arcade, at the apex of which is a roundel containing a bust of the evangelist as a human scribe. The latter is labelled by the inscription '*hic lucam in humanitate*' ('here is Luke in his human form') and the bull is labelled '*hic lucam forman accepit vituli*' ('here Luke accepts the form of a calf/bull'). This curious choice of vocabulary references Philippians 2:7–8, in which Christ 'made himself nothing by taking the very nature/form of a servant, being made in human likeness. And being found in appearance as a man, he humbled himself by becoming obedient to death – even death on a cross.' By this simple but clever means, the meaning of the evangelist symbol is made apparent – the bull signifying Christ as the sacrificial victim at the Crucifixion – in accordance with the commentaries of Gregory the Great, Augustine of Hippo and Bede. The same strategy is employed in the other three miniatures. This is a sophisticated little package. By the same token, the use of a limited palette of locally available pigments, simply applied, is at odds with the use of expensive powdered 'shell gold', applied with a brush, which uses far more of the precious metal than gold leaf, which belies its somewhat provincial, if engaging, style.

The St Luke evangelist portrait also carries a multicoloured acrostic verse, on the other side of the leaf, which, if you read the first letter of each line vertically down the page, names Æthelwald. His earlier namesake, Bishop Æthilwald (note the different Northumbrian dialect spelling with an 'i') of Lindisfarne (722–40) is also named as the source of an abbreviated Psalter contained further on in the book, along with another item thought to be of Lindisfarne origin around that time, namely the earliest surviving example of liturgical drama – a Harrowing of Hell with responsorial spoken parts, in which Christ liberates Adam and Eve and others gone before who did not have the benefit of his Word. The rest of the original volume consists of a suite of selected prayers, some composed by the earlier church fathers of the East and of the West, such as Augustine and Ephrem the Syrian, and by more recent local authors such as Prince Loding/Laidcenn of Ireland, and has a contemporary Old English gloss to its Latin text. The

*Book of Cerne (*CUL, MS *Ll.1.10), evangelist miniatures of Matthew the Man/Angel (f. 2v), Mark the Lion (f. 12v), Luke the Calf/Bull (f. 21v) and John the Eagle (f. 31v).*

HIC MA
THEUS

HIC MAR
CUS

HIC
LUCAS

HIC
Iohannis

style of the figural decoration in Cerne is whimsical and this is heightened by its endearing zoomorphic initials, with letters formed of creatures, and a Brontosaurus-like menagerie of ornamental line-fillers and terminals to letter strokes, which munch contentedly upon parts of adjacent words, as if ruminating upon the text.

The psalms – the age-old cry 'de profundis' and the jubilant shout of joy that encompass human experience in whatever period – were the mainstay of both public and private prayer throughout the Middle Ages. In this early period priests were expected to be *psalteratus*, to have memorized the whole of the psalms by heart. The earliest example of handwriting from these islands after the Roman period are the Springmount Bog Tablets, a set of long, thin wooden tablets (like shallow trays) covered with wax (in Roman fashion), with extracts from the psalms incised into them with a pointed metal or bone stylus. Some early monastic rules advise the monks to spend their spare time, including when travelling, learning these poetic songs, which were sung at the divine office, eight times every day and night throughout the year. Presumably the monks were not to become so immersed in them that they toppled into the peat bog they were crossing, which served to preserve this otherwise perishable organic object (peat and deserts inhibit the bacterial action that causes organic materials to decay, as they produce an anaerobic environment). Bede is known to have produced an abbreviated psalter for devotional recitation, and probably for teaching, and the one ascribed to Bishop Æthilwald of Lindisfarne, his contemporary, may have been influenced by it – or may even be it.

Æthelwald of Lichfield was one of several reforming bishops in the early ninth century who were inspired by their Carolingian peers on the Continent to attempt to reassert their rights and those of the Church in the face of encroachment by secular rulers and their representatives. Charlemagne's imperial ambitions had been reflected in England by those of King Offa of Mercia, who extended Mercia's overlordship across most of southern and central England in the second half of the eighth century. In his attempts to secure his dynasty, Offa assassinated many of his competitors, including his own family members, but his son outlived him by only a few months. Offa's own mortuary chapel on the banks of the River Ouse is reputed to have been washed away and disappeared as completely as his dynastic schemes, leaving the throne to pass to another king-worthy line in western Mercia. Offa's successor, King Cenwulf of Mercia, set about defusing the situation, restoring Canterbury's status and privileges as the primatial see (Offa having established his own, more biddable archbishopric at Lichfield).

Bishop Æthelwald's efforts therefore focused upon reconciliation and upon celebrating the role of the cathedral's founder, St Chad of Lindisfarne, in converting Mercia. His prayerbook echoes the style and colouring of the Lichfield Angel, a fragment of the painted stone shrine of St Chad, while the bull of its St Luke miniature resembles a pantomime cow, with mismatched upper and hind quarters. This is because its upper half was modelled upon a half-length evangelist symbol in a famous earlier book, the St Augustine Gospels, thought to have accompanied the missionary Augustine from Rome to Canterbury in 597. They share features such as the stiffly gelled hair ridges between their horns, one quoting the other in a visual homage. The St Augustine Gospels bull would be quoted visually again in the Royal Bible, made in Canterbury during Æthelwald's time. That book is only a part of the whole, having suffered at the hands of the Viking raiders who began devastating Kent and its church libraries after sacking the Isle of Sheppey in 835. One even scratched some graffiti, including a fine Urnes-style Viking great beast, into one of the Royal Bible's grand Byzanto-Carolingian purple-dyed pages. This splendid if mutilated volume, made in Canterbury in the 840s and '50s, marks the final flourish of Insular illuminated manuscript production. Its grandeur, emulating the great Tours Bibles begun by Alcuin and conflating stylistic and iconographic elements from early Christian, Byzantine, Carolingian and Insular art, belies the claims of some scholars that Insular culture was already in decline and was simply dealt the *coup de grâce* by the Viking age. Rather, it was still vibrant, ambitious and erudite in its wide-ranging sources.

The Royal Bible still contains grand full-page titles, painted in gold and silver inks on imperial purple pages, indicating that it once contained full-page facing images, including the annunciation to Zachariah of John the Baptist's birth and the Quadriga horsemen of the Apocalypse. Like the Tiberius Bede, some of its ornament recalls contemporary Mercian silver-niello metalwork with a distinctive style of animal ornament known as the 'Trewhiddle' style, after a hoard of silverwork buried on a site in Cornwall that is now a caravan park. The hoard was never redeemed by the Vikings who presumably plundered and concealed it for later retrieval. Unlike the earlier zoomorphic interlace that characterizes the Lindisfarne Gospels, Trewhiddle and Tiberius Group beasties are complete, independent creatures (in Mercian 'heraldic' fashion). They are often quite whimsical, looking back, archly, over their shoulders. Their sculptural equivalents can be found on some pieces of Mercian stone carving, such as the Cropthorne cross-head and the remarkably rich assembly of sculptures, including architectural friezes that combine Insular ornament with Byzantinizing and near eastern figures, centaurs and Syriac lion hunts, at the church of Breedon on the Hill in Leicestershire.

The Lichfield Angel is a painted sculpture of a Hellenistic-style angel, related to a similar one at Breedon and, like it, dating to around the year 800. Offa's reign had been characterized by wide-ranging, exotic cultural references, emphasizing the international extent of his economic and political aspirations. The angel was found during archaeological excavations in 2003 beneath the crossing of Lichfield Cathedral, which revealed a porch/crypt at the west end of one of the two early gemini churches. Burials had clustered therein around what is thought to be the remains of a shrine, perhaps that of St Chad of Lindisfarne, who founded the cathedral in 669–72. The angel formed part of the gable-end of a house-shaped shrine, in early Christian fashion, and looks as if it has just landed from heaven, via Constantinople. It has an elaborate bouffant coiffure, clinging dampfold drapery revealing the form beneath, as if fresh from the shower, and splendid feathered wings. It probably formed half of the end panel of the stone shrine, as part of an Annunciation to the Virgin. Much of its original paintwork survives, for although the shrine had been broken up someone had placed this fragment face down in this sacred site and buried it, to protect it. The palette consists of shades of purple to white, perhaps referencing both the imperial dignity accorded to purple and also the exegesis of Bede, which linked the shades of purple of the hangings in the Temple to the

stages of the journey of the just soul. The colouring and treatment of the angel's wings are closely echoed in those of the eagle evangelist symbol in the Book of Cerne's St John miniature, which may have been designed consciously to emulate St Chad's shrine, while the emphasis on purple in the palette also recalls that of the mid-eighth-century St Chad Gospels, which may have been displayed at the altar adjacent to the shrine's original location.

The refurbishment of Chad's shrine in the early ninth century may conceivably be related to the cathedral's demotion back to episcopal status, from its temporary elevation to archiepiscopal rank under Offa. King Cenwulf may have thus honoured the shrine in recompense for his restitution to Canterbury of its dignity and properties, acknowledging the undiminished sanctity of Mercia's key cathedral, or the community and bishop may themselves have done so. By visually alluding to the shrine, Bishop Æthelwald's prayerbook would have served as an eloquent visual reminder of his episcopal succession from the cathedral's founder, St Chad of Holy Island.

Another important sculpture, from the eighth century, was found at Repton in Derbyshire. It depicts an impressively moustachioed and armed mounted warrior wearing a diadem, who is thought perhaps to be the Mercian King Æthelbald, who was buried in the eighth-century crypt-cum-baptistry at Repton church in 757. It was remodelled in the ninth century, probably to serve as the mausoleum for further Mercian royalty, gaining impressive barley-twist stone columns modelled upon those in

Opposite: *The Lichfield Angel, part of a house-shaped shrine of St Chad,* c. *800 (Lichfield Cathedral).* Above: *St Chad Gospels (also known as the Lichfield or Llandeilo Gospels), evangelist miniature of St Luke (Lichfield Cathedral Library,* MS *1, p. 218). Probably made in Lichfield in the mid-8th century, the volume was in Wales a century later. The marginal inscription records that it was swapped by Welshman Gelhi, in return for his best white horse, and presented by him to the shrine of St Teilo at Llandeilo Fawr, where documents, including manumissions freeing slaves, were added in its margins – the earliest extant Welsh handwriting.*

St Peter's in Rome, having received the burials of King Wiglaf (d. 839), who spent his reign combatting the Vikings and the expansionism of King Ecgberht of Wessex, and his grandson, the saintly prince Wystan/Wigstan. The latter resigned his claim to the throne in favour of the religious life but was nonetheless killed by a kinsman about 840; his shrine there became a place of pilgrimage. The crypt was later filled in and lost sight of until the 1770s, when a workman fell through its ceiling. In the 1970s and '80s excavations were conducted in the church and in the neighbouring vicarage garden by Harold Taylor and Martin and Birthe Biddle, who were intrigued by a report submitted to the Society of Antiquaries in the eighteenth century of a gravedigger's claims to have found a giant's burial there. These were dismissed as drunken fabrication. However, the dig revealed in the garden an Anglo-Saxon chapel full of the bones of around three hundred individuals – mostly young and middle-aged men but around 20 per cent were women and children – and the remains of a very large, tall individual at their midst. Was this a charnel house filled with the remains of the prominent double monastery and its young charges, or the remains of the Viking Great Army, which overwintered at Repton after attacking it in 873, and either their camp followers or some of the monastery's nuns and the children committed to their care? Analysis revealed it to be the latter. The excavations also revealed the slipways constructed to haul the Viking longships ashore for the winter, during which the army was decimated by plague. The ground still holds many secrets of this remarkable age, but the manuscripts that have survived also repay careful excavation, to unlock the various forms of evidence that these most complex of artefacts contain.

The other three surviving Mercian prayerbooks are all today in the British Library: Harley MS 7653 (the Harleian Prayerbook), Harley MS 2965 (the Book of Nunnaminster) and Royal MS 2 A XX (the Royal Prayerbook). All were made in western Mercia, in the area around Worcester and Winchcombe (where the Mercian royal archives were kept by its abbess), with the Book of Cerne, the last of them, being made in Lichfield for its bishop in the 820s. The other three date from circa 790 to 820 and all show signs of having been made by and/or for women. Together, they provide the most tangible evidence for female literacy and book manufacture in the all-too-slight surviving material evidence. Further notable examples of such women involved in books at this time include Abbess Eadburh of Minster-in-Thanet, who was a good friend to St Boniface, Apostle to the Germans, and who supplied books for his mission to the Germanic homelands in answer to his letters during the second quarter of the eighth century. In these he requested that she and her nuns provide him with books decorated with gold to wow the locals (the visual and aural theatrical panoply of worship being designed to impress long enough to give the opportunity of preaching and conversion) and written in large writing (uncial script), rather than the small 'joined-up' writing (minuscule), for his eyesight was no longer so good.

A copy of the Acts of the Apostles, thought to have been copied at Minster-in-Thanet at this time (Oxford, Bodleian Library, MS Selden Supra 30), even bears what I have interpreted as the proofreading marks of Abbess Eadburh, presumably in her own hand, scratched with a stylus into the lower margin of one of its leaves (p. 47), reading 'EADB LEX'. The learned abbess was evidently very hands on.

As my work and that of Rosamond McKitterick on Merovingian and Carolingian Gaul has shown, women were responsible for making luxury manuscripts not only for the mission fields (where women such as Boniface's kinswoman, Leoba, who was lauded as the greatest poet of the age but none of whose work is known to survive, were active on the perilous front line) but for the great high altars of the day. Another early instance of the probable work of a female Mercian scribe is the section added around 700 in uncial script to a copy of Jerome's Commentary on Ecclesiastes, an Italian manuscript of about 500, containing an inscription that indicates ownership by Abbess Cuthswith of Inkberrow, Worcestershire (Universitätsbibliothek Würzburg, M.p.th.q.2, f. 1).

Although claimed as Canterbury products, where their provenance indicates they were later in the Middle Ages and whence Minster-in-Thanet's properties passed as a result of the Viking raids, the opulent earlier manuscripts of the Southumbrian Tiberius Group – the Vespasian Psalter (British Library, Cotton MS Vespasian A I) of the 730s, which contains the earliest historiated/story-telling initials that would become such an important feature of medieval illumination, and the Stockholm Codex Aureus (Stockholm, Royal Library, MS A.135 – are dripping with gold leaf, with classicizing figural forms, and are penned in elegant uncials,

Overleaf: *David composing the Psalms, the Vespasian Psalter, Psalm 27 (BL, Cotton MS Vespasian A I, ff. 30v–31r), made in Canterbury or Minster-in-Thanet, Kent, in the 730s. It features the earliest historiated initials (the one here depicting David and Jonathan shaking hands) and has an Old English interlinear gloss, added in the mid-9th century.*

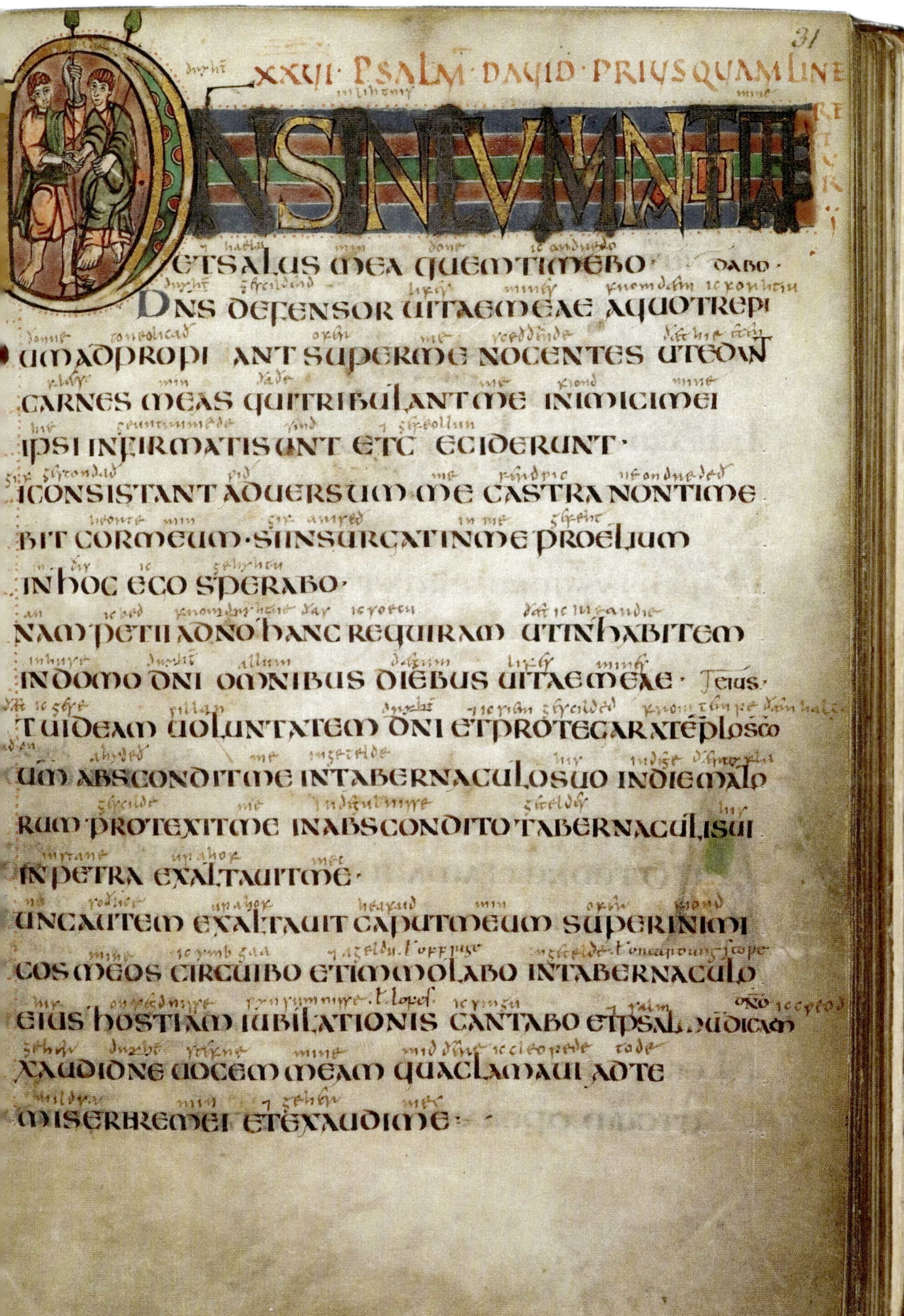

XXVI· PSALM· DAUID· PRIUSQUAM LINE RETUR

DNS INLUMINATIO MEA

ETSALUS MEA QUEM TIMEBO· DABO·
DNS DEFENSOR UITAE MEAE A QUO TREPI
UM ADPROPI ANT SUPER ME NOCENTES UT EDANT
CARNES MEAS QUI TRIBULANT ME INIMICI MEI
IPSI INFIRMATI SUNT ET CECIDERUNT·
SI CONSISTANT ADUERSUM ME CASTRA NON TIME
BIT COR MEUM· SI INSURGAT IN ME PROELIUM
IN HOC EGO SPERABO·
UNAM PETII A DNO HANC REQUIRAM UT INHABITEM
IN DOMO DNI OMNIBUS DIEBUS UITAE MEAE· T EIUS·
UT UIDEAM UOLUNTATEM DNI ET PROTEGAR A TEMPLO SCO
UM ABSCONDIT ME IN TABERNACULO SUO IN DIE MALO
RUM PROTEXIT ME IN ABSCONDITO TABERNACULI SUI
IN PETRA EXALTAUIT ME·
NUNC AUTEM EXALTAUIT CAPUT MEUM SUPER INIMI
COS MEOS CIRCUIBO ET IMMOLABO IN TABERNACULO
EIUS HOSTIAM IUBILATIONIS CANTABO ET PSALMUM DICAM DNO
EXAUDI DNE UOCEM MEAM QUA CLAMAUI AD TE
MISERERE MEI ET EXAUDI ME·

fitting the specification for Boniface's contemporary commissions to Abbess Eadburh and conceivably made in Minster-in-Thanet. They are both written in elegant uncials (some of the Codex Aureus's pages being purple-dyed in imperial style) and the figure-style is well modelled and naturalistic, in Roman and Syriac fashion. The Vespasian Psalter features a miniature depicting David, his musicians and scribes composing the Psalms, in which the king plays a lyre that is very like that found in the Sutton Hoo ship mound a century earlier, fusing the Germanic and Antique legacies that these new 'heirs of Rome' had inherited. They also contain the other ingredients of Insular art – La Tène ornament, zoomorphic ornament (but in the form of independent 'heraldic' beasts rather than zoomorphic interlace), Byzantine blossom, Greek key patterns and other Antique ornaments – but these occur independently, rather than woven into a whole in the manner of the Northumbrian and Irish manuscripts.

I reached the conclusion that these three prayerbooks were women's books by analysing the thematic nature of their textual compilations, by studying their language and by their provenances (the evidence for the biography of the book – where it has been and whom it has met between its production and the present). The Harleian Prayerbook is now but a fragment of its former self, yet, like the other two, it nonetheless evinces signs of adaptation of some of its Latin linguistics to female use. For example, even prayers that are ascribed to male authors may begin in the masculine voice and drift in mid-course into the feminine voice. Thus, a *peccator* (male sinner) ends as a *peccatrice* (female sinner), as if the power of oral recitation by women has overcome the primacy of the written source in a male voice. The Royal Prayerbook also reveals a female reader-focus in its choice of components to group around

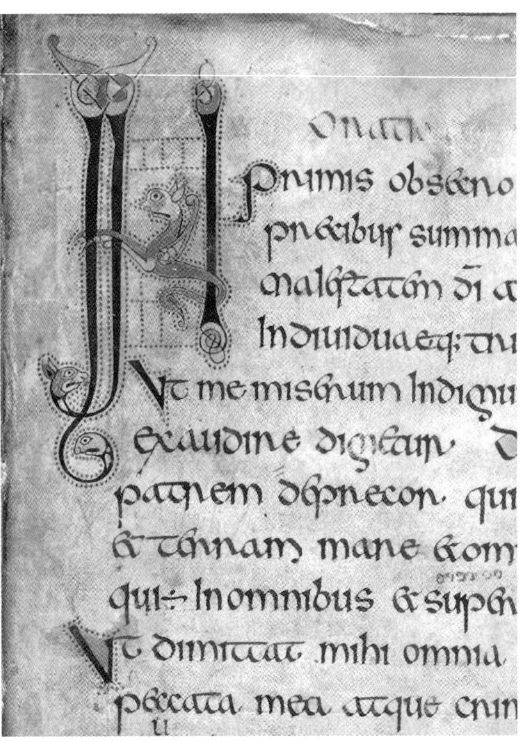

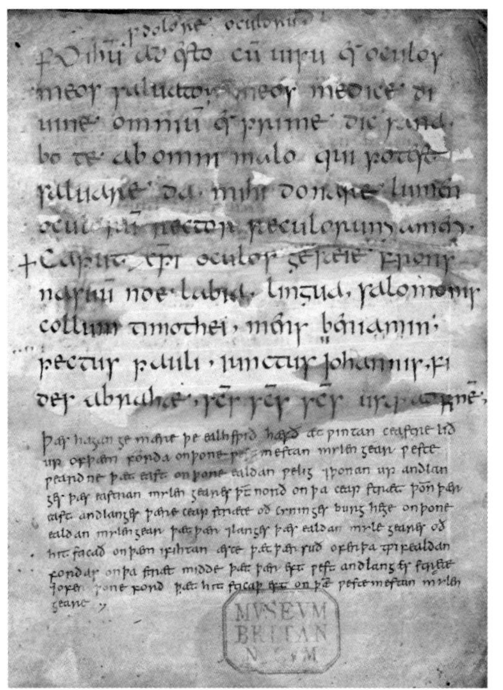

its central theme: Christ as the *sanus et salus*, the health and salvation of the world. Its opening Gospel extracts focus upon miracles of healing, several featuring women, such as the raising of Jairus's daughter and the healing of the woman with the flow of blood. Its prayers and charms revolve around spiritual and physical healing and it is possible that it was made for a female physician who was perhaps a nun. Its decoration features a senmurv, an unusual beast of Persian origin, which is a hybrid of mammal, bird and fish, symbolizing the union of the elements of earth, air and water – another example of Mercian Eastern exoticism.

The Book of Nunnaminster also displays feminine linguistic elements and has a strong provenance indicating female ownership. In a blank space on its final page is written a record of 'Lands that Ealhswith had in Wintonceastre'. Ealhswith (d. 902) was the Mercian noblewoman who married King Alfred the Great in 868, while he was heir apparent. Her mother was Eadburh, a member of the Mercian royal family, and it is likely that she was descended from King Cenwulf, which would have served to legitimize, or at least render more palatable, the West Saxon overlordship of Mercia. Ealhswith may have been given or bequeathed the volume by her mother or another Mercian noblewoman. She herself is said to have founded a nunnery, the Nunnaminster next to the New Minster, in what is now the cathedral close, at Winchester. When it was excavated by the Biddles,

Opposite: *The Royal Prayerbook* (BL, *Royal* MS 2 A XX, *f. 17r), a female physician's prayerbook from early 9th-century western Mercia. This folio detail features a playful initial with a Persian senmurv, combining the elements of mammal, fish and bird, one of many exotic influences apparent in Mercia at this time.* Above: *The Book of Nunnaminster* (BL, *Harley* MS *2965, f. 40v), the end of the early 9th-century prayerbook with a land grant added below at the start of the 10th century recording the property owned by Ealhswith, wife of Alfred the Great, who founded the Nunnaminster in Winchester and who probably owned this book.*

the area in which it sits was found to correspond to the land boundaries cited in the Book of Nunnaminster's record. It is probable that the book was bequeathed by the dowager queen to her nunnery, where Benedictine devotional and liturgical annotations were added by tenth-century nuns, and that it was considered a suitably sacred text in which to enter the record of her important foundation gift, rendering it both additionally legally binding and an acceptable gift to God. Presumably the book was left to it along with other of her properties, to sustain and inspire other women for the spiritual resistance to the pagan Viking onslaught that Ealhswith's offspring by Alfred sought to repel.

The presence of earlier books evacuated from parts of southern and central England overrun by the Danes, especially those from Mercia, into Wessex, free western Mercia and the Welsh Marches served to influence the style of pointed cursive minuscule script and zoomorphic initials employed by King Alfred and the scholarly equipe he assembled during the 880s, after he had retaken London and established the demarcation line of the border with the Danelaw, which he immediately sought to push back.

A copy of the Old English translation of Pope Gregory the Great's *Cura pastoralis* (Pastoral Care) was sent by Alfred to his Mercian tutor Bishop Werferth of Worcester, along with an *aestel* (Old English for a spear or pointer, from the Latin *hasta*) made of precious metals and jewels/enamels, known as the Alfred Jewel (now in the Ashmolean Museum, Oxford). The *aestel* was probably intended to function like a Jewish liturgical *yad*, the bone pointer that would have been inserted into the 'jewel' helping the reader to follow the lines of the text without touching them. It would also have served as a metaphor for the pastoral guidance of the bishops, leading their people along the paths of righteousness and strengthening their spiritual and moral fibre for the fight against the pagan Viking forces. At the centre of the jewel, protected by its rock crystal covering, is an enamel in the Byzantine cloisonné technique, depicting a front-facing, half-length male figure holding a rod and staff (in the manner of ancient rulers, as referred to by the psalmist: 'your rod and your staff, they comfort me'). This is thought to represent sight or vision. The book that it accompanied is known as the Hatton Pastoral Care (Bodleian, Hatton MS 20) and was made in Winchester in the 990s. Its script and initials are indebted to earlier Mercian work. Several smaller *aestels* have also been found (for example, at Minster Lovell and Salisbury) and presumably accompanied copies for other bishops.

Alfred assembled a group of scholars, as Charlemagne had done at Aachen a century earlier, including his tutor, Bishop Werferth, and his fellow Mercians, Ethelstan, Plegmund and Werwulf, John the Old Saxon, Grimbald the Frank and Alfred's biographer, Bishop Asser of St David's in Wales, whom he made Bishop of Sherborne. Together, and with Alfred perhaps participating himself and the work spilling over into his son's reign, they embarked on a programme of translating into Old English some key works, designed to bolster the resistance of the English to the pagan influx and to improve their faith. These included the *Consolation of Philosophy* by Boethius, St Augustine's *Soliloquies*, Pope Gregory's *Pastoral Care* and the first fifty psalms of the Psalter, which Alfred is credited with translating himself, Orosius's *Histories Against the Pagans*, Bede's *Ecclesiastical History*, and the annals of his own people (including those of Mercia) in the *Anglo-Saxon Chronicle*, which was made for someone in his circle, but probably not a royal initiative.

Welsh readers will, I am sad to say, be disappointed to learn that the two illuminated manuscripts that have often been thought to have been made in Wales, the St Chad Gospels (known in Wales as the Llandeilo Gospels) and the Hereford Gospels (MS P.I. 2), probably were not, although relations with Wales have played a big part in their stories and the St Chad Gospels does contain what may be the earliest Welsh handwriting to have survived. There are, of course, unilluminated Welsh books and there would have been others. The earliest extant Welsh illuminated book is the Ricemarch Psalter (Trinity College Dublin MS 50), which was made between 1064 and 1082 by the scribe Ithael and the artist John in the scriptorium at Llanbadarn Fawr and given by Ithael to his brother Rhygyfarch/Ricemarch, who lived at the school at St David's. Their father, Sulien, became Bishop of St David's in 1072 and had spent some thirteen years studying in Ireland, which is reflected in the style of the illumination and lettering in the contemporary Hiberno-Norse style, which harks back to that of the Insular period.

The early ninth-century Hereford Gospels, which has also sometimes been attributed to Wales, likewise exhibits cultural affinities with Hiberno-Saxon manuscripts, contemporary Irish script and art styles, and Mercian manuscript culture of primarily western Mercian character, while alluding visually to works such as the Barberini Gospels from the farthest eastern fenland reaches of Mercia around 800 (where there is a related group of sculptures around Peterborough). What might this suggest concerning its origins?

The Hereford Gospels' closest relative, in many ways, is the St Chad Gospels, which was probably made for the shrine of St Chad at Lichfield in the mid-eighth century. The only extant example of script likely, demonstrably, to be from Hereford itself at this period is a charter that remains in Hereford Cathedral Archives (HCA 4067). This is a charter of Bishop Cuthwulf of Hereford, renting an estate on the River Frome to the ealdorman Ælfstan, dated 840–52. The Hereford scriptorium is the probable source of this document, which is written in an elegant Phase II pointed minuscule that

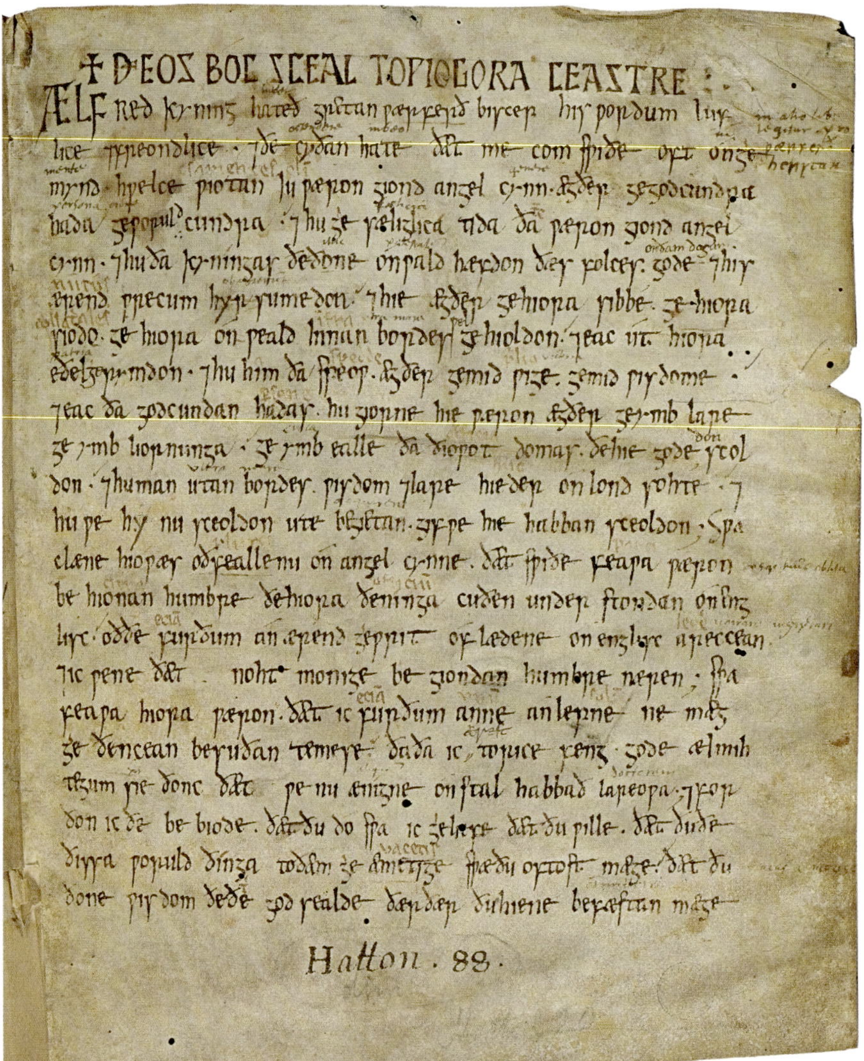

The Pastoral Care *(opposite), composed by Gregory the Great in Latin and translated into Old English in the late 9th century by or for King Alfred the Great (Bodleian Library,* MS *Hatton 20, f. 1r). This copy was sent by Alfred to his tutor, Bishop Werferth of Worcester, along with an* aestel *(pointer), thought to have been the Alfred Jewel (above), which is inscribed 'Alfred had me made' in Old English. Other copies and* aestels *were sent to other bishops to encourage them to direct the English people in the way towards God and to strengthen their resolve against the pagan Vikings.*

finds its closest parallels in Mercian charters of the second quarter of the ninth century and in the Book of Cerne. The influence of Lichfield's scriptorium evidently continued to be exerted at Hereford, and it seems possible that its Gospel book was in fact made at Hereford as part of the developmental phase of book production associated with western Mercia from about 780 to 820. After this, Mercian practices were modernized in response to developments at the Canterbury Cathedral scriptorium, begun by Archbishop Wulfred (805–32), who was himself a scribe. Although a Mercian noble, he was intent upon restoring Canterbury's privileges, which had been rescinded by King Offa in favour of his new, and more amenable, if short-lived, archbishopric of Lichfield. Script reform, to produce more impressive-looking documents, was part of this agenda. The Hereford Gospels belongs to the preceding phase of script development and is probably of late eighth- or, more likely, early ninth-century date and made in Hereford.

It is intriguing, and may be telling, that the eastern Mercian artistic milieu of the Barberini Gospels, which I have suggested was made at Peterborough (Medeshamstede) around the year 800, should also be reflected in some aspects of the decoration of the Hereford Gospels. If the latter was indeed made at Hereford, the establishment there of a shrine dedicated to the cult of St Ethelbert the King during the early ninth century would fit well as a context for contact with eastern Mercia/ East Anglia and provides a possible context for production of the Hereford Gospels.

The origins of Hereford Cathedral are uncertain. There had been missionary activity in the region by figures who feature in Wales (and further afield) – saints David and Dyfrig – and St Chad of Holy Island was active in Mercia from 669, moving his *cathedra* (bishop's seat) from Repton to Lichfield, where a cathedral was built about 700. In 672, the year of Chad's death, Archbishop Theodore of Tarsus restructured the Mercian diocese, splitting it into five parts, with the Magonsaete in southwest Mercia (established *c.* 676) corresponding to what became the Hereford diocese and the diocese of the Hwicce to Worcester. It may be that it took a while for Hereford itself, at a much-frequented ford of the River Wye, to rise to prominence within the existing landscape of church activity. Hereford Cathedral is said to have been (re)founded by Putta (d. 688), who settled there around 676 after he was driven from Rochester by Æthelred of Mercia. Close by the medieval cathedral site is a minster dedicated to St Guthlac (673–714), a princely Mercian warrior turned hermit-monk who trained at Repton and established a hermitage at Crowland in the Fens and whose associations extend from the western to the eastern extremities of Mercia.

Opposite: *The earliest extant Welsh illuminated manuscript, the Ricemarch Psalter (Psalm 1), made in Llanbadarn Fawr, Wales,* c. *1080 (Trinity College Dublin,* MS 50, *fol. 35r).* Above: *Luke miniature from the Book of Deer (*CUL, MS Ii.6.32, *f. 29v), Monastery of Deer, Aberdeenshire, 10th century. This is the earliest extant book from Scotland, other than those that were probably made on Iona.*

The Hereford Gospels (Hereford Cathedral Library, MS P.I. 2, *ff. 35v–36r), Mark incipit opening and chained binding, added when the book was incorporated into the famous 17th-century chained library at Hereford Cathedral, early 8th century.*

Hereford Cathedral is dedicated to two saints, St Mary the Virgin and St Ethelbert the King. The latter was king of East Anglia in the late eighth century. We know little about his reign, other than that he minted his own coinage, featuring images of Romulus and Remus, the founders of Rome, which may indicate an ancestral connection with the Wuffingas dynasty, of Sutton Hoo fame, which also used that iconography, and an aspiration for diplomatic links with Rome. Such expressions of independence may have led to him being beheaded by Offa, king of Mercia, in the year 794. This is said to have taken place at Sutton Walls, near Hereford, during Ethelbert's visit to conclude his proposed marriage to Offa's daughter, Ælfthyth/Alfreda (who is said subsequently to have become a recluse at Crowland before heading to Rome on pilgrimage, thereby signalling either that she had not been complicit in his murder or that she felt the need to expiate the sin of her father in this regard through her own spiritual devotion).

Ethelbert's body is said to have been brought to Hereford by 'a pious monk' and was buried there. The first reliably recorded bishop of Hereford,

Wulfheard, appears in 803. Miracles occurred at the site during the early ninth century and by about 830, around the time that the ancient ford was being transformed into a fortified centre, Milfrid, a Mercian nobleman, is said to have been moved by them to construct a stone cathedral and shrine on the site of the little wooden church that stood there, and to dedicate it to the sainted king.

It was in this period that the shrine of St Chad of Holy Island, the founder-figure of Lichfield Cathedral, was being upgraded (some 130 kilometres (80 mi.) from Hereford) and the Lichfield Angel polychrome sculpture was being carved as part of a new tomb-shaped shrine. Its decoration echoes that of the mid-eighth-century St Chad Gospels, and I have suggested that this cross-media visual referencing was extended during the 820s to the illuminated prayerbook made at Lichfield for its bishop, Æthelwald.

Might the Hereford Gospels, with its own complementary references to the Hiberno-Saxon saints of the past and to the western and eastern Mercian churches of the present, actually have been made at Hereford during the early ninth century, under the cultural stimulus of recent developments at Lichfield, for the shrine of St Ethelbert the King or for the bishop of Hereford? William of Malmesbury, writing in the early twelfth century, refers to royal and episcopal Saxon tombs and a cross adjacent to Hereford Cathedral.

The manufacture of the Barberini Gospels at Peterborough Cathedral around 800 might also have been related in part to these political events, but rather than associating itself stylistically and culturally with the Hiberno-Saxon idiom (as the Hereford Gospels does), it wears instead a fashionable Southumbrian stylistic cloak of Italo-Byzantine artistic influences combined with contemporary Mercian Tiberius Group influences. The visual rhetoric of the Hereford Gospels on the other hand, despite some signs of influence from such grand artistic trends, retains a provincial 'Celtic' feel consistent with its Welsh border location, and bears similarities in appearance to the earlier great Insular books of the high altar, notably the St Chad Gospels (probably then still at Lichfield), and to the grander of the Irish pocket Gospel books, notably the MacDurnan Gospels, which I have suggested was made at Armagh in the early ninth century as a replacement for a book associated with the cult of St Patrick.

The scale of the Hereford Gospels places it, like the Book of Durrow, in an intermediate position between the full-size Insular Gospel books and the Irish pocket Gospel books. It may have served as the portable Gospels of a leading prelate or have been intended to honour the influence of Irish ecclesiastical influence in Wales and the border area. The scale of its decoration and its probable use as a 'book of the high altar', in which important legal transactions were recorded to confer additional sacrality upon their status, situates it more in the realm of those Insular Gospel books that served a liturgical role in worship in leading centres, often associated with the cults of saintly figures.

Returning to the Hereford historical context, the eighth century saw the rise of the kingdom of Mercia to a position of political supremacy in southern England. The dynasty of kings Æthelbald and Offa was focused upon Tamworth and the Midlands, but expanded its influence and overlordship by the late ninth century to form what might be considered 'Greater Mercia', incorporating Kent, East Anglia and Wessex. From the end of the century the seat of power in Mercia moved to western Mercia, focusing upon centres such as Winchcombe (80 kilometres (50 mi.) from Hereford), where the abbey was the repository for the royal archives.

The first of the rulers from this area, King Cenwulf of Mercia (r. 796–821), was at pains to distance himself from much of Offa's policy and a rapprochement with East Anglia and Kent is marked during his reign. He restored to Canterbury many of the rights, lands and privileges that Offa had transferred to his more compliant short-lived archbishopric of Lichfield, but also ensured that it, and other ecclesiastical centres in his own western Mercian homeland, continued to enjoy his support and that of the Mercian aristocracy. It is possible that Beonna, who was elected Bishop of Hereford at the Synod of Clofesho in 824 and who remained in office until 830, was the same person of that name who was abbot of Medeshamstede in the late eighth and early ninth centuries and who disappears from view around 805.

Milfrid's patronage of Hereford would fit into such a scenario, prior to the escalation of Viking incursions into England. His stone church would have contained the shrine, and both would have needed a copy of Scripture as a focal point. Given its historical and cultural associations and its relatively modest political and economic status as a Mercian border bishopric – one that was well aware of the need to preserve a visual rhetoric of association with its Celtic neighbours and antecedents – we would expect its book of the high altar to look something like the Hereford Gospels.

In the late ninth century the Hereford diocese passed from Mercian rule to that of the new West Saxon rulers of later Anglo-Saxon England and would have formed part of the kingdom's western boundary. William of Malmesbury later records Hereford as the place where King Athelstan (r. 924–39) compelled the rulers of the northern Britons to meet and pay him tribute. That, and the reconquest of the Danelaw begun by his grandfather, father and aunt, would allow Athelstan to claim to be king not only of Wessex, but of all England.

3

THE TENTH CENTURY: KING ATHELSTAN'S OFFERING TO A SHRINE

BEDE'S *LIVES OF ST CUTHBERT* (CORPUS CHRISTI COLLEGE, CAMBRIDGE, MS 183)

King Athelstan (*c.* 894–939), the 'princely rock', was the grandson of King Alfred and Ealhswith, by Edward the Elder and his first wife, Ecgwynn. Alfred was succeeded by his son, Edward the Elder, in 899 and he ruled until 924, consolidating his father's policies and eating further into the Danelaw. His younger son, Ælfweard of Wessex, may have followed him for a few weeks but upon his premature death in 924 his older half-brother Athelstan became king. There seems to have been some resistance to this, however, and he was not crowned until September 925. It may be that there were those in Wessex who found rule by someone raised in Mercia objectionable. Scholars have also debated whether his legitimacy may have been questioned as not much is known about his mother (William of Malmesbury later relates that a nobleman called Alfred plotted to blind Athelstan because of his possible illegitimacy). Such tensions may also have played a role in his statesmanlike arrangements in preparing the ground for his own successor, by consciously not marrying or producing an heir.

Athelstan proclaimed himself King of the Anglo-Saxons from 924 to 927 (a title adopted by Alfred in 886) and King of the English from 927 to his death in 939, acknowledging his territorial gains and the hoped-for process of integration of the Danes. The considerable corpus of Anglo-Scandinavian sculptures from tenth- and eleventh-century England help to chart this process, as the styles and iconographies of English and Scandinavian culture interbred. The Nunburnholme Cross in Yorkshire, for example, shows signs of being a prehistoric standing stone that was carved with the Crucifixion and Insular ornament and received the image of a seated Viking warlord in the tenth century. At Gosforth in Cumbria, in the tenth century, a tall, slender cross was erected juxtaposing the iconographies of Sigurd, Odin and Christ, and a Viking hogback tombstone modelled on their feasting halls has the Crucifixion carved on its end wall.

Athelstan was responsible for extending and consolidating the gains made by his forebears in regaining territory and compelled the rulers of neighbouring Celtic realms to acknowledge his overlordship. He was also one of the most significant royal bibliophiles of the early Middle Ages. His formative years as a youth were spent in the household of his aunt, Alfred's daughter Æthelflæd, Lady of the Mercians, who had married Æthelred, ruler of western Mercia. There, on the volatile borderland with Wales, he learned the art of diplomacy and the strategy of warfare, especially from his aunt, who was so instrumental in the pushback against the Danes and in maintaining peace in the Marches. Æthelflæd died in 918 and was briefly succeeded by her daughter Ælfwynn, but Edward rapidly deposed her and took direct control of Mercia. Ongoing tensions between Wessex and Mercia, and the perennial competition for the succession to power, may have prompted Athelstan's decision not to marry and not to pre-determine his successor and thereby potentially undermine the future of the fragile united England with a single monarchy, which he was instrumental in creating. His sexual or asexual preferences are unknown, though many have speculated, but like his grandfather Alfred he was of a scholarly, pious persuasion and may have viewed his single state as part of a lay quasi-religious vocation. He was, in 2021, voted in a poll run by historians Tom Holland and Dominic Sandbrook (on their podcast *The Rest Is History*) as the most successful ruler of England (although it is uncertain which six Anglo-Saxonists were consulted, as his has not exactly been a household name, worthy though he was).

In 927 he conquered the last remaining Viking kingdom, York, which he seized upon the death of its ruler, Sihtric, to whom Athelstan had married his sister, and became the first Anglo-Saxon ruler of England in its entirety. At Eamont, near Penrith, on 12 July 927, King Constantine II of Alba, King Hywel Dda of Deheubarth, Ealdred of Bamburgh and King Owain of Strathclyde (or Morgan ap Owain of Gwent) all accepted Athelstan's overlordship (making him the first southern ruler to exert overlordship in the North and, through the legacy of his aunt and uncle, in Wales), inaugurating seven years of peace in the North. He set about taking measures towards centralizing government and invited more of his leading subjects, including the Welsh kings who increasingly attended his councils and to whom he accorded precedence over others present. Under Athelstan the royal Witan (royal council) started its journey towards a national assembly and is sometimes seen as a proto-Parliament. The border with Wales was set by him along the River Wye and that with Cornwall along the Tamar, also establishing a bishopric for Cornwall just over that side of the river, at St Germans. In 934 he took a force to Scotland – stopping en route to visit the shrine of St Cuthbert (who was so respected in the North) – to impel its king, Constantine II, to submit to him. Resentment at the extension of Athelstan's overlordship led the Scots and Vikings to unite, along with some Britons, to invade England, only to be decisively defeated at the Battle of Brunanburh in 937, which won Athelstan great repute in Britain and abroad.

After taking York, Athelstan issued new coinage, known as the 'circumscription cross' type, which bore the inscription *Rex totius Britanniae* (King of all Britain). This was followed in the early 930s by the 'crowned bust' type, depicting the king wearing a crown with three prongs, which is how Athelstan is depicted in the miniature showing him with St Cuthbert. The Vikings seized back York after his death, however, and it was not regained until 954.

Athelstan was a great lawgiver, building upon the law code of King Alfred and adding ordinances of his own, such as the Ordinance on Charities, involving the Church more in the law (drawing upon the advice of Archbishop Wulfhelm and his bishops in clerical matters) and making provision against robbery (which he was the first to equate with disloyalty towards the king's person) and for the maintenance of the poor, also freeing a number of those condemned to penal slavery each year. The pace of legal change also indicates the amount of unrest that Athelstan sought to curb.

If his grandfather can be credited with assembling the greatest scholarly equipe since Charlemagne's, then Athelstan can be thanked for establishing the bedrock of royal bibliophilia. He assembled a collection of his own and, encouraged by the Celtic and Carolingian practices of gift-giving books and by the practice of presenting sacred books to shrines, he bestowed several earlier Gospel books to key ancient Celtic and Anglo-Saxon churches, such as Canterbury and Bodmin.

Another such gift was the illuminated copy of Bede's prose and verse lives of St Cuthbert, which he had made in Winchester specifically as a gift to the shrine of St Cuthbert, which was now at Chester-le-Street and had been proving instrumental in conducting a pincer movement with Wessex to ensure the survival of Christianity in the North and fostering diplomacy with the Danelaw. He presented it to the shrine in 934, during his strategic visit there. He also brought a gift of fine textiles, including an exquisitely embroidered stole and maniple (liturgical vestments), which bear the inscription (in translation), 'Aelflaed ordered this to be made' and 'for the pious bishop Frithstan'. Aelflaed was the second wife of Edward the Elder and died in 916; Frithstan was Bishop of Winchester from 909 to 931: the items, therefore, were made between 909 and 916. Athelstan is depicted in the book, cloaked and crowned as the rightful king, presenting this very book to the saint, who stands before his church-shrine and holds a smaller book (perhaps intended to represent the St Cuthbert Gospel, British Library, Add. MS 89000, which is thought to have been placed in his coffin). The frame of the picture contains birds and other creatures inhabiting an elegant vine scroll of white on a dark ink ground, which is reminiscent of both silver-niello metalwork, sculptures and walrus ivory carvings of the period (it particularly resembles an ivory pen case of the period, now in the British Museum), for this 'Winchester Style' can be found across the artistic media.

William of Malmesbury wrote that Athelstan was 'a boy of astonishing beauty and graceful manners' and that Alfred the Great honoured his grandson with a ceremony in which he gave him a purple/crimson cloak, a belt set with gems and a sword with a gilded scabbard, perhaps acknowledging him thereby as a king-worthy potential heir. In the miniature opposite Athelstan wears just such a cloak (the sword and belt may have been deemed inappropriate to depict in the saint's presence). This is the first certain portrait of an English monarch (other than on coins) and served to signal to the North that its most prominent saint conferred divine authority upon his rule, just as he acknowledged the authority of the saint by saying 'this is your life' and bestowing the book containing it upon him. This clever piece of visual royal public relations was indebted to the Carolingian and Ottonian imperial development of ruler imagery, since the time of Charlemagne and Charles the Bald, whose daughter Judith had been King Alfred's stepmother. Athelstan cultivated relations with the Continent, bestowing gifts upon churches in Saxony (it is possible that one of his early tutors was John the Old Saxon, one of the scholars who participated in the Alfredian revival of learning) and receiving books and relics in return from his Ottonian in-laws. He established new ecclesiastical foundations in England, such as Muchelney and Milton Abbas, and probably served as a conduit for ideas concerning the Benedictine Reform movement in England. Two leading figures in the Benedictine monastic reform of Edgar's reign, Dunstan and Æthelwold, served at Athelstan's court early in their careers and were ordained at Winchester at his request.

A great lawgiver and enforcer, Athelstan also set great store by his administration and by the appearance of its output, designed to impress. He appointed a master scribe, known now as Athelstan A, with a fine hand, to pen major charters. An eighth-century Anglo-Saxon Gospel book that he gave to Canterbury Cathedral (British Library, Royal MS I B VII) contains a manumission in Old English, recording that Athelstan freed a family of slaves, at the behest of his mass priest, to mark his accession to the throne.

King Athelstan says 'this is your life' to St Cuthbert (Corpus Christi College (CCC), Cambridge, MS 183, f. 1v) during his visit to the shrine in 934. The king presents St Cuthbert with a copy of Bede's prose and verse lives of the saint made at Winchester in the 930s. The white lead used for the flesh tone has turned silver-black, owing to oxidization.

About 927 or 936 Athelstan is said to have advanced on Cornwall, which was showing signs of making alliances with the Vikings who posed a threat to England. He and his troops went as far as West Penwith, where he put down a Cornish 'last stand' at the Battle of Boleigh (near Lamorna, at the threshold of one of Cornwall's most sacred ancient landscapes around the Merry Maidens stone circle and other prehistoric monuments and the early monastery of St Buryan). He is also said to have 'conquered' the Isles of Scilly, placing the powerful symbol of an iron standard at Land's End (perhaps on the rock formation known as the 'armed knight'). He subsequently took a 'softly, softly' approach, patronizing the cults of St Buriana and St Petroc as part of a policy of peaceful assimilation, giving them enhanced property and power. He is said to have established a college of canons at the Irish St Buriana's sixth-century Irish foundation of St Buryan to celebrate annexing the Isles of Scilly, giving Exeter (to which it then became affiliated) a foothold in the far west and seeking to win hearts and minds by celebrating its Celtic roots. The earliest land grant in Cornwall is a bequest from him to St Buryan, enacted four years after his death. He also gave a Breton Gospel book to the altar of St Petroc in Bodmin, which contains the oldest Cornish place and personal names in the manumissions that were enacted there in the 930s onwards and were recorded in the margins of the sacred book, now known as the Bodmin Gospels (British Library, Add. MS 9381).

Athelstan may have been influenced in adopting this practice of granting manumissions and of having the records of legal transactions that were sworn to by oath before an altar written into the pages of a Gospel book – what I have termed a 'book of the high altar' in the context of such books at the shrines of saints – by the example of contemporary Welsh ruler Hywel Dda, whose epithet 'the Good' was earned by his commitment to justice. He may, in turn, have been influenced by the presence near to his citadel of a mid-eighth-century Gospel book from Lindisfarne or its daughter-house Lichfield, now known as the St Chad Gospels (or the Llandeilo or Lichfield Gospels; Lichfield Cathedral MS 1), which was obtained in the mid-ninth century by the Welshman Gelhi in return for his best white horse and presented by him to the altar of St Teilo in Llandeilo Fawr (Carmarthenshire), where legal transactions including manumissions were entered in its margins as offerings to God. Gelhi also took advantage of the opportunity to swear an oath upon the book and to record in it that his family had not obtained a local gold mine dishonestly. The redemption of books taken hostage, in this case one probably having been taken or evacuated from Lichfield during Viking raids, was an eastern early Christian practice of Armenian origin that was considered to benefit the soul.

Athelstan also obtained books once owned by renowned early centres, such as the MacDurnan Gospels (Lambeth Palace Library, MS 1370) from Armagh, to which a colophon (f. 3v) was added for King Athelstan, recording his gift of the volume to Christ Church, Canterbury. It also commemorates the book's former owner, Maelbright MacDurnan, abbot of Armagh and Raphoe, who died in 927. Charters were entered into the volume at Canterbury during the early eleventh century. At least one Irish cleric from that area, Bishop Dub Innse of Bangor in the north of Ireland, spent time at Athelstan's court and as such may have been the conduit for a precious Armagh pocket Gospel book (the grandest of its type) coming to him as a gift. The Irish bishop met others attracted to Athelstan's scholarly court. An Irish Gospel book of about 1140 contains the statement: 'Here begins the Gospel Dice [Game] which Dub Innse, bishop of Bangor, brought from the English king, that is

Left: *Manumission freeing slaves in the Bodmin Gospels (*BL*, Add.* MS *9381, f. 13r), a Breton Gospels* c. 900 *that was given to Athelstan by Landévennec Monastery and presented by him to the altar of St Petroc in Bodmin, Cornwall.* Right: *Manumission in Old English, added in a blank space in an 8th-century Northumbrian Gospel book, recording that to mark his accession Athelstan freed a family of slaves at the behest of his mass-priest. He presented the book to Canterbury Cathedral (*BL*, Royal* MS *1 B VII, f. 15v).*

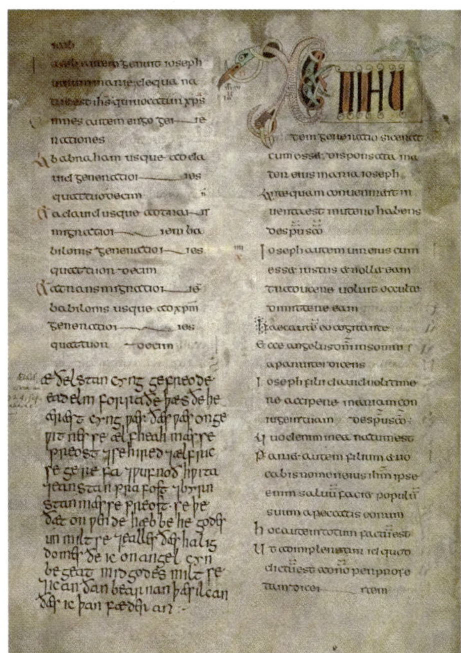

from the household of Æthelstan, King of England, drawn by a certain Franco [or Frank] and by a Roman scholar, that is Israel.'

The latter was Israel the Grammarian, whose origins are debated (Brittany, Wales, Ireland and Trier have all been proposed) but who later became an imperial tutor and then a monk at Trier. He was a practitioner of the complicated hermeneutic Latin style of writing that Aldhelm had made popular in intellectual circles in the seventh century and which enjoyed a revival at Athelstan's court, not only in poetry but in the complex, grandiose language employed in legal documents by the anonymous but influential scribe Athelstan A.

Another strand of poetry of the period is the 'Battle of Brunanburh' poem – preserved in four of the nine copies of the *Anglo-Saxon Chronicle* – which praises the victory of Athelstan and his brother Edmund I in the style of early Germanic epic battle verse and of the Norse sagas. Poetry of this sort, which includes works such as the 'Battle of Maldon' and *Beowulf*, would have appealed to the Anglo-Saxons and the Anglo-Scandinavian populace alike and would have served to reaffirm their shared Germanic roots. By the end of the tenth century these and other great works of secular and religious vernacular poetry were being collected into anthologies such as the Exeter Book, the Vercelli Book, the Caedmon Genesis and the Nowell Codex.

Athelstan was also given many books and relics by way of thanks by the Breton monastery of Landévennec, which enjoyed early connections with Cornwall and which he had sought to protect from Viking raids. He also received book-ambassadors, such as the Athelstan Psalter (British Library, MS Cotton Galba A XVIII) from Carolingia, which was made in northern France during the ninth century and which was 'modernized', probably at Winchester to judge by the stylistic similarity of the added figures to a fragmentary fresco from the Old Minster there. An illuminated calendar was added, along with miniatures depicting Christ in Majesty, surrounded by the ranks of the blessed, and another depicting the Virgin and Apostles, the martyrs and the ranks of angels set beneath Christ in Majesty. The style favours quite solid little figures with round faces and wide-open eyes (looking back to the Old Minster fresco and late ninth-century works such as the Fuller Brooch and the Alfred Jewel) and lacks the flying draperies, agitation and courtliness of the fully developed Winchester Style that was to come.

The board game Gospel Dice, played at the court of King Athelstan, in a 12th-century Irish Gospel Book (Corpus Christi College, Oxford, MS 122, f. 5v).

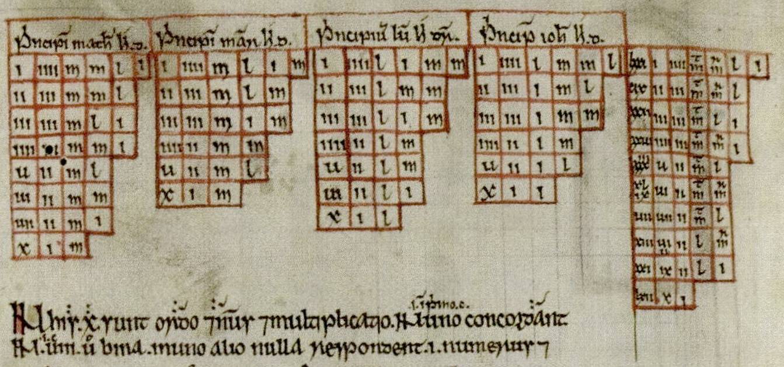

Hi sunt .x. fuit ordo et numerus et multiplicatio. H. in uno concordant. M. iiii. uel bina. in uno alio nulla respondent. i. numerus et multiplicatio. ordo uero corruptus est quia lucas in secundo canone posuit ante marcum.

Incipit alea euangelii quam dubinsi episcopus bennchorensis detulit a rege anglorum id est a domu adalstani regis anglorum. depicta a quodam francone et a romano sapiente id est israel.

Si quis uoluerit scire hanc aleam plene. illi ante omnia huius disciplinae documenta haec .vii. scire in animo necesse est. duces scilicet et comites. propugnatores et impugnatores. ciuitatem et ciuitatulam. et .ix. gradus bis.

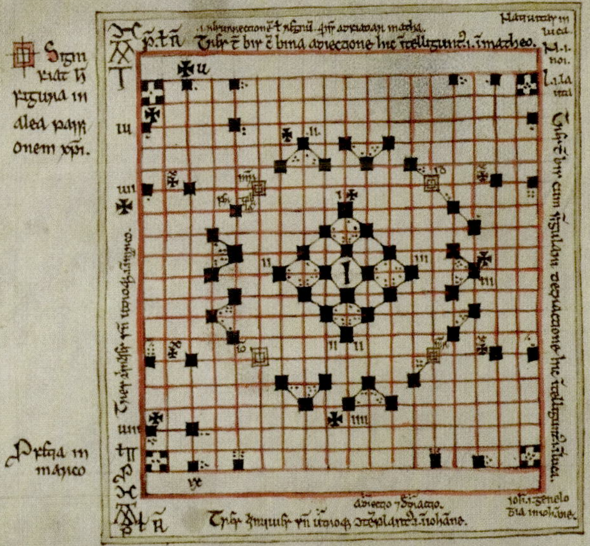

Below: *St Mark miniature, the Coronation Gospels (*BL*, Cotton* MS *Tiberius* A II*, f. 74v), a gift to Athelstan from his brother-in-law, Emperor Otto* I*, and his mother. This book was used by the early kings of England to swear their coronation oaths upon.* Opposite: *Christ in Majesty with the choirs of the blessed, one of the leaves added in the early 10th century to the Athelstan Psalter, perhaps at Winchester, to a 9th-century Carolingian manuscript (*BL*, Cotton* MS *Galba* A XVIII*, f. 21r).*

OMNIS CHORVS
MARTYRVM
OMNIS CHORV
CONFESSORVM
VIRGINVM
OMNIS CHO

The Coronation Gospels (British Library, Cotton MS Tiberius A II, perhaps made at Lobbes, Belgium, sometime between 875 and 925), a diminutive but beautifully illuminated manuscript, was sent as a gift by the founder of the Ottonian dynasty, Emperor Otto I (who had married one of Athelstan's half-sisters, Eadgyth), and his mother, Matilda. This book was subsequently used at the coronation of the English monarchs, who swore their oaths of allegiance upon it, a theory advanced by the great bibliophile Sir Robert Cotton, who bore it triumphantly to the landing stage at the Palace of Westminster when a new ruler, Charles I, came to take up his throne – only to see the royal barge pass him to land at the next jetty, a conscious royal snub that heralded his fall from favour. He would soon find the door of his beloved library, which contained many important medieval books that he had salvaged from the wreckage of the Dissolution of the Monasteries, barred to him as he languished under house arrest on a trumped-up charge of attempted rape concocted by his enemies. In 1731 this superb library would be decimated by a fire that swept through Ashburnham House in Westminster, where it was then housed. It is a mercy that so many of the priceless tomes survived. Another prominent collector of Anglo-Saxon manuscripts was Matthew Parker, Archbishop of Canterbury from 1559 to 1575, much of whose library passed to Corpus Christi College, Cambridge, as part of his attempts to provide a backstory for the newly established Church of England by emphasizing its origins in the early Church in England.

Duke Hugh of the Franks, seeking the hand of Eadhild, Athelstan's half-sister, sent Athelstan relics, which included the Lance of Charlemagne, thought to be that which pierced the side of Christ at the Crucifixion, and the Sword of Constantine, which incorporated fragments of the True Cross and one of the nails of the Crucifixion. Athelstan bestowed these precious relics, and land, upon Malmesbury Abbey, where he was laid to rest following his death in 939. He was succeeded by his half-brother, Edmund I (r. 939–46).

After Athelstan's death Anlaf Guthfrithson became king of York and reclaimed the Viking Five Boroughs of northeast Mercia. Most of Edmund's reign was occupied with the fight-back, which culminated in him expelling the Viking kings of York in 944. He also had trouble with North Wales and with the British kingdom of Strathclyde, which he invaded in 945 but then ceded to King Malcolm I of Scotland. On his way north, Edmund emulated Athelstan and stopped to pray at the shrine of St Cuthbert and to bestow gifts, probably including the Byzantine 'Nature Goddess' silk found in Cuthbert's coffin.

Despite these military priorities, Edmund perpetuated the learning of Alfred and Athelstan's reigns, reintroducing several Mercian personnel, as well as Welsh and continental books and scholars, such as the renowned poet Frithegod. He also continued to foster and extend the law (his preoccupations being loyalty to the Crown, regulation of relationships within state and kindred, curtailing vendettas and ensuring payment of *wergild*, 'blood money', and cattle rustling). He also nurtured the early Benedictine movement, appointing Dunstan and Æthelwold to Glastonbury Abbey (although at one point Edmund was persuaded to expel Dunstan from the kingdom, but relented), while also patronizing non-Benedictine houses.

Athelstan, Edmund and Eadred all encouraged a rising trend of aristocratic women embracing the monastic life once more, following the Viking upheavals, by endowing several nunneries. Edmund also continued to cultivate continental diplomatic contacts with Otto I and Louis IV and is recorded in the confraternity book of Pfäfers Abbey in Switzerland, on the well-trodden route across the Alps to Rome.

The post-Conquest chronicler John of Worcester wrote:

> While the glorious Edmund, king of the English, was at the royal township called Pucklechurch in English, in seeking to rescue his steward from Leofa, a most wicked thief, lest he be killed, was himself killed by the same man on the feast of St Augustine, teacher of the English, on Tuesday, 26 May, in the fourth indiction, having completed five years and seven months of his reign. He was borne to Glastonbury, and buried by the abbot, St Dunstan.

His sons being young, Edmund was succeeded by his brother Eadred (r. 946–55). The north continued to present problems and York produced further revolts during Eadred's reign. It was not fully conquered by him until 954. He suffered from ill health and died at just over the age of thirty, unmarried and without children. He was succeeded by Edmund's sons, first Eadwig and then Edgar.

Eadwig (r. 955–9) was fifteen when he became king and twenty when he died. The number of charters issued by him suggests that he may have been buying support and he certainly fell out with Abbot Dunstan, whom he exiled to Flanders. In 957 his brother Edgar took the kingdom north of the Thames, leaving Eadwig that to the south. That year or the next Archbishop Oda forced Eadwig and his wife, Ælfgifu, to separate on grounds of consanguinity.

It is likely that their union fell foul of the political cliques of the day. Ælfgifu and her mother were later portrayed in lives of St Dunstan and St Oswald, of the reforming party, as debauching scandalously together with the young king in his chamber while he should have been attending to court business. If she was the same Ælfgifu named in a will that survives today, she can be seen to have been a generous benefactress of the Old and New Minster at Winchester and a respected member of King Edgar's court.

Eadwig's choice of friends did not always commend him to the reformers. Ælfsige, Bishop of Winchester, was one of his closest allies, a member of the West Saxon aristocracy, wealthy, married and a father. This was not unknown but was not the profile of a bishop calculated to conform to the standards of Dunstan, Æthelwold and Oswald. Upon Archbishop Oda's death in 958, Eadwig appointed Ælfsige to the post, but he froze to death in the Alps en route to Rome to receive the pallium from the pope. When Edgar succeeded to the throne, he dismissed the next archbishop and appointed Dunstan in his place.

Edgar reigned from 959 to 975, a period often presented as a golden age not only because it fell during a lull in Viking hostilities, but because of Edgar's governmental measures such as a standardized coinage system introduced in the 970s and for his support of the English Benedictine Reform, along continental lines, which fostered a religious, social and cultural flowering.

Two illuminated manuscripts symbolize this era visually. The first is the New Minster Charter of 966 (British Library, Cotton MS Vespasian A VIII, drawn up by Bishop Æthelwold of Winchester and issued by Edgar to the New Minster (which had been founded alongside the Old Minster in Alfred's reign as the West Saxon royal mausoleum) to mark the Reform. The miniature that opens the text is painted upon a purple page (now faded), in Roman and Byzantine imperial fashion, and framed by a typical Winchester-style exuberant border composed largely of acanthus foliage on a golden trellis. It frames an image of Christ in Majesty, set in a mandorla supported by angels, beneath which is King Edgar flanked by the Virgin, who holds a martyr's palm leaf and a golden cross, and St Peter, who holds a book and his symbol, the key, up to heaven. The king holds a book – the charter itself, which actually

The New Minster Charter, made in Winchester in 966, depicting King Edgar, flanked by the Virgin and St Peter, presenting to Christ in Majesty the foundation charter of the English Benedictine Reform movement (BL, Cotton MS Vespasian A VIII, f. 2v). The opulent Winchester-style illumination, with its gilded acanthus borders, is set upon a purple-dyed page, in imperial fashion.

takes the form of a slim codex – and wears a purple-blue, gold-bordered cloak and a crimson tunic. He appears to be dancing, but it is likely that the artist was trying to depict him lying prostrate before Christ, to whom he presents the charter and his intention to reform His Church – to give His Bride, the Church, her white robe of good works. The figures wear 'damp-fold' drapery, which articulates their forms beneath, with agitated hemlines known as 'flying drapery', this and the border being a fine example of what has become known as the Winchester or 'First' Style of later Anglo-Saxon art. The whole is painted in full colour and scintillates with gold leaf. The effect of candlelight upon the appearance of such works would have animated them still further, even if its effect upon the eyes of the artist sapped his animation.

The other manuscript, the *Regularis Concordia*, contains a miniature depicting King Edgar seated between St Æthelwold and St Dunstan (British Library, Cotton, Tiberius A III, f. 2v). The surviving manuscript dates to the eleventh century but is thought to be an accurate copy of a tenth-century original. The king and his key prelates hold a scroll, which represents the contents of the book – the agreement of the English Church to follow the Benedictine Rule – and this is received by the acquiescent figure of a Benedictine monk beneath. The image is executed in a delicate tinted drawing version of the Winchester style, akin to that employed earlier in St Dunstan's Classbook (Bodleian Library, MS. Auct. F. 4. 32), the abbot's own personal florilegium of chosen learned texts, made while he was at Glastonbury from 940 to 957. This features Dunstan's own hand in parts of the drawing and captions that depict him kneeling before Christ at the opening of the book (f. 1r). Dunstan was known to be a gifted artist-scribe, metalworker, bell-founder and musician.

These two influential pieces of royal iconography, probably devised by Bishop Æthelwold, served to identify Edgar as

Christ's chosen viceregent on Earth, as in Carolingian and Ottonian iconography, and the collaboration of Church and State.

Æthelwold also oversaw the production of a splendid illuminated book of his own, the Benedictional of St Æthelwold (British Library, Add. MS 49598), the supreme masterpiece of the fully blown Winchester Style, made at Winchester sometime between 963 and 984, probably during the 970s. A prefatory poem in gold ink, by the scribe Godeman, records that the 'son of thunder' – a term bestowed by Jesus on the apostles James and John (Mark 3:17) but here used to refer to Æthelwold – told him to use plenty of gold and colours in his book. A benedictional contains the blessings that only the bishop can pronounce on the major feast days throughout the year. One of the many miniatures that adorn this opulent volume (f. 118v), along with historiated and decorated initials, depicts Æthelwold reading from the book during a service in the New Minster. He and the book are shown fully painted and the surrounding architecture and congregation are in ethereal coloured outline drawing. This may mean that this page is unfinished, but I have suggested that the use of different techniques was employed here (and in the Eadui Psalter, to be encountered in the next chapter) to distinguish between the painted and gilded celestial realm and the ethereal lightly drawn temporal world of the present. The splendour of this book, used by Bishop Æthelwold in major services in the royal cathedral/mausoleum of the New Minster, where he would be seen performing the public theatre of the liturgy, would have affirmed both his current and eternal status.

Another of the images in this remarkable book depicts the women encountering the angel at Christ's empty tomb on Easter Sunday. The tomb looks rather like a wardrobe and may be intended to depict a prop used in liturgical drama at Easter (of the sort known since the fifth century and first encountered in Britain in a text from eighth-century Lindisfarne preserved in the ninth-century Mercian Book of Cerne). The 'women' have singularly square jaws and this may likewise also indicate that they would have been played by monks in such dramas.

Oswald, Bishop of Worcester (961–92) and Archbishop of York (972–92), was also a leading reformer and commissioner of illuminated manuscripts. Of Danish stock, he was sent by his uncle, Archbishop Oda, to become a monk at

King Edgar seated between St Æthelwold and St Dunstan (BL, Cotton MS Tiberius A III, f. 2v), from the Regularis Concordia. *The surviving manuscript dates to the 11th century but is thought to be an accurate copy of the original, issued in 970. The king and his key prelates hold a scroll, which represents the agreement of the English Church to follow the Benedictine Rule, received by the monk underneath them.*

Fleury. He later returned and was taken up by Dunstan. He founded Ramsey Abbey, where he brought Abbo of Fleury to teach, and reformed several others. The Ramsey Psalter artist-scribe, who is discussed in the next chapter, may have been a monk of Ramsey Abbey or of Winchester and travelled on the Continent, where he undertook work in several scriptoria, including that at Fleury, while visiting and perhaps accompanying an important churchman on his travels. There he became proficient in the Carolingian Reimsian style of drawing, which, coupled with the strong tradition of penmanship and drawing already prevalent in Britain, led to the development of the Utrecht Psalter Style or 'Second Style' of Anglo-Saxon art in the late tenth and eleventh centuries (to be encountered in the next chapter). Oswald died of natural causes while washing the feet of the poor and was soon proclaimed a saint.

Edgar's support of the Reform movement does not necessarily vouch for his own spiritual condition. Of his three wives he is only certainly known to have married the third, Ælfthryth, widow of Ealdorman Æthelwold, whom he married in 964. Their surviving son, Æthelred 'the Unready', was to have a

Left: *The Benedictional of St Æthelwold, the Women at the Tomb* (BL, *Add.* MS *49598, f. 51v), made at Winchester,* c. *963–84, for its great reforming bishop. The tomb may be depicted like a prop used in liturgical drama at Easter and the women would be played by monks in such plays.*
Right: *Miniature of St Æthelwold pronouncing an episcopal blessing on a congregation of monks and clerics* (BL, *Add.* MS *49598, f. 118v). The bishop is fully painted and celestial, while the temporal congregation is in outline drawing.*

troubled reign (978–1013 and 1014–16), but fared better than his half-brother Edward the Martyr, who succeeded Edgar in 975 but had been murdered by 978. He is said in one source to have been by Edgar's first consort, a nun whom he seduced. Other rumours suggest that his stepmother, Ælfthryth, had a hand in arranging his premature death at one of her properties, Corfe Castle.

In 966 she witnessed the New Minster Charter as the 'legitimate wife' of the king, and her recently born elder son Edmund attested as his 'legitimate son', whereas Edward was described as 'begotten by the same king', but it is uncertain whether this was on the king's instruction, which would indicate that he wished to cut Edward out of the succession, or was ordered by Bishop Æthelwold, who was a friend and ally of Ælfthryth. She was consecrated as queen in 973 and thereafter attested charters as *regina*, the first West Saxon queen to do so on a regular basis. Her consecration was a major change in status, because previous West Saxon kings' consorts had only been described as the king's wife, whereas she also had the status of 'the queen'. Ælfthryth seems to have manoeuvred her own son, Æthelred the Unready, to the throne and was a formidable queen mother – a foretaste of things to come in the next century.

Edgar's strong and stable rule had been secured at a cost. A late tenth-century hagiographer, Lantfred of Winchester, wrote at the end of the king's reign:

> At the command of the glorious King Edgar, a law . . . was promulgated throughout England, to serve as a deterrent against all sorts of crime . . . that if any thief or robber were found anywhere in the patria, he would be tortured at length by having his eyes put out, his hands cut off, his ears torn off, his nostrils carved open and his feet removed; and finally, with the skin and hair of his head shaved off, he would be abandoned in the open fields dead in respect of nearly all his limbs, to be devoured by wild beasts and birds and hounds of the night.

Although not found in his known laws, the code designated as IV Edgar refers to a list, now lost, of punishments; a code of the Scandinavian king, Cnut, who seized the English throne from the weak Æthelred in 1016, says that it is based upon Edgar's law and contains a similar set of dire punishments. The elegant artistic culture and the piety of the age, some genuine and some assumed, formed a thin veneer covering the bloodshed that lurked beneath the surface.

4

THE ELEVENTH CENTURY: QUEEN EMMA'S 'APOLOGIA'

ENCOMIUM EMMAE REGINAE (BRITISH LIBRARY, ADD. MS 33241)

The eleventh century was a time of conquests. The Viking Age had become a significant factor in European history from the late eighth century onwards and extended from new colonies such as L'Anse aux Meadows in Newfoundland to Constantinople, where Vikings served as the imperial Varangian Guard, whose graffiti is still there, carved on the marble balustrades of the gallery of Hagia Sophia.

The initial raids, settlements and trade had given way to full-scale military conquest during the second half of the ninth century. The Danes (the 'black strangers') were successful in carving out the Danelaw with its Five Boroughs in England and the Norse (the 'white strangers') settled the Highlands and Islands and west coast of Scotland and northern England and established the first towns in Ireland as major trading centres: Dublin, Wicklow, Waterford, Wexford, Cork and Limerick.

Despite processes of integration and conversion to Christianity, Scandinavian ambitions in these islands continued to grow. The reign of King Æthelred 'the Unready' ('Unræd', the 'ill-advised') lacked the vision and strength of his father, King Edgar the Peaceable, and raids resumed, leading to demands for Danegeld – protection money or tribute. When this was paid, Scandinavian royal military campaigns ensued.

An Old English poem, 'The Battle of Maldon', commemorates what may have been a real event that took place in 991 on the River Blackwater outside the town of that name on the Essex coast, in which Byrhtnoth (whose name means 'bright courage'), an Anglo-Saxon ealdorman of Essex (the local representative of royal government), heard of Viking raiders landing on an offshore island and rallied troops to withstand them. In the poem, the strangers demand tribute and Byrhtnoth refuses but gallantly allows them to cross the causeway to fight in the open, instead of pursuing his advantage, leading to the slaughter of him and his men. It is a celebration of Germanic heroism and loyalty to one's lord. It may have been written soon after the battle and the earliest manuscript of it (British Library, Cotton MS Otho A.xii) was burnt in the Cotton Library fire in Ashburnham House (now the site of Westminster School) in 1731; fortunately, a transcript had already been made around 1724. In 1953 Tolkien published his own sequel, 'The Homecoming of Beorhtnoth Beorhthelm's Son'.

England came under the control of Sweyn Forkbeard, king of Denmark and Norway, after he invaded in 1013, in response to which Æthelred abandoned the throne and went into exile in Normandy. Sweyn

Here is an extract from 'The Battle of Maldon',
translated by Jonathan Glenn, quoted with his kind permission:

Then on the bank stood a Viking messenger,
called out stoutly, spoke with words,
boastfully brought the seafarers' errand
to that land's earl where he stood on shore:
'Seamen sent me quickly to you,
ordered me tell you to send rings at once,
wealth for defence: better for all of you
that you with tribute this spear-rush forgo
than that we share so bitter a war.
Nor need we kill each other if you perform it;
for gold we will fasten a truce with you.
If you determine it, the mightiest here,
that you for your people ransom will pay –
give to the seamen at their own choosing
wealth for a truce and take peace from us –
we with that payment shall to our ships,
on ocean fare, hold peace with you.'

Byrhtnoth spoke, lifted shield,
shook slender ash-spear, with words spoke,
angry and one-minded gave him answer:
'Hear you, seafarer, what this folk says?
Spears will they give you, ash-spears as tribute,
poisonous point, old sword –
an armor-tax useless to you in war.
Seamen's messenger, bear word back again;
tell your people much loathlier tale:
that here stands a good earl with his war-band,
who will defend this homeland,
Æthelred's land, land of my prince,
folk and fold. At battle, now,
heathen must fall. Too shameful it seems
that you, unfought, should go to ship
bearing our wealth, now that thus far
you have come into our land.
Not so softly shall you carry off riches:
point must, and edge, reconcile us first,
grim battle-play, before we give tribute.'

He bade them take shield then go,
so that warriors all stood on the bank.
One band could not to the other for water:
there came flowing the flood after ebb-tide;
streams locked. Too long it seemed
till they might bear spears together.
With tumult they stood along Pante's stream,
the van of the East-Saxons and the ash-army;
nor might any bring harm to the other,
but those who through flane-flight took death.

The flood went out. The seamen stood ready,
many a Viking, eager for war.
Then bade men's protector to hold the bridge
a war-hardened hero – he was called Wulfstan –
who with his spear slew the first man
who most boldly there on the bridge stepped.
There with Wulfstan stood warriors unfrightened,
Ælfere and Maccus, brave twain,
who would not at the ford flight work,
but fast against fiends defended themselves,
the while they could wield weapons.
When they perceived and saw clearly
that they found the bridge-wards there bitter,
those loathly strangers began to use guile,
asked for free landing, passage to shore,
to fare over the ford leading foot-troops.

Then the earl for his arrogance
left too much land to a hostile people.
Then over cold water Byrhthelm's son
began to call (men listened):
'Now you have room: come quickly to us,
warriors to war. God alone knows
who may master this battlefield.'

Slaughter-wolves waded then, heeded not water;
the Viking band, west over Pante,
over bright water, bore their shields;
seamen to land linden bore.

There against anger Byrhtnoth stood ready,
surrounded by warriors. He bade them with shields
build the battle-hedge, hold that troop
fast against foes. Then was the fight near,
glory in battle. The time had come
when fey men must fall there.
Clamor was raised there. Ravens circled,
eagles, eager for carrion. There was uproar on earth.
From hands then they released file-hard spears;
ground spears [, grim ones,] flew.
Bows were busy; shield took spear-point.
Bitter that battle-rush! Warriors fell;
on either hand young men lay.
Wounded was Wulfmaer, chose slaughter-bed,
Byrhtnoth's kinsman; he was with swords,
his sister-son, badly hewn.
There to the Vikings requital was given:
I heard that Eadweard slew one
fiercely with sword, withheld not its swinging,
that at his feet a fey warrior fell;
for that his lord thanked him,
his bower-thegn, when he could.
So the stout-thinkers stood firm,
young men at battle, eagerly vied
who with spear-point soonest might
in fey man life conquer there,
warrior with weapons. Slain fell on earth.
Steadfast they stood. Byrhtnoth directed them,
bade each young man think on the battle,
who against Danes would win glory in fight.

Then one strode, battle-hard, lifted his weapon,
his shield as defence, and against that man stepped.
So the earl moved toward the churl:
either to other evil intended.
Then hurled the sea-warrior a southern spear
so that wounded was warrior's lord.
He shoved then with shield so the shaft burst –
the spear broke and sprang back.
Enraged was that warrior: he with spear stung
the proud Viking who gave him the wound.
Wise was that fyrd-warrior: he let his spear wade
through the youth's neck, hand guided it,
so that it reached life in the ravager.
Then he another speedily shot
so that the byrnie burst; he was wounded in breast
through the ring-locked mail; in him at heart stood
poisoned point. The earl was the blither:
the brave man laughed then, said thanks to Metod
for the day-work God gave him.
Then a certain warrior let a hand-dart
fly from his hand, so that it went forth
through that noble, Æthelred's thegn.
By his side stood an ungrown youth,
a lad in the battle, who full valiantly
drew from the man the bloody spear,
Wulfstan's son, Wulfmaer the Young.
He let tempered shaft fare back again:
the point sank in so he on earth lay
who had his lord so grievously reached.
An armed man then went to the earl:
he wished to fetch wealth of that warrior –
spoil and rings and adorned sword.

Then Byrhtnoth drew his bill from its sheath,
broad and bright-edged, and struck against byrnie.
Too quickly one of the seamen stopped him
when he marred the earl's arm.
Then to the ground fell the fallow-hilt sword,
nor could he hold hard blade,
wield weapon. Then yet this word spoke
that hoar battler, encouraged the young men,
bade them go forth with good company.
He could not stand fast on foot any longer;
he looked to the heavens:
'I thank thee, Wielder of peoples,
for all those joys I had in the world.
Now have I, mild Measurer, most need
that you grant to my spirit goodness,
that my soul may journey now to thee,
into thy wielding, Lord of the angels,
depart in peace. I am entreating thee
that no hell-scathers harm it.'
Then heathen men hewed him,
and the men who had stood by him,
Ælfnoth and Wulfmaer, both lay there,
when close to their lord they their lives gave.

died a mere 41 days later, on 3 February 1014, in Gainsborough, Lincolnshire. Æthelred returned and resumed his reign until his death in 1016, when the people of London and the Witan chose as his successor Edmund Ironside, his son by his first wife, Ælfgifu of York, despite the efforts of his second wife, a Norman princess named Emma, to have her eldest son Edward (later 'the Confessor') succeed his father.

After fighting the decisive Battle of Assandun on 18 October 1016, King Edmund and Cnut signed a treaty by which all of England except for Wessex would be controlled by Cnut. Edmund died soon after on 30 November (under unclear and perhaps suspicious circumstances) and Cnut went on to reign throughout England for nineteen years, until his death in 1035, during which time it formed part of his massive Scandinavian trading empire.

Despite his major achievements, Cnut (Canute the Great) is best remembered in popular culture for his doomed attempts to turn the tide. This tale was first related by Henry of Huntingdon in the early twelfth century in his *Historia Anglorum:*

> When he was at the height of his ascendancy, he ordered his chair to be placed on the seashore as the tide was coming in. Then he said to the rising tide, 'You are subject to me, as the land on which I am sitting is mine, and no one has resisted my overlordship with impunity. I command you, therefore, not to rise on to my land, nor to presume to wet the clothing or limbs of your master.' But the sea came up as usual, and disrespectfully drenched the king's feet and shins. So jumping back, the king cried, 'Let all the world know that the power of kings is empty and worthless, and there is no king worthy of the name save Him by whose will heaven, earth and the sea obey eternal laws.'

This tale was once viewed as synonymous with arrogant folly but is now interpreted as a demonstration to his followers of political realism and of Cnut's Christian acknowledgement of God's ultimate authority.

After his accession Cnut promptly married King Æthelred's widow, Emma, who was also known in English as Ælfgifu. A number of royal/noble brides bore that name, which in Old English means 'elf gift' or 'spirit gift', the Christian equivalent of which became Godgifu ('gift of God', the name of Æthelred and Emma's daughter), so it may have been something of a generic name bestowed upon important brides, as their lord's helpmate, in which case Emma would have welcomed receiving it alongside her own given name. Cnut's first marriage was set aside, which was permitted as it had been conducted by the pagan custom of handfasting, rather than the Christian sacrament, but there is no sign that he repudiated his first wife, who continued to fulfil an important strategic dynastic role and whose sons remained as his co-heirs. Emma's three sons, Edward and Ælfred by Æthelred and Harthacnut by Cnut, were also claimants to the English throne.

Our next book was made abroad for Emma, this powerful queen of England (*c.* 984–1052) who had been wife to two kings of England. Æthelred's inability to repel a second wave of Scandinavian attacks, this time royally sponsored, did not impress his queen, herself of Viking Norman stock, and after his death in 1016 she seems to have embraced her second marriage the following year with alacrity. Wedding the royal widow bestowed legitimacy upon Cnut's reign and together they made a formidable pair. They sought to buy back the favour of the great and the good of Church and State by presenting gifts, notably books. In one, the *Liber Vitae* of New Minster and Hyde Abbey (British Library, Stowe MS 944), in which the names of benefactors and notables to be remembered in prayer there were inscribed, they are depicted in an elegant ink line drawing presenting a large golden cross to the high altar. Cnut is depicted as king and Emma clutches her drapery before her belly – a Byzantine iconographic gesture conveying virginity – as a born-again virgin bride-queen. Powerful royal iconography!

In this image, Emma is captioned with her Old English name, Ælfgifu. This may have been a convenient ambiguity, on occasion, but it is certainly a source of confusion for the historian (and perhaps for some contemporaries), for that was also the name of Cnut's first wife, Ælfgifu of Northampton, a Mercian noblewoman. Her father, Ælfhelm, ealdorman of southern Northumbria, was killed in 1006, probably by order of King Æthelred the Unready, and her brothers, Ufegeat and Wulfheah, were blinded. This enmity may have prompted the family to agree to Ælfgifu's marriage to the young son of Sweyn Forkbeard, Cnut, after Sweyn's invasion of England in 1013. The marriage may have served to consolidate the allegiance of the Anglo-Viking population. Cnut had to flee to Denmark following Sweyn's death and Ælfgifu followed with Sweyn's body and her young son by Cnut, Svein (later to become king of Norway). She soon gave birth to another son, Harold Harefoot (the 'fleet of foot'?), whose paternity

CNUT REX

was later questioned in the dynastic machinations and conflicts that were to follow. Ælfgifu may have governed part of Denmark on behalf of her husband and was later regent of Norway on behalf of her son from 1030 to 1035, a time remembered for her harsh rule and punitive taxation.

In England Cnut and Emma followed Athelstan's earlier practice of appointing a skilled scribe, who travelled with the court, to write their most impressive land grants and documents – and to pen many of the impressive illuminated Gospel books and psalters that they gave as gifts in order to try to regain the favour of leading nobles and churchmen after Cnut's coup. One such manuscript, the York Gospels (York Minster MS. Add. 1), was given to Archbishop Wulfstan of York, known as 'the Wolf' for his polemics encouraging the English to withstand the Scandinavian takeover. This even contains Cnut's 'Letter to the English', in which he essentially apologized for any unpleasantness (that is, the bloodshed, the land-grab and the 'Danegeld' protection money) and promised to look after the English in future. The pastel-coloured illumination, which exudes peace and goodwill, was by their favoured artist-scribe. This was a monk of Canterbury Cathedral, who was also a gifted illuminator, named Eadui Basan (Eadui the Fat). He is known to have written charters from around 1016 until the late 1020s and signed the Eadui Gospels (Hanover, Kestner-Museum, WM XXIa, 36), now in Hanover. He also left us a self-portrait in the Eadui Psalter (British Library, Arundel MS 155, f. 133r), kneeling at the feet of St Benedict, the founder of his Order. The rest of the Christ Church Canterbury monks hover nearby, executed in tinted drawing, while St Benedict is fully painted and gilded and occupies eternal time. Eadui is painted likewise, even his bottom, which protrudes into the earthly zone. It might be he whom a contemporary in the Canterbury community, Ælfric Bata, had in mind when he wrote of the equivalent of a rock-star scribe, out on the road having fun and earning rewards instead of staying where he belonged, teaching and writing in the monastic scriptorium.

Eadui did work in that scriptorium for part of his career, though, and collaborated in the making of the Harley Psalter (British Library, Harley MS 603). This sought to make a version of a famous Carolingian book made in the diocese of Reims in the 830s, the Utrecht Psalter (Utrecht University Library), which the Archbishop of Canterbury had obtained as an exemplar.

King Cnut and Queen Emma presenting a gold cross to the high altar in the New Minster and Hyde Liber Vitae *(BL, Stowe MS 944, f. 6r).*

Both books survive, permitting a detailed study to be made of the similarities and conscious differences, making it a case study in the interaction of tradition and innovation. It also permits us to witness the interaction of scribes and artists at close quarters, for the Carolingian Utrecht Psalter employed the Gallicanum version of the Psalms, written in stately classical Roman-style rustic capitals, whereas in Canterbury the text had to be changed to the Romanum edition used there, penned in a more compact English version of the Caroline minuscule script developed by the Carolingians in the late eighth century as a multi-purpose script. This meant that the amount of space allotted to the text by the scribes, who were usually responsible for establishing the layout of a book, needed to be different in each book. As a result, the spaces left for the artists to add the lively pen drawings to illustrate the text became squeezed, so much so that you can tell where they seized the initiative and took over designing the layout themselves, compressing the space available for the scribes and leaving them equally frustrated. As both artist and scribe, Eadui must have been conflicted. A century and a half later the Christ Church Canterbury scriptorium was still working on the Harley Psalter and had embarked upon two further 'copies' of it in the meantime. In the process, its personnel learned a tremendous amount about how protracted text and image cycles worked together and had composed others of their own.

It was probably also within Cnut and Emma's reign that the Christ Church Canterbury scriptorium produced a volume known as the 'Anglo-Saxon Scientific Miscellany' (British Library, Cotton MS Tiberius B V/I). This compilation of material relating to computus, astronomy, astrology and geography – including calendrical matter, Cicero's *Aratea* on the constellations, the *Physiologus* (or Marvels of the East), the *Periegesis* of Priscian (a schoolbook relating a voyage by a Greek/North African, written in Alexandria in the second or third century AD) and Archbishop Sigeric's pilgrimage itinerary from Canterbury to Rome (*c.* 990) – also features the earliest *mappa mundi* (world map) of the post-Roman world. Herein the legacy of classical geographers is joined by more detailed observation of the coastlines of Britain, Ireland, the northern isles, Iceland and Scandinavia gleaned through the navigational experience of the

Eadui Basan before St Benedict, with the Christ Church Canterbury monks receiving the Benedictine Rule (BL, Arundel MS 155, f. 133r). Eadui, like St Benedict, has a stubble beard (sign of humility) and is fully painted and in the celestial realm, while the other monks are in the temporal zone and in outline drawing.

William Howarde
SCS BENEDICTUS PATER MONACHORUM ET DUX
TIMOR DEI
Qui vos audit me audit
Obedientes estote preceptis meis
Ausculta o fili precepta

international Scandinavian trading empire, of which Britain temporarily formed a part.

In parts of this book can also be seen a curious phenomenon of late Anglo-Saxon book production, namely the use of bilingual parallel Latin and Old English versions of texts, written in different scripts by the same scribe. The Latin is penned in English Caroline minuscule (introduced earlier, in the tenth century) and the Old English is in Anglo-Saxon minuscule (descended ultimately from Insular minuscule scripts). In a typically English reaction to being part of a continental European mainstream, the new script was increasingly confined to the international currency of Latin, while England's own script was used for its own language.

By the time of the making of the Hereford *mappa mundi*, about 1300, the monstrous races and beasts of the *Physiologus*, an Early Christian text dealing with the mythical peoples and animals of Africa and Asia, probably written in Alexandria in the fourth century, had migrated from the pages of books such as this onto the map image itself, as a visual encyclopaedic world view which may have served as an altar retable. Eastern references and Christological virtues inherent in the symbolism of the images abound. It contains curious details such as a passage describing ants the size of dogs, which live beyond the River Gorgoneus and dig up gold from the earth. Men seeking gold are described crossing the river with their camels, leaving the young tied on their own side; the she-camels are laden with gold and return to their young, but the male camels are left behind for the ants to devour, enabling the thieves to escape.

Following Cnut's death in 1035, his two 'elf-given' wives and their sons vied for the throne. The fullest contemporary comment comes from Manuscript E of the *Anglo-Saxon Chronicle*:

> 1036 [for 1035]: Here Cnut died at Shaftesbury. And he is buried in Winchester in the Old Minster . . . And soon after his passing, there was a meeting of all the councillors at Oxford, and Earl Leofric and almost all the thegns north of the Thames, and the men of the fleet in London, chose Harold as regent of all England, for himself and his half-brother Harthacnut who was in Denmark. And Earl Godwin and all the foremost men in Wessex opposed it just as long as they

World map from the 'Anglo-Saxon Scientific Miscellany', Canterbury, 1020s–30s (BL, Cotton MS Tiberius B V/1, f. 56v), one of the earliest medieval mappae mundi.

> could, but they could not contrive anything against it. And then it was decided that Ælfgifu, Harold's mother, should settle in Winchester with the king her son's housecarls, and hold all Wessex in hand for him; and Earl Godwin was their most loyal man. Some men said of Harold that he was son of King Cnut and Ælfgifu, daughter of Ealdorman Ælfhelm, but to many men it seemed quite unbelievable; nevertheless he was full king over all England.

Emma's attempts to ensure the succession of her progeny by her virile Viking, rather than by her English first husband, led to tensions nationally and within the family. Her older son by Æthelred, Edward (later known as the Confessor), eventually accused her of conspiring to have him and his brother Ælfred Ætheling assassinated in 1036 when they returned from exile in Normandy to visit her, successfully in the case of Ælfred, who died from a red-hot iron being laid on his eyes. The *Encomium Emmae Reginae* places the blame for this treachery upon Harold Harefoot, but Earl Godwin of Wessex, who was accompanying the brothers, has also attracted suspicion. This event nonetheless led to Edward and his earls (including Godwin) depriving his formidable mother of her property and power in 1043 after he came to the throne (she had been the most wealthy and powerful woman in England until her namesake and son Harold seized her treasure along with Winchester).

It was then that Emma seems to have commissioned a monk, probably from the monastery of St Bertin at Saint-Omer in western Flanders, to write the *Encomium Emmae Reginae* or *Gesta Cnutonis Regis*. This related Emma's version of events, glossing over her first marriage and sons, presenting herself and Cnut in a good light, advancing their son Harthacnut (who reigned from 1040 to 1042 and for whom she served as regent while he was occupied in Norway) as the rightful heir and contesting the claim of Harold Harefoot to the English throne, blaming his mother for Ælfred's death and suggesting that she was responsible for sending a forged letter to Normandy inviting him back to England. The *Encomium* also claimed that Ælfgifu's son Harold was actually the son of a servant. These complex family feuds were to have a direct bearing upon the events leading to the Norman Conquest of England in 1066. It may have been the bitter rivalry between the two royal mothers that ensured the stalemate between Cnut's sons, which led, following their deaths, to the restoration of the Anglo-Saxon house of Wessex, in the form of King Edward the Confessor, who reigned from 1042 to 1066.

The *Encomium* is in three parts: the first deals with Sweyn Forkbeard's conquest of England; the second focuses on Cnut and relates the defeat of Æthelred and Edmund Ironside, his son by his first wife, Cnut's marriage to Emma (not mentioning her marriage to Æthelred) and Cnut's kingship. The third addresses events after Cnut's death: the seizing of the royal treasury, and the treachery of Earl Godwin. The author begins 'May our Lord Jesus Christ preserve you, O Queen, who excel all those of your sex in the amiability of your way of life,' and further on calls her 'the most distinguished woman of her time for delightful beauty and wisdom'. Her intellectual interests, or those of the author, may account for Virgil and the *Aeneid* being cited in the prefatory letter and in Book I, while influences from Sallust, Lucan, Ovid, Horace, Juvenal and Lucretius are also to be found.

In the prefatory image to the *Encomium*, Emma is shown enthroned receiving the book from its author, who kneels before her. Her sons Harthacnut and Edward stand behind him, in the wings, emphasizing that Emma is the source of their claims to the throne that she, as regent, is occupying. She wears an elaborate crown, a distinctive form seen elsewhere in Anglo-Saxon depictions of Lady Philosophy, who appears in Boethius's *Consolation of Philosophy* to comfort the wrongfully accused philosopher Boethius (d. *c.* 526) in his prison cell, having been unjustly imprisoned by

Queen Emma receiving the Encomium Emmae Reginae, *her version of her life and the events she had been implicated in, from the author, a monk of Saint-Omer in western Flanders (BL, Add. MS 33241, f. 1v).*

the heretical Ostrogothic usurpers of the Roman Empire's power in parts of Italy. This piece of visual propaganda surely had Emma's input, presenting her as the very embodiment of philosophical endurance of the injustice inflicted upon her by usurpers. Emma may not have been the scribe or even the author of the book, per se, but she was certainly writing – or rewriting – history.

Normandy originated as a kingdom when King Charles III ('the Simple') of West Francia granted the territory around Rouen to the Viking warlord Rollo, who had taken it in 876 as a dukedom after he had unsuccessfully besieged Chartres. The ensuing treaty of Saint-Clair-sur-Epte (911) is the foundational document of the Duchy of Normandy, designed to secure Rollo's loyalty and to stave off Viking attacks on the area, which had begun in the 840s. Normandy was often used as a base for those attacks and extortion, however, especially against England. As a result of this Æthelred launched a failed attempt to kidnap Richard II ('the Good'), Duke of Normandy, Emma's brother. His marriage to Emma in 1002 was probably intended to ease tensions, launching Emma on a career as queen of England (twice over), Denmark and Norway. She owned, in her own right, properties in Winchester, Exeter, Devonshire, Suffolk, Oxfordshire and Rutland.

When Sweyn invaded in 1013, Emma fled with her family to Normandy. After Cnut invaded in 1015, she worked to keep control of London until he won the crown in 1016 and then concluded her marriage to him a year later. She probably thereby saved her English sons from elimination, a tactic that Cnut often employed against rival claimants to power. They were packed off to Normandy for safekeeping. She later championed the right of her son by Cnut, Harthacnut, to the crown. In 1039 he sailed to England with a fleet, had the body of his opponent, King Harold Harefoot, disinterred and cast into a ditch and restored his mother Emma's position. He had no offspring and it may have been Emma who then sought to appease her eldest English son by persuading Harthacnut to appoint him his successor. After becoming king, Edward and his foremost earls deprived her of property and influence, but Edward later relented.

Through Emma Normandy thus had a twofold claim to the English throne. We can imagine how, having been restored to Edward's favour, Emma would have sought to influence her pious, childless son in favour of appointing her kinsman, Duke William of Normandy, to the English throne and how she would have opposed the rival claim advanced to Earl Godwin's son, Harold Godwinson.

Despite Harold's visit to William in Normandy, the battle lines were being drawn and culminated in the Battle of Hastings in 1066, so graphically recorded in the Bayeux Tapestry, sewn by Englishwomen for William the Conqueror's half-brother, Bishop Odo of Bayeux, and depicting the Norman version of events. The tapestry itself is virtually a graphic novel, with its lively images – drawn in thread – and captions deriving from the narrative strip illustrations of some illuminated manuscripts. One such was the Old English Hexateuch (British Library, Cotton MS Claudius B IV), which relates the biblical narrative of the first six books of the Bible, accompanied by lengthy captions in Old English (those for the first five books being by the famous homilist Ælfric of Cerne Abbas), and includes a depiction of Noah's Ark with Viking dragon-headed prow and stern. The core of it was composed by Ælfric the Homilist (d. 1010), but the earliest manuscript copy (British Library, Cotton MS Claudius B IV). was made (and amplified) in the second quarter of the eleventh century at St Augustine's, Canterbury.

I have conjectured that one section of the Bayeux Tapestry may perhaps depict Emma. A heavily draped woman stands beneath an architectural arch resembling a church, while a tonsured cleric slaps her round the face. The audio-guide to the Tapestry, on display in Bayeux, describes this as an otherwise unknown betrothal ritual, but I suggest that a glance at the border beneath the scene may suggest another meaning. It shows a squatting naked priapic male figure. Might this passage therefore allude to Emma's infatuation with her virile Viking husband and matters arising that led to her detention and silencing by her son Edward when he came to the throne, with the assistance of the earls and Church? It was kinship to Emma and her advancement of the cause of the Northmen (as the Vikings and Normans were known) that gave Duke William of Normandy his claim to the English throne, his reason to invade and the opportunity to turn Normandy, with the aid of English resources and advanced bureaucracy, into what would become the Angevin Empire.

After her death in 1052 Emma was interred alongside Cnut and Harthacnut in the Old Minster at Winchester and later translated to the Norman cathedral. Their remains were desecrated by the Roundheads during the Civil War in the mid-seventeenth century, their bones jumbled up together on the cathedral floor and later reburied together – perhaps a fitting conclusion to their shared quest to gain and retain the throne.

Emma was one of several powerful Normans at the English court in the pre-Conquest era. Another was Robert of Jumièges, prior of the Abbey of St Ouen at Rouen in Normandy and then abbot of Jumièges Abbey from 1037. He became a close friend and adviser to Edward the Confessor, who appointed him Bishop of London in 1044 and Archbishop of Canterbury in 1051. He crossed Earl Godwin (whose daughter, Edith, had married Edward) and is said, in a Norman chronicle, to have been sent by Edward in 1051 to offer William the throne, which has been hotly contested. The next year he was exiled to Normandy, where he died.

Robert was an architectural patron and had been responsible for the impressive early Romanesque abbey at Jumièges and he may have had a hand

The Bayeux Tapestry scene perhaps relating to Queen Emma's interventions in the dynastic succession conflict that led to the Battle of Hastings in 1066. Emma may be being silenced by a cleric while confined in a church. Might the priapic figure in the lower margin and the dragon of evil allude to her relationship with Cnut?

in Edward the Confessor's construction of Westminster Abbey, depicted in the Bayeux Tapestry. He also owned a splendid sacramentary known as the Missal of Robert of Jumièges (Rouen, Bibliothèque municipale, MS 274 (Y 6)), inscribed by his own hand with his gift of it to the abbey of Jumièges while he was Bishop of London. He may also have owned the equally splendid pontifical known as the Benedictional of Archbishop Robert (Rouen, Bibliothèque municipale, MS 369 (Y 7)), although this might also have been Archbishop Robert of Rouen, Emma's brother, to whom she is known to have given a magnificent psalter. Both books are illuminated in a flamboyant, expressionistic late version (the Mixed or 'Third Style' of later Anglo-Saxon art) of the renowned Anglo-Saxon Winchester School style, which had reached a height of perfection in the Benedictional of St Æthelwold (British Library, Add. MS 49598, made in Winchester in the 970s) and the late tenth-century Ramsey Psalter (British Library, Harley MS 2904, made in Winchester or Ramsey Abbey, Cambridgeshire). The Ramsey Psalter artist-scribe was highly skilled in both the fully painted and gilded Winchester style and in the elegant outline or tinted drawing version of it that became increasingly popular when the continental Reims style of drawing arrived in England, further stimulating its own tradition of fine drawing and penmanship that stemmed from the Insular period. The Ramsey Psalter hand also wrote a very elegant, rounded version of Caroline minuscule, elevating it to new calligraphic standards. This inspired Edward Johnston, the 'father of modern calligraphy', to use it as the basis for his 'foundational hand', used to teach and revive handwriting in Britain and North America in the early twentieth century.

The work of the Ramsey Psalter hand is to be found in several continental scriptoria and it may be that he travelled in the entourage of a prince, of Church or state, and contributed to the work of the scriptoria where they stopped, such as Fleury, where he contributed the elegant tinted drawings of the constellations to a copy of Cicero's *Aratea* written by scribes there. He may have been instrumental in transmitting Carolingian influences back to England and vice versa.

Early Norman art was influenced by a number of sources, including Anglo-Saxon book production. Manuscripts made in post-Conquest England and in Normandy are stylistically related; the term 'channel school' was coined in reference to this link. Anglo-Saxon influence can be found in the Franco-Flemish area and in parts of northern and western France from the late tenth century. The Jumièges Psalter and the Préaux Gospels, made after the Conquest, show how deeply the Winchester style had penetrated post-Conquest Normandy. German/Flemish influence can be detected in the hard, metallic style of the mid-century English Caligula Troper (British Library, Cotton MS Caligula A XIV), while the Judith of Flanders Gospels (Morgan Library and Museum, New York, MS M.708) introduced English style to the scriptorium of Weingarten Abbey in Swabia. Three of Judith's illuminated manuscripts survive and her Gospels are adorned by a magnificent jewelled treasure binding. She also donated property and artworks to Durham Cathedral.

Judith was Countess of Flanders and was married to Tostig, Earl of Northumbria and brother of Harold Godwinson. Tostig died on 25 September 1066 at the Battle of Stamford Bridge, at which King Harald Hardrada of Norway sought to assert his claim as Harthacnut's heir to the English throne. They were defeated there by Harold Godwinson (who had been elected as Edward's successor by the Anglo-Saxon royal Witan), but he and his exhausted troops then had a long march south to engage with Duke William of Normandy on 14 October at what became known subsequently as Battle, near Hastings on the Sussex coast. There Harold and the flower of Anglo-Saxon manhood perished. The Norman Conquest had arrived. The Witan immediately elected a new king of their own – Edgar Ætheling, the son of Edward the Exile and grandson of Edmund Ironside – but he was unable to resist William, who was duly crowned King William I of England on Christmas Day 1066, in the Confessor's Westminster Abbey. Henceforth, the royal court would be based in London, rather than Winchester, and William would rule until his death in 1087.

Another notable female bibliophile was St Margaret of Scotland (1046–1093), the sister of Edgar Ætheling, who had been born in exile in Hungary and had returned to England. She fled north at the Norman Conquest and was wed to Malcolm III (Canmore), king of Scotland, who, although himself illiterate, was proud of his wife's learning and piety and commissioned treasure bindings for her books. One of these, the St Margaret Gospels (Bodleian Library, Lat. liturg. f. 5), was made in southern England during the second quarter of the century and later survived 'death by drowning' when accidentally dropped into a river that the queen was crossing, which demonstrated the power of a saint who owned such books that could survive immersion in water. Margaret went on to reform the churches of Scotland.

These were some of the two-way streets of cultural influence that gave birth to the international Romanesque style, which was to spread throughout Europe. Through such ecclesiastical reform and via the expansion of Norman knights through Wales and Ireland and to the Holy Land, it would spread to the far west and to the Near East in the following century.

The events of 1066 were followed by the expansion of Norman power throughout England, accompanied by a programme of building castles, cathedrals and churches. William and his wife, Matilda, were both great architectural patrons in Normandy and they extended such benefaction to England. Many Anglo-Saxon manorial estates passed into Norman hands, as William bestowed the expected rewards upon his supporters and mercenaries. By the 1080s most of the positions of power in Church and State had passed to Norman personnel. Resistance in Northumbria was brutally crushed in a bloody series of campaigns in 1069–70 and a punitive repressive aftermath, known as the Harrying of the North. The need to control the north would lead to the rise of the powerful Prince-Bishops of Durham.

A firm but relatively fair hand at the helm of the Church in England came in the form of Lanfranc (*c.* 1005–1089), who had left his legal career in Pavia to become a monk at Bec in Normandy. Following the deposition of the Anglo-Saxon Archbishop of Canterbury, Stigand, in 1070 Lanfranc was appointed in his place. He immediately set about reforming and reorganizing the English Church and, with William, protected its independence. He also reasserted the primacy of the archdiocese of Canterbury and sought to weed out corruption, to reinforce the monastic vocation, spirituality and education among the clergy and to serve as an advocate for the new fashion of requiring celibacy from the clergy. His served as a restraining hand upon the harsher aspects of William's reign and he sometimes served as viceregent during the king's absences.

The fruits of a massive audit to formalize the Norman land-grab was enshrined in 1086 in a tax census known, appropriately, as Domesday Book, from Doomsday, the day of the Last Judgement in religious terms (now in the National Archives, Kew), which comprises two parts: 'little Domesday' (covering Essex, Suffolk and Norfolk) and 'greater Domesday'. This was conducted by William's royal agents and surveys the property, land, livestock and resources of most of England (excluding the northeast and northwest) and parts of Wales. The 268,984 households listed (which give the heads of households, mostly tenants-in-chief and their tenants, thereby excluding most urban dwellers, the landless and the poorest in society) are thought perhaps to indicate a total English population of 1.2 to 1.6 million. It names 13,418 places and often indicates who held the land (both secular and religious) before the Conquest and who held it after – the latter often being Normans or their supporters. The pattern here and in office-holding shows both an immediate purging of opponents and then a gradual replacement of those in positions of wealth, responsibility and power by the Norman coterie. Its purpose was to indicate the level of taxes and services due to the Crown.

William I was succeeded by his third son, Wiliam II (William Rufus, 'the Red'), who ruled from 1087 to 1100 and was by all accounts a rough and difficult man who died unmarried and without an heir. He did, however, assert his overlordship in Normandy and Scotland and made in-roads of Norman authority into Wales.

Lanfranc was succeeded in 1093 as Archbishop of Canterbury by Anselm of Aosta, another monk of Bec, who was in office until 1109. As its prior, this gifted philosopher and theologian made Bec a premier seat of learning and has been seen as one of the initiators of scholasticism. His *Prayers and Meditations*, which have been called 'a searching exploration of the state of the soul and a lament on the loss of purity', show us the depth of his spirituality. A popular and respected man, he was tipped to become the next Archbishop of Canterbury after Lanfranc, but this was delayed by William Rufus attempting to take control himself for a while, until popular pressure forced him to allow Anselm to be installed and to have Canterbury's lands and rights returned.

This was enacted against the backdrop of the Investiture Controversy (1076–1122) begun by Pope Gregory VII and Emperor Henry IV, in which the Church and secular rulers in Europe struggled for control of the right to appoint abbots, bishops and even the pope himself. Anselm had managed to hold the balance against William Rufus, even though it was at the cost of him being twice exiled, but the scene was set for an ongoing contest that would lead to the martyrdom of Thomas Becket a century later in the cathedral at Canterbury, the extension and remodelling of which had been started by Lanfranc and Anselm. It would rumble on until the rift between Thomas Wolsey and Henry VIII.

These early Norman church leaders did not achieve church unity in Britain and encountered challenges from the archdiocese of York and the Welsh bishops, but they forwarded the monastic life and the further development of the parish system. Under them the creation of illuminated manuscripts continued, combining the earlier Anglo-Saxon styles with the emerging international Romanesque. The zoomorphic, inhabited, gymnastic and historiated initials found in late eleventh- and twelfth-century books thus fused the legacy of the Insular manuscripts of Britain's past with the elegant and contorted forms of the sculptured capitals and cloisters of Normandy, Burgundy, Italy and Iberia. The 'barbaric' but vigorous and decorative tastes of the Northmen surely played a role in this.

William II's eldest brother, Robert Curthose, inherited Normandy. His second brother, Richard, died in a hunting accident in the New Forest. The brothers had a rumbustious and competitive relationship, and when William II was also shot with an arrow while hunting in the New Forest (which, by this time, some must have nicknamed the 'new king forest') some suspicion fell upon his younger brother, Henry Beauclerc, who duly succeeded him as King Henry I of England in 1100. The *Anglo-Saxon Chronicle* noted laconically that the king was 'shot by an arrow by one of his own men' and a later addition names a nobleman, Walter Tirel. The royal corpse was found by a charcoal burner, who brought it to Winchester. A bloody end to a turbulent century.

5

THE TWELFTH CENTURY I: CHRISTINA OF MARKYATE'S GIFT

THE ST ALBANS PSALTER (DOMBIBLIOTHEK HILDESHEIM, MS ST. GOD. 1)

King William II died unmarried and was succeeded in 1100 by his brother, Henry I, who ruled until his own death in 1135, leaving no legitimate male heir, as his son William Adelin had drowned in the sinking of the *White Ship* off the coast of Normandy in 1120. Of the three hundred onboard, many of them Anglo-Norman royalty and nobles, only one survived, a butcher named Berold, from Rouen, according to the account by Orderic Vitalis. This prestigious new state-of-the-art vessel was attempting to overtake the king's ship ahead of them, in an act of bravura, when it struck a submerged rock. William Adelin had escaped onto a small boat, but turned back to try to save his half-sister, Matilda, upon hearing her crying for help. His boat was swamped by others seeking safety and everyone drowned, in an incident that has some prescient overtones of the tragic sinking of the *Titanic* nearly eight centuries later.

Henry I's death provoked a succession crisis that triggered a vicious period of civil war in England, known as the Anarchy (1135–53). The flower of the English aristocracy had been lost with the *White Ship* and Henry left only one legitimate offspring, another daughter named Matilda (sometimes also referred to as Maud), who was married to Geoffrey V, Count of Anjou. He was her second husband, the first having been the Holy Roman Emperor, Henry V, hence her sometimes being referred to as empress. Despite Henry having made them swear an oath of allegiance to Matilda, his barons could not stomach the idea of being ruled by a woman, especially one with Geoffrey at her side, for whom they harboured a traditional enmity. Henry's nephew, Stephen of Blois (whom Orderic recounts only narrowly missed sailing on the *White Ship* due to a bout of diarrhoea), jumped into the breach with a counterclaim, landing on Sennen Beach – the catflap to the realm – in the far west of Cornwall and having himself crowned king. He was opposed militarily by Matilda and Geoffrey. A bloody and treacherous period of fifteen years of conflict ensued, mostly enacted in southern and central England but also on the Continent. In the late twentieth century, Ellis Peters enshrined this period in the popular imagination with her Brother Cadfael novels, set in Shrewsbury on the border between England and Wales.

Matilda (1102–1167) gained control of England for a few months in 1141 and was effectively monarch for 209 days but was never crowned; she died 26 years later, in Rouen. Stephen tried to have his son, Count Eustace IV of Boulogne, crowned co-ruler in 1152 but this was prevented by the pope as an uncanonical Norman practice and Eustace died the following year, upon which Stephen agreed the Treaty of Wallingford (also known as the Treaty of Winchester or Westminster) with Matilda, appointing her son by Geoffrey as his heir to the English throne. That son duly became King Henry II of England (r. 1154–89). He and his sons, Richard and John, became known as the Angevin kings, from Geoffrey's title to Anjou. From the time of the accession of Henry III, John's son, in 1216, England's rulers were known as the Plantagenets, from Geoffrey's badge the *planta genista* (broom), and reigned until the Tudors came to power at the Battle of Bosworth in 1485. Having lost most of their continental territories, the Plantagenet rulers, unlike their Norman and Angevin precursors, spent more time in England and focused primarily upon affairs in these islands. This did not deter them from continuing at times to pursue their ambitions in France.

The twelfth century was a time when people, trade goods, art and ideas were on the move. The Crusades began when Pope Urban II called for Crusade at the Council of Clermont in 1095, which also issued a series of canons, among them one that renewed the Peace of God, designed to protect the vulnerable during travel, and another that granted a plenary indulgence (the remission of all penance for sin) to those who went to the aid of Christians in the East. This mobilized large western military forces on a protracted quest to regain the 'Holy Land' from Muslim control and expansion, which had taken effect from the mid-seventh century and which had spread around the 'fertile crescent' of the eastern and southern Mediterranean, taking root even in western territories such as Sicily and Iberia. Such was the response to the initial call at Clermont that not only did knights 'take the cross', but a people's crusade was also launched. These converged upon Constantinople, which had appealed for assistance against Muslim threat. In 1097 hordes of uncouth westerners soon ran amok in that ancient city, so iconic of the Christian faith of Byzantium, as graphically and poignantly related by an eyewitness, the emperor's daughter Anna Comnena, in her *Alexiad*. In 1204 the Fourth Crusade culminated in the Sack of Constantinople and the carving up of the city and much Byzantine territory between the crusaders.

On his way home from the Third Crusade in 1192, Richard Cœur de Lion ('the Lionheart'), king of England, was captured by his enemy Duke Leopold of Austria near Vienna, who gave him over to Emperor Henry VI, who demanded that England pay an extortionate ransom of 150,000 marks. Richard returned to England in 1194 and was crowned a second time to secure his throne. He then promptly returned to the

Continent to spend his final five years fighting King Philip II of France. Given his protracted absences, it might be questioned whether the English people got their money's worth and whether Richard deserves his dashing place in the national historical memory, which has been bolstered by his role in the legends of Robin Hood. Richard lies in the Abbey of Fontevraud, alongside his parents, King Henry II and Queen Eleanor, in the Angevin heartland.

Henry II had embarked upon a contest for control of the Church in England – or at least its wealth – with the pope, in which the king's close confidante and former drinking partner, Thomas Becket (*c.* 1119–1170), the son of merchants living on Cheapside in the heart of the City of London and who became his chancellor, became entangled. As part of his strategy Henry had Thomas appointed Archbishop of Canterbury in 1162, little counting upon the new sense of responsibility and spirituality that this inspired in the Londoner, which led him to withstand attempted royal encroachment upon the rights and authority of the Church and efforts to achieve less proximity to the papacy. This would lead to Thomas escaping England when Henry issued the resulting Constitutions of Clarendon in 1164, to seek papal intervention which duly saw him reinstalled at Canterbury. There, on 29 December 1170, a small group of knights led by Reginald FitzUrse obeyed the king's drunken wish to be freed from 'this turbulent priest' (as an eighteenth-century tradition came to report it) and spliced the archbishop's skull in two as he knelt at the transept altar of the cathedral. They thereby started one of the biggest cults and pilgrimage destinations in Europe, sealed by Becket's rapid canonization some two years later. A manuscript depicting his martyrdom was illuminated for Cirencester Abbey in the 1180s in a volume containing Becket's collected letters by Alan of Tewkesbury and his *Life* by John of Salisbury (British Library, Cotton MS Claudius B II, f. 341r). This became a popular image, repeated on items such as the Becket Chasse, one of several similar relic caskets decorated with Limoges enamels, and on alabaster panels from Nottingham; it was also recounted in Gerald of Wales's *Expugnatio Hibernica* (Conquest of Ireland) in 1189. Henry subsequently humbled himself at Becket's tomb, in public penance, and one of Becket's slayers, Richard de Luci, founded in expiation Lesnes Abbey at Abbey Wood, in what are now the outskirts of southeast London (where its ruins can be seen alongside ancient woodland).

Successive popes continued to preach Crusade, as imams preached jihad. There was even a disastrous western 'children's crusade' in 1212 in which some 30,000 children from France and Germany (probably two

& exercendi circa karissimũ filium tuũ illustrẽ regẽ anglorũ aplice uiscera caritatis. ut ei respondeat mane iusticia sua. humilisq; & prompta

deuotio. quã uob & ecclẽ romane tẽpe oportuno exhibuit i sinũ suũ aplico modãmine cuertat. Explicit epla octogesima. Incipit octogesima prima. ·ii·

Robes sarisbiensis eccla amico suo.

Ex inspato & in cõsuetũ m̃ dei gr̃a ppiciante nup innotuit: qd ad uos e rat lator psentiũ cõsti tut. Gauisus ḡ diuini

minilstrata occasione scribendi ad amicũ. eã grant arripui: arbitratus in longe calamitatis magnũ da

solatiũ. qd in tuis aurib; liceat an gustiarũ cumulũ deplorare S; unde sumet exordiũ: Nã dicendi pariv inopia; materia copiosa & exuberans. & quisi tẽpe nro malitia exercuis set ad sũmũ: fidẽ excedit. Publicas angustias an domesticas deplorabo: S; generales mundus agnouit. sua queq; miseria pun acũ: n forte

rt

separate, parallel movements) attempted unsuccessfully to reach the Holy Land, many of them dying or being trafficked into slavery in North Africa en route. The Crusades continued in the East until 1291, when the last crusader state, Acre, finally fell. This was an age of heightened and often extremist religious fervour in both East and West. Abuses of power and costly renders demanded by both Church and State, around Europe, led to widespread discontent and to the rise of schismatic or heretical groups such as the Cathars, who were persecuted during the Albigensian Crusade in Languedoc in southern France from 1209 to 1229. Local scores were also often settled, including pogroms against the Jews in the Rhineland and France, which were opposed by the Church.

Pilgrimage routes had proliferated in both East and West since Antiquity. In western Europe these ranged from local routes such as St Kevin's Way in Ireland to the Via Francigena and other routes to Rome and the Camino de Santiago de Compostela, which ran from various points in Europe to the northern Spanish coast and the shrine of St James in western Galicia. The last developed from the late eighth century as a boost to the strength of the Christian tradition and to international relations and solidarity, largely in response to the spread of Islam throughout Iberia, which threatened to traverse the Pyrenees into Carolingian Frankia. Amazing Apocalypse manuscripts were made throughout northern Spain in the eleventh and twelfth centuries, emphasizing the impending peril of the end times and painted in a highly stylized manner that Picasso would later draw upon for his *Guernica*, painted in response to the destruction of Guernica, the Basque national focal point on the Camino that was devastated by saturation bombing by Nazi and Spanish fascist forces in 1937.

Elsewhere in Spain – especially in Andalusia in the south – southern Italy and Norman Sicily and in the Latin Kingdom of Jerusalem, increased interaction between Christian, Muslim and Jewish communities led to the development of interesting hybrid cultures, characterized by tolerance (if sadly only for a time), and of mutual learning, which fostered an age of intellectual and experimental enquiry known in the West as 'scholasticism'.

Scientific and medical knowledge progressed significantly in the West through contact with Islam – and the works of Aristotle, lost to the West through the wreckage of the Roman Empire and the expansion of

The earliest known representation of the murder of St Thomas Becket, from a manuscript of John of Salisbury, Life of St Thomas Becket, c. *1180 (BL, Cotton MS Claudius B II, f. 341r).*

Islam, were recovered. Scholasticism began to thrive, towns grew and in the West universities (from the Latin *universitas magistrorum et scholarium*, meaning 'community of teachers and scholars') emerged. The earliest was Bologna in Italy, which specialized in Civil and Canon Law, where teaching began around 1088 and which was organized into a university in the late twelfth century. To the south, Salerno, which specialized in medicine *inter alia* and was founded in the eighth century, grew out of the Schola Medica Salernitana, and reached its peak between the tenth and thirteenth centuries, benefitting from encounters with Muslim scientific thought. The works of Avicenna (Ibn Sina, *c.* 980–1037, the 'father of early modern medicine', who served the rulers of Iran during the Islamic 'golden age') and the philosopher Averroes (Ibn Rushd, 1126–1198, the 'father of rationalism', a scientific polymath and jurist in Andalusia) began to circulate in the West, alongside those of Aristotle, Plato and other Greek thinkers to whom they were indebted.

In Paris the cathedral and abbey schools flourished with the aid of stellar teachers such as Peter Lombard and Hugh of St Victor and attracted aspirant laymen and churchmen, including the new mendicant orders of friars. The early book trade was centred upon the neighbourhoods linked by the Petit Pont, following the line of the lively late twelfth-century schools linking the Ile de la Cité and the Left Bank. John of Garland's *Dictionarius*, written for arts students in Paris around 1220, states that booksellers were to be found 'beak by jowl' with poultry sellers on the 'parvisus', the square or place 'to be seen' in front of the cathedral of Notre Dame.

This intellectual nexus developed into the University of Paris, the statutes of which were officially recognized by Pope Innocent III in 1215, followed rapidly by other notable seats of learning such as Oxford, where teaching had been taking place from at least 1096 and which was organized into a university between 1200 and 1214. Cambridge University began as an offshoot of Oxford, some of whose teachers relocated there for a while following a dispute in 1209. Other Italian and Iberian universities arose in the thirteenth century, with Poland, Austria and parts of Germany following suit in the fourteenth century. London, by contrast, retained its medieval series of schools of theology, law and music, clustered around St Paul's Cathedral and the Inns of Court (which still remain at the heart of England and Wales's legal profession). What is now University College London was established in 1826 as London University, but the University of London was established by royal charter in 1836 as a degree-awarding examination board for students holding certificates from University College London and other colleges in the London area and then moved to a federal structure with constituent colleges in 1900.

By the 1170s numerous glossed bibles, with wrap-round commentaries for study – a complex layout designed to enable two or more texts to be read in tandem, somewhat in the manner of modern tablet technology – were already being made in Paris. This effectively marked the start of the Paris book trade, with the scriptorium of the Abbey of St Victor making them initially and then subcontracting out the work to neighbouring lay scribes and illuminators as demand grew (for example, a document dated 1213 records that the abbey provided an exemplar of Ptolemy's *Almagest* to a commercial producer).

The reputation of Parisian schools and their books attracted patrons and trade grew commensurately. Some patrons sent their own scribes there to copy texts, such as the scribe Michael who was sent to Paris by Archbishop Hartwich of Hamburg-Bremen (a missionary archdiocese, requiring books for the mission fields in northern Germany and Scandinavia), including Peter Lombard's 'Sentences' and his *magna glossatura* commentary on the Pauline epistles (the oldest known of which was copied in 1166 by Michael). Hartwich left some thirty such books copied from Parisian exemplars to the church in Bremen.

Book production flourished in many ways in this period of cultural and intellectual exchange and of reaffirmation of faith traditions in the twelfth and thirteenth centuries. Artistic interaction between East and West contributed to the development of international Romanesque art and architecture, influenced by Antique and Byzantine traditions and by those encountered along the pilgrimage routes.

The monastic and other ecclesiastical scriptoria carried on producing books during the later eleventh and twelfth centuries and beyond. Large-format Romanesque or 'Atlantic' Bibles, usually divided into two or three parts, were made in the monastic scriptoria of the Rhine and Meuse. Particularly fine examples include the Floreffe and Stavelot Bibles. Heavily illustrated and beautifully painted versions were also made in England, such as the Bury, Lambeth and Dover Bibles. One of the other great works of English Romanesque manuscript illumination, the Winchester Bible (Winchester Cathedral Library), which was made there for Bishop Henry of Blois, brother of King Stephen, is the work of several very gifted artists who also display a wide-ranging set of cultural influences. Some of them were also responsible for a series of superb frescoes at the royal monastery of Sigena in Aragon, on the Camino de Santiago de Compostela, one of the major pilgrimage routes in the West. These were sadly mutilated in the Spanish Civil War of 1936–9 and exist now as mere ghosts of their former selves. The artist of a splendid, now detached, leaf depicting scenes from the life of King David, now in the Morgan Library and Museum in New York and known as the Morgan Leaf, was one of them and may also have visited Norman Sicily, as his work exhibits the influence of mosaics there.

Another of Henry's books, the Psalter of Henry of Blois (British Library, Cotton MS Nero C.iv, also known as the Winchester Psalter) reflects his eastern-facing interests born of the Crusades, and features what is essentially a manuscript icon of the Virgin and Child in Byzantine style. The marriage of Ottonian emperor Otto II to the Byzantine princess Theophano in 972 had provided another important route for the transmission of eastern artistic influences into western sacred art. A further illuminated book that epitomizes international collaboration is the Melisende Psalter (British Library, Egerton MS 1139), made around 1135 for the queen of that name, an Armenian who was married to the crusader Fulk of Anjou. Produced in the Latin kingdom of Jerusalem, its hybrid style is the work of artists from the local region, Byzantium and the Latin West, while its covers are plates of ivory carved with delicate foliate tendrils, which have an almost oriental look, forming roundels containing imagery relating to King David.

Psalters remained the principal vehicle for private devotion. Particularly opulent illuminated copies include the St Albans Psalter, perhaps made in the second quarter of the twelfth century and given by the monastic community to anchoress Christina of Markyate. Prayer books were also made from at least the late eighth century, as we have seen, and by the 1230s the first books of hours began to appear in the context of urban book production, becoming the main vehicle for personal devotions and a medieval bestseller. For personal devotions were also on the rise, as were anchorites and mystics.

The Morgan Leaf depicting scenes from the life of King David (Morgan Library and Museum, New York, MS M.619). This is a detached leaf from the largest, most magnificent English Romanesque Bible, the Winchester Bible, probably made in two campaigns between 1160 and 1190 in the Winchester Cathedral scriptorium. The artist responsible for this splendid leaf is one of those who also travelled to Spain to paint a series of frescoes at the royal monastery of Sigena in Aragon, on the Camino de Santiago de Compostela pilgrimage route. These were very badly damaged in the Spanish Civil War, and the remaining damaged fresco was moved to the Museu Nacional d'Art de Catalunya in Barcelona in 1936.

The *Ancrene Wisse* is one of the earliest extant prose works in Middle English to have been composed after the Norman Conquest, probably in the thirteenth century. It contained instruction for women wishing to pursue the solitary life of the anchoress, which served to popularize the earlier trend for recluses and carried it into the high Middle Ages.

A forerunner of this trend was Christina of Markyate, who was born in Huntingdon sometime between 1096 and 1098 and died around 1155, a year after the election of the only English pope, Adrian IV (Nicholas Breakspear, who as cardinal had been instrumental in establishing the Church in Scandinavia). She was born into a wealthy Anglo-Saxon family that was trying to come to terms with Norman rule at that time and she was first named Theodora, but later took the name Christina in honour of her Christian faith. She is said to have made a personal vow, during a childhood visit to St Albans Abbey, to dedicate herself to her faith and to remain chaste. She later fled on her wedding night and sought shelter with a series of hermits, the last of whom was Roger, a hermit and sub-deacon of St Albans Abbey whose cell was at Markyate. While there she embroidered vestments, had visions, became a trusted advisor of the abbot of St Albans, and went on to take her monastic vows and to found Markyate Priory, becoming its prioress.

The *Life of Christina of Markyate* (British Library, Cotton MS Tiberius E I), which may have been commissioned by Geoffrey de Gorham or Gorron, who became abbot of St Albans from 1119, relates that they were close platonic friends and that 'while [Geoffrey] busied himself in supplying the maiden's needs, [Christina] strove to enrich the man in virtue.' Christina served as his advisor on ecclesiastical matters and even considerately provided underwear for his pilgrimage to Rome in 1136 or 1139, although she did not want him to leave. Their friendship was such that he is said to have altered the St Albans Psalter's original programme of decoration as a gift for her, by having an illuminated 'C' containing a depiction of her (in the same style as the rest of the book's illumination) pasted in over a previous initial at the beginning of Psalm 105. It depicts the saintly Christina being presented to Christ as their intercessor by the St Albans monks, with Geoffrey probably the figure depicted at the forefront. There were evidently changes to plan during the making of this beautiful copy of the Psalter, but even if this initial was an addition it may be that it was a further adaptation to an original scheme that had already been constructed with reference to Christina. For I would propose that other unusual features of its iconography also point to them having been designed with her in mind, either as a devotional gift to her or to affirm and celebrate her connection to St Albans Abbey and to promote her as a patron saint, along with St Alban.

The book is known as the Albani Psalter or Psalter of Christina of Markyate and is one of the most extensively and beautifully illuminated Romanesque Psalters. It has been owned, since the nineteenth century, by the church of St Godehard in Hildesheim, in Lower Saxony in northwestern Germany, but is kept in the Hildesheim Cathedral Library (Dombibliothek). A detached single leaf from it is at the Schnütgen Museum in Cologne. In addition to the Psalms, it contains a Calendar, Canticles, Litany and Collects, which allow it to function liturgically and devotionally (fulfilling its two major functions as the mainstay of both public and private prayer), and is adorned with no less than forty full-page miniatures in the most engaging style of Romanesque art. Its elegant, attenuated figures and damp-style drapery reflect the influence of a mannered phase of Byzantine art and the inherited decorative stylization of early northern European cultures, with the figures looking as if they have just stepped out of the shower, with a 'wet T-shirt' look, revealing their stylized, elongated underlying anatomy.

These mesmerizingly attractive and decorative images also contain some innovative iconographies. As part of its programme of illumination there is a prefatory cycle of miniatures relating scenes from the Life of Christ (a late Anglo-Saxon iconographic introduction, thought to reflect earlier Christological scenes in ninth- to tenth-century Byzantine Psalters). In one of these miniatures the news that Christ is risen from the tomb is conveyed to his disciples by a woman, Mary Magdalene, who in the Renaissance would come to be viewed as a prostitute. Here, as one of his most faithful followers, it is she who proclaims the truth of the Resurrection to eternal life to the men, who cower in an upper room, clutching the books containing their acts of witness but hiding from the authorities. Mary raises her finger in instruction

Overleaf, left: *St Albans Psalter, miniature with an unusual depiction of the scene in which Christ dines with Simon the Pharisee and his feet are anointed with perfumed oil, presaging his death, given by Mary Magdalene who dries his feet with her hair (Dombibliothek Hildesheim,* MS *St. God. 1, p. 36). Judas, challenging the two-dimensionality of the frame, steps through it to remonstrate with Christ about the expense of the oil being expended upon him.* Overleaf, right: *St Albans Psalter, miniature of Mary Magdalene announcing the Resurrection to Christ's disciples, emphasizing women's role in teaching and proclaiming the Gospel (Dombibliothek Hildesheim,* MS *St. God. 1, p. 51). This beautiful book may have been made or amplified as a gift to Christina of Markyate at St Albans Abbey,* c. *1123–35.*

and perhaps also in admonition, encouraging them to come out, go forth and proclaim the Good News (Old English *Godspel* – Gospel). This may have been designed as a tribute to Christina's own contribution to this process.

The onus of responsibility upon believers to engage in sharing the Gospel is further emphasized by the inclusion of three miniatures depicting the Encounter at Emmaus, where some of Christ's followers encounter a stranger on the road, whom they do not recognize until the act of breaking bread together (the Eucharist) reveals him to them as the Messiah.

Other instances of the original illumination of the book containing iconography that may have been intended to reference Christina is the initial 'S' opening Psalm 136/137 ('Super flumina'), which is an alternative treatment of the biblical episode treated by Boney M in their hit song 'By the Rivers of Babylon'. The body of the initial forms a river, inhabited by a charming shoal of little fishes, guided by a larger fish (the fish is an ancient symbol of Christianity and the big fish may be intended to represent Christ, or even Christina leading her people). On the banks sit the people, in contemporary Romanesque dress, lolling lethargically, lamenting and exchanging gossip during their exile from the Promised Land, while at the top, others of their number fell wood in order to reconstruct the Temple. They are supervised by a veiled woman who examines some of the timber to approve it: I suggest that this is Christina overseeing the building of her temple to shelter and proclaim the Word of God – the priory at Markyate, near St Albans.

The iconographic customization is completed by an illuminated bifolium depicting King David and his musicians composing and playing the Psalms opposite an image of the martyrdom of St Alban. There is also a full complement of historiated initials and smaller images. Perhaps in explanation or even vindication of such a lavish scheme, the manuscript also contains a text composed around 600, namely Pope Gregory the Great's defence of the use of images, in the original Latin and in the Anglo-Norman court French of the day, with elements of English incorporated.

The book also contains the earliest surviving example of French vernacular literature, the *Chanson de St Alexis* or *Vie de St Alexis*, thought

St Albans Psalter, 'By the Rivers of Babylon' (Psalm 136), with, perhaps, Christina shown at the top of the initial S selecting timber to build her priory at Markyate to lead God's people back to the Promised Land (Dombibliothek Hildesheim, MS *St. God. 1, p. 350).*

SUP̄ FLUMINA
babilonis illic
sedim⁹ & fleuimus:
dum recordarem̄
sion.
In salicib; in medio ei⁹:
suspendim⁹ organa nr̄a
Quia illic interro-
gauerunt nos: q̄
captiuos duxer̄t nos
uerba cantionū.
Et qui abduxerunt nos:
ymnū cantate nob de canticis sion.
Quom̄ cantabim⁹ canticū dn̄i: intra alienā.
Si oblit⁹ fuero tui ierusalem:
obliuioni detur dextera mea.
Adhereat lingua mea faucib; meis:
si non meminero tui.
Si non proposuero ierusalem:
in pn̄cipio letitie mee.
Memor esto dn̄e filiorū edom:

to have been composed in a Norman religious house (although the inclusion of English linguistic components suggests an English origin) during the second half of the eleventh century or early twelfth. St Alexis (d. *c.* 404) was the son of a Roman senator who, when forced into marriage rather than a calling to prayer and chastity, fled on his wedding night and, having given his possessions to the poor, went to Edessa in Syria and from there wandered as a beggar for seventeen years. Returning eventually to Rome, he lived, unrecognized, beneath his parents' staircase for a further seventeen years, until his body was found bearing a scroll recording his life (related in the *Chanson*, along with miracles subsequently performed by his relics). He he was lamented and mourned by them, as related in the lengthy poem, of which this is a verse relating his mother's sorrow:

O bele boche, bels vis, bele faiture, Com
vei mudede vostre bele figure!
More your amai than no creature.
Si grant dolor ui m'est apareüde!
Mielz me venist, friends, que morte fusse.

(O beautiful mouth, beautiful face, beautiful body, How
I perceive your beautiful appearance changed!
I loved you more than any creature.
How great is the sorrow revealed to me this day!
It would have been better, my friends, if I had died.)

The parallels with Christina's own life cannot but present themselves and the text may have been included as a tribute to her and/or to support the case for her own sanctification. If the abbot and community were pushing for canonization, this might account for the image being added, in the pasted-in initial, to stress Christina's efficacy as a saintly patroness and intercessor, for she is shown humbly, arms outstretched, being presented by the community to Christ. The gathering containing the Alexis material seems to be an addition to the book's original codicological plan and may reflect discussions between Christina and Geoffrey concerning its relevance to them. It has even been suggested that its scribe (Scribe 3) may have been Geoffrey himself. Its illumination is by a particularly gifted artist known, thereby, as 'the Alexis Master' and this whole section of the book would therefore seem to represent a particularly customized endeavour.

To recap and conclude, this book is a special, customized package, made in the St Albans scriptorium by at least six scribes (with signs of a possible continental background for at least one of them) and four artists, and adapted and expanded as a programme during production. Scholarly consensus would now tend to favour this having occurred while Geoffrey de Gorham was abbot (1119–46) and considers that it was possibly owned by Christina and may have been made for her at Geoffrey's behest or have been adapted in her honour, with the addition of the replacement initial C depicting her, as a gift. Entries in the calendar and other additions also indicate that it was probably owned by Christina until her death. Perhaps the book was commenced in connection with the new shrine of St Alban that Abbot Geoffrey was establishing in 1124–9 and its programme grew and was adapted to incorporate an emerging, more recent additional patron saint – Christina – who would have catered to the rising trend among pilgrims for an eremitic asceticism and for female devotion.

The Romanesque was an international style, practised (with local variations) throughout much of Europe and the Near East, owing to the expansion of the Angevin Empire, with England and Wales and Normandy at its heart, the Crusades and the growth in numbers travelling long-distance pilgrim routes. Stylistic influences travelled as well as people and are reflected in the art of the age.

The work of Master Hugo, who was responsible for some of the stellar miniatures in the Bury Bible (Corpus Christi College, Cambridge, MS 2; one of the great Romanesque refectory or lectern Bibles, placed on a lectern and used for reading to monastic communities during meals), blends influences from southern Italy and probably also from Cyprus, Byzantium and the Holy Land, suggesting that he may have travelled. He was also adept in other artistic media and is recorded as having designed and cast a bell and the bronze west doors of Bury St Edmunds Abbey. He also carved in wood and perhaps ivory (the Bury St Edmunds Cross in the Cloisters Museum, New York, is attributed to him).

These artists are all thought to have been religious personnel, but another English illuminator of the age, who worked on the Dover Bible (Corpus Christi College, Cambridge, MS 3 and MS 4), depicts himself in the act of painting one initial, his squirrel-hair brush delineating its outline, while his young assistant grinds mineral-based pigments with a muller. The artist is an older man with an elegant well-trimmed beard and fine clothes, including a bejewelled hat. These proclaim him to be a layman, as is his assistant, who

Parce tuis quesо
monachis clementia ihu;
ONFITEMINI
dño quoniam bonus:
qm in sclm miscdia ei.
Quis loquetur poten
tias dñi: auditas
faciet omis laudes ei.
Beati qui custodiunt
iudicium: & faciunt
iustitiam in omni tempore.

bonu testimoniu phibet cu frib; uniuersis.
Explic argumentum.
Incipit epl'a tertia.
ENIOR
GAIO karo. que ego
diligo in ueritate ca
ritatis. Jdo in omib;
orationem facio pspe
te ingredi. & ualere.
sicut pspe agit ani
ma tua. Gauisus su
ualde uenientib; frib;

wears the traditional lay workman's cap. The community had obviously felt it necessary to bring in, or to farm some of the work out to, a secular artist from the town or elsewhere. The reason for this unusual image may have been, I would propose, to explain a problem with materials. The background on which the initial letter and the artist stand is blue, but instead of being the deep solid blue often found, this (and some of that elsewhere in the Dover Bible) is a wishy-washy pale and patchy light blue, reminiscent of over-enthusiastically stone-washed jeans. Pigment examination has shown it to be made from lapis lazuli, mined in Badakhshan in Afghanistan, on the Silk Road. Centuries earlier, Bishop Eadfrith had successfully faked it using local woad plant dye and gum, knowing of and valuing its properties and exoticism, but unable to obtain it. But getting your hands on this precious substance was not enough, you needed to have the recipe to prepare it as a pigment. This entailed grinding it and suspending the particles into water and skimming them off until the right particle size was obtained to give the vibrant jewel-like blue. Get it wrong and the pale imitation seen in parts of the Dover Bible is the result. Our artist is evidently blaming this waste of an expensive material upon the lack of expertise on the part of his assistant in preparing it!

The twelfth century was not only a time of religious fervour, of pilgrimage, of mystics and of Crusade, it was a time of romanticism and the rise of courtly love. A key theme at the core of this was the Arthurian legends, appropriated many times across the centuries as a means of legitimizing new or upcoming regimes (even extending to the Tudors and to John F. Kennedy's Camelot and retold by George Lucas in the original *Star Wars* film). Britain, the home of the origins of the genre and of its historical roots, played a leading role in this.

A key contributor to this was Geoffrey of Monmouth (*c.* 1095–1155), who is thought perhaps to have been a Breton living on the Welsh borders. His major work was the *Historia Regum Britanniae* (The History of the Kings

Opposite, above: *St Albans Psalter, a pasted-in initial C (Psalm 105) containing a depiction of the saintly Christina of Markyate being presented to Christ by the St Albans abbot and monks, as an intercessor for them (Dombibliothek Hildesheim,* MS *St. God. 1, p. 285).* Opposite, below: *The Dover Bible, detail of an artist painting an initial S while his assistant is grinding pigments (*CCC*, Cambridge,* MS *4, vol. II, f. 242v). They are both laymen, although the book was probably made in the scriptorium of Christ Church Canterbury for its dependent priory at Dover in the 1150s. This pictorial colophon may have been intended to explain why the expensive lapis lazuli from Badakhshan in Afghanistan had only yielded a washed-out pale blue rather than the deep blue it was famed for – because the artist's assistant had not followed the recipe closely when preparing it and had not ground the granules to the correct size.*

of Britain), which relates in Latin the purported history of Britain, from its first settlement by Brutus of Troy, a descendant of Trojan hero Aeneas, to the death of Cadwaladr in the seventh century, covering Julius Caesar's invasions of Britain, kings Leir and Cymbeline and developed narratives of Arthur.

Much of this is based on the sixth- to ninth-century works of Gildas, Bede and Nennius, expanded with material from bardic oral tradition and genealogical tracts, and embellished by Geoffrey's own imagination. It is now thought to contain little reliable history. William of Newburgh wrote around 1190 that 'it is quite clear that everything this man wrote about Arthur and his successors, or indeed about his predecessors from Vortigern onwards, was made up, partly by himself and partly by others.'

Geoffrey's work was nevertheless widely disseminated throughout medieval western Europe and enjoyed a significant afterlife in a variety of forms. These included translations and adaptations such as Wace's Old Norman-French *Roman de Brut*, Layamon's Middle English *Brut*, and several anonymous Middle Welsh versions known as *Brut y Brenhinedd* ('Brut of the Kings'), where it was generally accepted as a true account.

It was largely Geoffrey's structuring and shaping of the Merlin and Arthur myths that ensured their enduring popularity, and he is considered to have established the canon of Arthurian literature. He was passionate about his subject-matter and called himself Galfridus Arturus (both names popular among the Breton lords of Monmouth).

From the twelfth century the Arthurian legends were embroidered by Geoffrey and his successors, contributing to the rise of the romance. This reflected the courtly culture of Angevin France and England, with works such as the Grail romances by Chrétien de Troyes placing the pursuit of honour and love at the centre of the romance genre: 'Through their kisses and caresses they experienced a joy and wonder the equal of which has never been known or heard of. But I shall be silent . . . for the rarest and most delectable pleasures are those which are hinted at, but never told.'

Chrétien de Troyes (*fl. c.* 1160–91), a French poet and troubadour, situated the Arthurian genre in the contemporary European literary mainstream, as a vehicle of the increasingly fashionable courtly romance, and he was the first to write about Lancelot, Percival and the Holy Grail. Chrétien's works include *Erec and Enide* (*c.* 1170); *Cligès* (*c.* 1176); *Yvain, the Knight of the Lion* and *Lancelot, the Knight of the Cart*, the last two written simultaneously between 1177 and 1181. *Yvain* is generally considered Chrétien's masterwork. His final romance was *Perceval, the Story of the Grail,* written between 1181 and 1190 but left unfinished, which was dedicated to Philip, Count of Flanders, to whose court Chrétien may have been attached in his last years. Other authors, including Robert de Boron and Wolfram, soon wrote of Perceval too.

Chrétien also established a new kind of vernacular poem, set in the (fake historical) Arthurian world of Geoffrey of Monmouth and Wace, but with the addition of wonders and marvels inspired by Celtic literature. Among his major sources were the Celtic *Mabinogion* and the *Matter of Brittany*.

Classical influences also occur in Chrétien's romances, with the *Iliad*, the *Aeneid* and the *Metamorphoses* being translated into the Old French vernacular during the 1150s. Foster Guyer argues that *Yvain, the Knight of the Lion* contains Ovidian influence:

> Yvain was filled with grief and showed the Ovidian love symptoms of weeping and sighing so bitterly that he could scarcely speak. He declared that he would never stay away a full year. Using words like those of Leander in the seventeenth of Ovid's Epistles he said: 'If only I had the wings of a dove/to fly back to you at will/Many and many a time I would come'.

Chrétien also deployed dramatic tension and climax to great effect, which has led to him being credited by some with pioneering the novel.

A complete cycle in a multi-volume collection on which H. O. Somner based his edition of the 'Vulgate Version' of the Arthurian romances is to be found in the British Library. Add. MSS 10292–10294 contains *Le Roman du Saint-Graal*, *Le Roman de Merlin* and *Le Roman de Lancelot du Lac, du Quete du Saint-Graal et de la Mort du Roi Artu*. This was written and illuminated in Picardy in France around 1316. It has been suggested that this was for a group of local men who had formed the medieval equivalent of a Rotary Club, convened for socializing and charitable works, who framed themselves as the knights of the round table. The romance of the central tale, however, is often parodied with harsh reality in the margins. The miniature set within the text depicting the first meeting of Queen Guinevere and Sir Lancelot at the feast with King Arthur, for example, contrasts with an image (by the same artist) in the margin depicting a ring (a wedding ring and an eternal circle/triangle, perhaps) with its two ends terminating and joined by the heads of the two lovers kissing, while a king, seen from the rear and squatting on the arc of the circle above, defecates upon them. That pretty much encapsulates the medieval attitude to the phenomenon of courtly love: it had its place and was a game and a social etiquette, but it was not to be condoned inappropriately or taken too seriously.

Eleanor of Aquitaine (*c.* 1122–1204) was queen to two kings and has long epitomized the twelfth-century era of romance and chivalry. It is said that Eleanor, upon separating from her second husband, Henry II of England, returned to her ancestral lands of Aquitaine in southwest France. There she found nobles rebellious, the people disorderly and all in desperate need of a firm hand. Eleanor rose to the challenge and set about bringing peace and order to her troubled realm.

She defiantly established her own court as a civilized haven of courtly manners and chivalric ideals in the notoriously illicit love nest of her grandparents, the Maubergeonne Tower, which still survives in Poitiers at the heart of the Palais de Justice. There knights and troubadours vied for her favour.

Eleanor's own colourful family background may have fostered her interest in unusual romances. Her maternal grandmother, Amauberge 'Dangereuse' de l'Isle Bouchard (1079–1151), was the mistress of her paternal grandfather. Dangereuse was an accomplished *trobiaritz* or female troubadour, a purveyor of 'unearthly music' who enraptured Crusade leader and troubadour William IX, Duke of Aquitaine, as he passed through Poitou in 1100 – the ultimate *liaison dangereuse*. Dangereuse, who had been married for seven years to Aimery I, Viscount of Châtellerault, was willingly abducted by the duke, who was promptly excommunicated, and spent the rest of her days as his mistress in the tower he built in her honour, Le Maubergeonne, at his castle in Poitiers.

When the duke's wife, Philippa, got home she was enraged to discover a rival in her palace. She appealed to friends at court and to the Church, but they could not prevail against William. When the papal legate Giraud (who was bald) complained and told the duke to return 'Dangereuse' to her husband, William simply humiliated him, by quipping, 'Curls will grow on your pate before I part with the Viscountess.' Philippa chose in 1116 to retire to the Abbey of Fontevraud, where she died in 1118. Ironically, that is where Eleanor's remains would also come to rest.

Eleanor and her graceful companions were said to have presided over a set of actual courts: the Courts of Love. During the sittings of these courts, knights brought their disputes over romance and love, whereupon the women would pronounce judgement, their decision final. Under Eleanor's careful guidance the ideas of courtly love flourished and knights learned how to be true knights: each devotedly pining for his mistress, pledging his affections to her alone as he strove to prove his worth by his deeds and gain her love. In short, while stories of Arthur and his gallant knights flourished throughout Christendom, Eleanor and her ladies were living the dream: Poitiers was little short of a real-life Camelot.

That is, at least, the most popular conception of the woman who is so often labelled as the queen of courtly love. Despite the enduring nature of the legend, how much truth is there in the deeds and ideas that have been ascribed to one of Europe's most romanticized women?

The ideas contained within the concept of 'courtly love', the noble and chivalric ideas on how a knight or suitor should behave to the object of his desire, had been in existence long before Eleanor's move to Poitiers. Indeed, they were part and parcel of the general move towards a more mannered, less chaotic society that was taking hold throughout the twelfth century, with an overall stress placed on virtue and nobility. There had also been talk of Courts of Love before her time – the idea of noble women pronouncing over affairs of the heart, while matters of state were dealt with by their husbands. Therefore, it seems that Eleanor cannot be credited with being the first to promote such ideas. In fact, there is little evidence for her having personally advanced the concept during her time at Poitiers at all. Likewise, the idea that Eleanor brought her civilized and cultured southern ideas to the barbarous north with her marriage to Louis VII of France, and again to the less-mannered English court in a precursor to the transformation effected in Poitiers, is on shaky ground.

Alas for legend, the French court, and Paris in particular, was already excelling in culture and the arts, and over her lifetime there is little evidence that Eleanor's patronage of the arts was any greater than other noblewomen of her era. It can be argued, therefore, that Eleanor's part in spreading the concept of everything courtly is as much a literary creation as the exploits of Arthur and his knights.

The spread of the legends of King Arthur and his knights also became entangled with that of Eleanor: made popular in the earlier half of the twelfth century with the advent of Geoffrey of Monmouth's history, the chivalrous group caught the imagination of many and, in a blending of traditions, it has been suggested Eleanor was in fact the inspiration behind some of the later emerging stories of Guinevere. She has been identified by many in works of the time, including those of Marie de France. The idea of Eleanor in the guise of Guinevere or Iseult is compelling enough to overcome the rationalizing that any number of women from the time could fit those roles and nothing stands out to link them to Eleanor. The literary work of Andreas Capellanus, in which Eleanor played such a part, was instrumental in influencing the late nineteenth-century scholar Gaston Paris, who in turn popularized the concept and legend of courtly love, and it was ultimately Eleanor's dramatic role in Capellanus's work that elevated her reputation into the realms of legend. Along with Capellanus and Paris, more recent works from current authors has done much to keep the image of Eleanor as the courtly queen alive and flourishing.

Rather like the figure of Arthur, it could be argued, given the enduring nature of the legend, that the lack of factual truth surrounding Eleanor's part in the creation of courtly love matters little to those who subscribe to the cult of Eleanor, and in fact the fabrications have been more influential than the woman herself ever was. In the popular imagination at least, Eleanor remains the queen of courtly love.

She may have inspired another woman, whom she probably knew (perhaps well) at the English court, Marie de France (*fl. c.* 1160–1215), a medieval poet who was probably born in France and lived in England during the late twelfth century. She lived and wrote at an unknown court, but she and her work were almost certainly known at the royal court of King Henry II of England. Virtually nothing is known of her life; both her given name and its geographical specification come from her manuscripts.

The real name of the author now known as Marie de France is a mystery; she acquired her nom de plume from a line in one of her works: 'Marie ai num, si sui de France' ('My name is Marie, and I am from France'). Some suggestions for the identity of this twelfth-century poet are Marie, Abbess of Shaftesbury and half-sister to Henry II, king of England; Marie, abbess of Reading; Marie I of Boulogne; Marie, abbess of Barking; and Marie de Meulan, wife of Hugh Talbot.

Marie wrote in Francien (which was a dialect found around Paris and the Île-de-France), but displays some Anglo-Norman influence, and she was proficient in Latin, English and possibly Breton. At a time when most educated scholars were usually male clerics, Marie was one of very few women to have achieved prowess with the pen.

The *Lais* are dedicated to a 'noble king', perhaps Henry II or his eldest son, Henry the Young King, and the *Fables* are dedicated to 'Count

William', possibly William of Mandeville or William Marshall. However, it has also been suggested that Count William may be William Longsword, a recognized illegitimate son of Henry II and Marie's nephew, if she was that monarch's half-sister.

Three of the five surviving manuscript copies of the *Lais* are written in continental French. That contained in British Library, Harley MS 978, written in Anglo-Norman French in the mid-thirteenth century, may reflect the dialect of the copyist. Its opening contains a rather vague rebuttal to some critics of Marie about whom we know nothing. The word 'Breton', used here, could equally well be applied to the inhabitants of Brittany in northwestern France or to Britons of England. Marie makes no clear distinction between the two, and authorities on both sides of the Channel have claimed her. The *Lais* are generally known as 'Breton lais'. Her most likely source was Anglo-Saxon, still spoken by many commoners in the twelfth century, with many of the tales probably having even earlier sources in Old Welsh.

Marie also translated Aesop's *Fables* from Middle English into Anglo-Norman French and wrote the *Espurgatoire seint Patriz* (Legend of the Purgatory of St Patrick), based upon a Latin text. Recently, she has been (tentatively) identified as the author of a saint's life, *The Life of St Audrey*. Her *Lais*, in particular, were and still are widely read and influenced the subsequent development of the romance/heroic literature genre.

Marie's Anglo-Norman French was an easy read in her own time and her verses were much shorter than those of her contemporaries such as Chrétien de Troyes. Her audience usually read them in French, although they were translated into various languages – including Old Norse, which allowed them to be read in Iceland.

Marie was therefore a popular part of a generation of writers who were in the process of inventing the French verse romance. Her favoured verse form is the octosyllabic couplet, consisting of eight-syllable lines in rhyming pairs, demonstrated in the prologue to the *Lais*, as translated by Judith P. Shoaf:

Ki Deus ad doné escïence
E de parler bon' eloquence
Ne s'en deit taisir ne celer,
Ainz se deit volunters mustrer.
Quant uns granz biens est mult oïz,
Dunc a primes est il fluriz,

E quant loëz est de plusurs,
Dunc ad espandues ses flurs.

(Whoever gets knowledge from God, science,
and a talent for speech, eloquence,
Shouldn't shut up or hide away;
No, that person should gladly display.
When everyone hears about some great good
Then it flourishes as it should;
When folks praise it at full power,
Then the good deed's in full flower.)

Marie's *lai* on the romance of Tristan (Tristram) and Iseult, here referred to simply as 'the Queen', is named *Chevrefoil*, a title that Shoaf suggests could have been chosen to highlight the destructive nature of honeysuckle or woodbine:

It's my pleasure and I want truly
For the lai men call Chevrefoil
(Honeysuckle), the truth to tell:
Why it was made, how it all befell.
More than one has told me or spoken,
And I've found it also written
About the Queen and Sir Tristram,
Their love so true, so pure, from
Which their sorrows multiplied –
Then, in a single day, both died.
King Mark was angry and then some –
Angry at his nephew Tristram;
He banished him beyond his border,
Because of the Queen, for he loved her.
He goes home to whence he hails –
He was born in South Wales.
He lives there for one whole year.
He could not go back to see her.
But then he's ready to risk it all –
Death, destruction, any downfall.
Don't be too surprised, really:
Any true love who loves loyally
Suffers, and depression haunts
Him when he can't have what he wants.
Tristram suffers, his thoughts roam,
So he slips himself away from home.
He goes straight into Cornwall,
There where the Queen is known to dwell.
He hid himself in the forest alone,
Wanting to be seen by none.
But he crept forth in the evening light
When men seek shelter for the night.
With peasants and the poorest folk
That night he his lodgings took.
He asked the news – just anything
About the doings of the King?
They told him then what they had heard:
The barons, summoned by the King's word,
Must come to Tintagel castle, where
The King wishes to hold court; there
At Pentecost, at Whitsunday,
They'll gather for joy, sport, and play.
The Queen, of course, will take part.

Tristram hears, joy fills his heart.
No way she can go to Tintagel
Without his seeing how she'll travel.
The day the king was on the move,
Sir Tristram came into a grove
Through which, he knew, the road lay
The crowd must use to pass this way.
He cut a hazel in half there,
Shaped and trimmed it, neatly square.
When he had prepared this staff,
He autographed it with his knife.
If the Queen saw this invention,
She would pay it great attention;
For this had all happened before –
She'd realized thus that he was there.
She'll recognize it, easy, quick,
As soon as she sees her lover's stick.
This is the gist of what he wrote,
The message he sent her, as he spoke:
That he'd stayed there for quite a while,
Waiting, lingering in exile,
Spying, trying to learn or hear
How he could find a way to see her,
For without her he cannot live.
For those two, it's just like with
The sweet honeysuckle vine
That on the hazel tree will twine:
When it fastens, slips itself right
Around the trunk, ties itself tight,
Then the two survive together.
But should anyone try to sever
Them, the hazel dies right away,
And the honeysuckle, the same day.
'Dear love, that's our story, too:
Never you without me, me without you!'

THE TWELFTH CENTURY II: GERALD OF WALES AND THE TOPOGRAPHY OF IRELAND

TOPOGRAPHIA HIBERNICA (BRITISH LIBRARY, ROYAL MS 13 B VIII)

The ambitions of the Angevin rulers and their knights did not stop at England. They looked eastwards to the Continent, the Mediterranean and the Holy Land and they also turned their attentions westwards, to the territories of their Celtic and Hiberno-Scandinavian neighbours. They were encouraged in this by the opportunities that internecine competition and hostilities among the local lords offered for mercenary employment, leading to the carving out of their own fiefdoms and even to conquest, in the case of Ireland. The great chronicler, and encourager, of this process in Wales and Ireland was Gerald of Wales, who wrote illustrated itineraries and descriptions of both, based on his own travels and upon local legend, and an account of the activities of Norman-Angevin knights that led ultimately to the royally sanctioned conquest of Ireland. Gerald's works were representative of the new sorts of text emerging from international scholasticism.

Our next focal book was, effectively, self-published as an illustrated edition by its author. Against the backdrop of the internationalism of a French-speaking aristocracy and a Latinate Church, Gerald of Wales (1146–1223), also known by his Latin name Giraldus Cambrensis, was, in the words of Robert Bartlett, 'a child of a frontier society at the edge of feudal Europe'. He was in turns a denigrator and champion of the Celtic peoples from whom he claimed part-ancestry, a sycophant and critic of kings and courts, an espouser of the militaristic feudal ideals of the Marcher knights of Wales (from whose ranks he sprang), and a reforming idealistic cleric intent upon the unity of Christendom and the independence of the Welsh Church.

Gerald's personal manifesto seems to have changed throughout his life, as he was disappointed or frustrated by each social set in turn. Gerald composed the *Topographia Hibernica* (Topography of Ireland) between 1186 and 1188, after his travels in Ireland in 1183 and with Prince John in 1185 to preach Crusade, and the *Expugnatio Hibernica* (The Conquest of Ireland) followed in 1189. In these and the *Descriptio Kambriae* (Welsh Itinerary and Description), this mass of contradictions in his own life led Gerald to attempt to integrate marginal communities (as perceived by the Anglo-Norman establishment) into the international scene by representing them as tangible historical communities with their own histories and structures, and to stress the mutual benefits of integration. Against the background of a strong British historical tradition, he produced innovative ethnographic writing in the footsteps of Gildas and Bede.

The grandson of an Anglo-Norman lord, Gerald of Windsor, and a beautiful Welsh princess, Nest ferch Rhys, the 'Helen of Wales', Gerald was the son of their daughter and a Norman knight, William de Barri; he was also nephew to the Bishop of St David's. He therefore faced many of the dilemmas posed to the Anglo-Irish of the early twentieth century. He is as much 'Gerald the Welshman' as George Bernard Shaw was 'Bernard the Irishman', the proverbial 'fish out of water' whose ethno-cultural affiliations were polarized in accordance with the circumstances – a '**** Welshman' when it suited the Anglo-Norman court and a '**** Englishman' to the Welsh and Irish.

In his *Descriptio Kambriae* Gerald described his birthplace, the castle of Manorbier on the south coast of Pembrokeshire in southwestern Wales, as a paradise on earth, suffused with a love of family, a people and a place. His depictions of Celtic harpists, in word and image, praise the beauty of Celtic music and imply that the Normans 'ain't got no rhythm'. Conversely, the Irish are lauded as the most naturally good-looking and affable of races and yet the most antagonistic and warlike.

Gerald was a born raconteur, a gifted embroiderer of spoken and written language, an inveterate textual 'fiddler'. The Howard Carter of his day, his lectures and after-dinner speeches seem to have called out for the slideshow to accompany them. In the illustrated copies of the *Topography* this is just what is provided, a lively, intriguing series of images that are elaborated in the same manner as the text, in all its various editions. As was the case with certain of the writings of Matthew Paris (*c.* 1200–1259), these tales of Gerald's, with their underlying agendas, were designed for recitation to an audience, preferably enriched by authorial digression, or for perusal, preferably enlivened by illustration. In the works of both authors, new programmes of illustration intimately related to the text were devised and set in the margins around the text block.

As we shall see shortly, the famous thirteenth-century chronicler-monk Matthew Paris is known to have planned and penned his own programmes; can the same be said to any extent of his predecessor, Gerald? If so, he deserves to be recognized as a key figure in the perception and development of marginal space as the vehicle for new programmes of illustration, a major contribution to book production and Gothic art.

This contribution would remain equally valid if Gerald acted in a supervisory capacity, instructing artists and scribes during the 'publication' of his works and intervening editorially during both text and image production. The textual recensions would certainly suggest that this was the case, showing that the author was dictating additions to the text as they were being written in the margins of the main text and with some of these additions being illustrated in the same way as points in the body of the text.

The medieval context for the authoring of texts should be borne in mind here. Authors would usually dictate their works, rather than penning them themselves. Authorial ventures into desktop publishing, such as those of Matthew Paris and Christine de Pizan, were the exceptions to the rule. Close authorial involvement and intervention in the processes of book manufacture may be considered virtually analogous to 'autograph' production in such a context. If Gerald need not have copied his own works in order to be considered to have published them personally, he can hardly be expected to have undertaken the even more specialized role of illuminator in order to be considered to have devised his own programme of illustration. With these caveats in mind it is worth noting, however, that these illustrations are not integrated into the text block as miniatures or column pictures, but are treated as textual accompaniments, or asides, within the lower margins. This might accord with the informality of authorial intervention rather than a more formally devised, established programme. The technique of tinted drawing used may also be indicative. Drawings with a light colour wash are easier to produce technically than full illumination with its complex processes of gilding and colour layering and are more amenable to the relative 'amateur', rather as watercolour was favoured during the nineteenth century.

There are 24 surviving manuscripts of the *Topography*, plus five fourteenth-century volumes containing, variously, excerpts, an abbreviated version and its Provençal translation. There are also early modern transcripts. Of the copies of the *Topography* proper, one is thought to date from the late twelfth century and fifteen from the thirteenth century. Of these thirteenth-century volumes, four are illustrated with a series of marginal tinted drawings: British Library, Royal MS 13 B VIII; Dublin, National Library of Ireland, MS 700; Bodleian Library, Laud. Misc. 720; and Cambridge University Library, F.I.27. Two further volumes in the British Library contain maps of Britain and Ireland, perhaps representing abbreviated extracts from a map of Europe in the Dublin manuscript: Arundel MS 14 (f. 27) and Add. MS 33991 (f. 26).

In such limited discussion of the illustrated copies as has already occurred the chronological sequence favours the London volume as the earliest, closely followed by Dublin, with the Oxford manuscript following a generation later. The Cambridge volume seems to have slipped through the art-historical net.

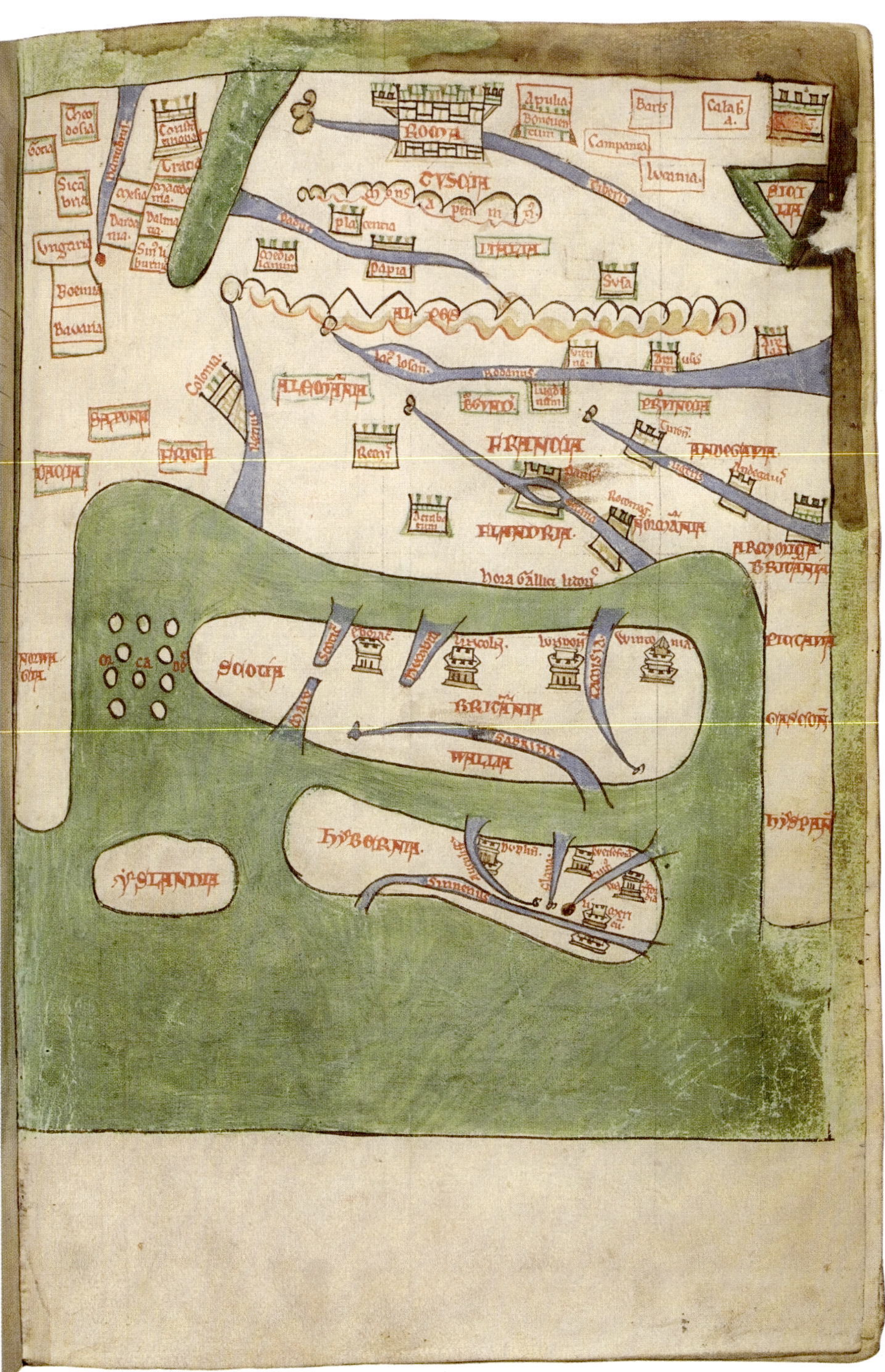

Gerald's role as the original artist behind the scheme has been questioned on the grounds that he does not mention any such talents in his own frequently self-promoting literary works, including his autobiography. Although such an omission would represent a surprisingly uncharacteristic degree of modesty for Gerald, the lack of such a reference in his surviving

Opposite: *A scholastic view: Giraldus Cambrensis's map of continental Europe, Britain, Ireland, the Orkneys and Iceland, in a manuscript from Lincoln, early 13th century, used to accompany his new topographical works on Ireland and Wales (National Library of Ireland, Dublin, MS 700, f. 48r).* Below: *An Irish scribe writing a book so wondrous that you would think it the work of angels, miniature from Giraldus Cambrensis,* Topography of Ireland, *c. 1196–1223 (BL, Royal MS 13 B VIII, f. 22r). Giraldus Cambrensis says he saw that book at Kildare and it sounds like the Book of Kildare was as amazing as the Book of Kells. This copy was made under Gerald's personal supervision at Lincoln Cathedral.*

literary output need not preclude his role in illustrating his autograph work, with whatever degree of aesthetic accomplishment, or in supervising the more professional illumination of copies of his work.

Chance statements in his writings do hint at the possibility. For example, he exhibits frustration at the limitations of verbal description (not normally a problem for Gerald) when describing, in his *Descriptio Kambriae*, the implement used in Wales for reaping, which he concludes with the passage, 'But since "Things imparted through the ears enliven the mind more slowly than things placed before our trustworthy eyes," you will understand the method better by seeing than by hearing,' perhaps implying that an illustration was envisaged. Pictures were of obvious benefit to the attempts to impart unfamiliar information, which characterized many new works of the twelfth and thirteenth centuries.

The Franciscan William of Rubruck, when writing an account of his mission to the Mongols in the 1250s, laments his lack of artistic ability, stating that 'The married women make beautiful wagons for themselves, which I don't know how to describe to you except through an illustration – indeed, I would illustrate everything for you, if I knew how to draw.' Gerald makes no such lament, and does in fact provide evidence in support of his draughtsmanship when he refers to his cartographic abilities in producing a now lost map of Wales. In his words, this map showed 'the tough mountains, bristling forests, lakes, rivers and high-raised castles; also the cathedral churches and many monasteries'.

The illustrations to Gerald's work show the same alert, detailed, loquacious spirit as his words. The simplified map of Europe in the Dublin volume (NLI MS 700, f. 48r) nonetheless contains quite a deal of visual information in its depictions of towns, mountains and other landmarks.

The passage in the *Topography* in which Gerald describes a marvellous Gospel book of such intricacy and subtlety of decoration that you would think it 'the work not of men, but of angels' is thought by some scholars to have been the famous Book of Kells, which was probably made on Iona around 800 and continued in Kells after the community of St Columba moved there to escape the Vikings following a particularly ferocious raid in 806, during which 68 monks were martyred. But Gerald is referring to a wondrous Book of Kildare, which suggests that the shrine of St Brigid had a similarly resplendent Gospel book as a focal point. What Gerald went on to say about the manner of its making may cast some light upon Gerald's personal experience of the processes of illumination.

He tells how an angel appeared to the scribe and 'showed him a drawing made on a tablet which he carried in his hand and said to him: "Do you think that you can make this drawing on the first page of the book that you are about to begin?" The scribe, not feeling that he was capable of an art so subtle and trusting little in his knowledge of something almost unknown, replied, "No".' But, with the assistance of the prayers of St Brigid, 'the angel came again and held before him the same and many other drawings. By the help of the divine grace, the scribe, taking particular notice of them all, and faithfully committing them to his memory, was able to reproduce them exactly in the suitable places in the book.' Substitute Gerald for the angel and we may be witnessing the genesis of the illustrated *Topography*. Just as Gerald's 'writing' of his texts may refer to dictation rather than penmanship, so his authorship of the illustrations may have assumed such an interventionist form. He would, nonetheless, remain their originator. Modesty was not one of Gerald's gifts and if he were a good artist himself, he would certainly have told us so.

Another of Ireland's early saints is celebrated by Gerald for his care of Creation, depicting a passage in one of the saint's 'lives' in which he was praying with his arms stretched out through the windows in his stone hut, when a blackbird nestled in his hand and laid her eggs. Kevin obligingly remained in prayer until the egg safely hatched.

I have proposed that the London and Dublin manuscripts are closely related and were made in the same scriptorium, which I think was that of Lincoln Cathedral, around the year 1200. Gerald spent the years 1196–8 there with his friend, the scholar Walter Map; both had studied in Paris, bought second-hand books on the 'parvisus' area in front of Notre Dame and would have had much in common. It is pleasing to think of Gerald enjoying his retirement in that beautiful building, with a good library and congenial company, reminiscing about the good old days as students in what, even then, was 'gay Paris'.

In the London manuscript events are generally subjected to a more episodic treatment with successive passages depicted, conflating time and space somewhat in the manner of Giotto. In 'Dublin' the images are simpler, if related in such detail as they do display. The later illustrated copies adhere to 'Dublin' for some images and 'London' for others, indicating that one scheme did not simply supplant the other.

'London' embroiders on the detail, drawn from the text. There are also signs in it of Gerald making authorial additions while the book was being

St Kevin of Glendalough, allowing a blackbird to hatch her young in his hand, which he had outstretched in prayer, miniature from Giraldus Cambrensis, Topography of Ireland, c. *1196–1223 (BL, Royal MS 13 B VIII, f. 20r). There is an original sewing repair to the torn vellum.*

made and the images in the margins respond to some of those changes. This suggests to me that Gerald was literally at the scribe and artist's elbow, telling them what to add in the margins as they worked: Gerald, in place of the Kildare angel!

This is most clearly demonstrated by the inclusion in the London volume of a depiction of the fish from Carlingford Lough with golden teeth, which is mentioned in Gerald's text. This image is accompanied by one of a deer with similar teeth, alongside one of a series of marginal annotations by the text scribe, carefully set and ruled for in the margins. This note draws attention to the analogy between the Carlingford fish and a deer captured in Dunholm wood, which displayed the same phenomenon.

This passage does not appear in Gerald's first edition of the text and seems to represent an embroidery upon it. The relationship of this note to the image implies that the cycle of illustration in this copy was being similarly embroidered and developed. A consideration of the text has led to the suggestion that this elaboration was undertaken within Gerald's circle, either during or as a result of his presence in its midst. Indeed, textual considerations suggest that it was conducted under Gerald's own supervision. It is interesting, therefore, to note that Dunholm, whence came the miraculous deer, is likely to be the wood that lies a mere 10 kilometres from Lincoln, where Gerald was resident from 1196 to 1198 and after 1207/8, when he retired to the cathedral. The closer the comparison between the images in the London and Dublin volumes, the more it becomes apparent that the London copy was being elaborated, in text and illustrations, and that 'Dublin', although physically slightly later in the style of its artwork and script, was closer to an original core programme.

A 'rough copy' of the *Topographia* and the *Expugnatio* was presented by Gerald to Hereford Cathedral, another centre with which he was closely associated, in 1218 (this may be the Dublin manuscript), and he promised to exchange it for an amended 'fair copy' in due course.

A particularly interesting detail concerns the depiction of an Irish musician to illustrate Gerald's eulogy of Celtic music. The Dublin and Cambridge manuscripts preserve an image of the characteristic Irish bard, a resplendent chap with elaborate garb, cloak, head-filet and flowing beard who plays a true Celtic harp, similar, for example, to 'Brian Boru's harp', a late medieval instrument now in Trinity College Dublin. Gerald, who criticized the Anglo-Normans for their boorish lack of appreciation of such music and lack of rhythm, was certainly familiar with such performers, and with other contemporary details of depiction.

Conversely, the episode of the rape of a woman in the taboo mill of St Fechin depicts a water mill of a design unknown in Ireland, but familiar in manorial England. This illustration only occurs in the latest of the illustrated copies, 'Cambridge', and probably represents a later addition to the original picture-cycle.

In his attempts to win recognition, and promotion, through his literary talents Gerald presented copies of his works to those in positions of power. The *Topography* was dedicated to Henry II, and Richard I received a presentation copy after his accession in 1189. During the 1190s he dedicated or presented works to William Longchamp, Bishop of Ely, Hubert Walter, Archbishop of Canterbury, and St Hugh, Bishop of Lincoln, and around 1220 Stephen Langton was also a recipient. Gerald's habit of presenting or circulating his works may have led him to produce or commission illustrated copies for the increased edification and admiration of his audience. This might also have led to the presence of illustrated copies in several centres, all reflecting the same ultimate scheme, or schemes, and style, from which further copies were generated.

Such provenance information as we possess concerning the surviving copies is not of great assistance. The London volume, probably made at Lincoln, was at St Augustine's, Canterbury, by the fifteenth century; 'Dublin' was given to Hereford Cathedral in 1438; 'Oxford' was owned by a prebendary of Durham in the early seventeenth century; 'Cambridge' was in the medieval library of Bury St Edmunds and may have been made there.

There was evidently a programme of illustration existing for the *Topography* before 'London' and 'Dublin' were made at the beginning of the thirteenth century. It was probably initiated by Gerald himself and circulated in several manuscripts, perhaps including presentation copies. 'Dublin', which is the second oldest copy to survive, is closest to the lost original cycle, which was already being elaborated at Lincoln, perhaps under Gerald's personal supervision, during the production of the 'London' volume, which is the oldest extant copy of the work. As already stated, 'Oxford' and 'Cambridge' preserve, variously, elements from both 'London' and 'Dublin' and, although a generation or more later, are surprisingly faithful to their style. It is unlikely that these later artists had access to both of the earlier volumes, indicating dependence on a further copy, or copies, now lost. Such intermediaries were partly influenced by the Lincoln-based expansion, as the later copies include the golden-toothed deer of Dunholm and the expanded images of the London volume.

The illustrative programme to the *Topography* seems to have been quite widespread and may have been influential in popularizing the genre of marginal illustration, especially in other 'historical' works, notably those of Matthew Paris. There was something of a pre-existing tradition of ad hoc marginal illustration known and practised in the British Isles. This would have rendered marginal space an obvious choice for the formulation of a new programme of illustrations to accompany a new sort of literary work, rather than integrating framed miniatures within the text block, especially when both text and image were undergoing continual editorial revision by the author and his circle. Against the background of the 'new naturalism' of the twelfth century and the growth of realistic observation, similar solutions were to be explored for other works, such as medical and scientific texts.

Stylistic parallels occur in early bestiaries (such as the Fitzwilliam Bestiary made in Lincoln) for certain images in the *Topography* are obviously indebted to them. For example, the image of the osprey diving into the sea to fish is probably derived from that of the eagle diving into the fountain in the bestiary tradition: likewise, the solemn little processions of beavers, badgers, foxes, lizards and insects and the golden-toothed deer.

Another image that is certainly related to the bestiary tradition is that of barnacle geese growing from a tree. However, in this instance Gerald's works are likely to have influenced the bestiary, rather than vice versa, as the *Topography* seems to be the earliest extant written source for the confusion of the birds with the crustaceans known as barnacles, which attach themselves to rocks. Two thirteenth-century bestiaries, Bodleian Library, Bodley 764 and British Library, Harley MS 4751, even borrowed Gerald's chapters on the barnacle goose, osprey, kingfisher and badger, while the list of eastern animals that Gerald inserted into the second edition of the *Topography* was taken from bestiaries. The bestiary itself became a popular illuminated genre of book from the late twelfth century among secular patrons and clerics alike, its iconographies and texts falling into different families. Among the most splendid are the Fitzwilliam Bestiary and the Aberdeen Bestiary.

The twelfth century also saw a rise in illustrated copies of earlier hagiographical works, such as Bede's *Life of St Cuthbert*, which existed in illustrated copies such as Oxford, University College, MS 165, a Durham work of the early twelfth century, and another lavish late twelfth-century Durham copy (British Library, Yates Thompson MS 26) or the Guthlac Roll (British Library, Harley Roll Y 6), which was made for Crowland Abbey, relatively near Lincoln, around 1200, which might also have served to stimulate the design of the figural scenes in the *Topography*.

Certain of the tales, especially the taller ones, are simply too good an opportunity to miss, such as the mare's stew kingship ritual, an image that persists essentially unaltered in all the surviving illustrated copies. Gerald's concern with bolstering the legitimacy and flagging splendour of Henry II's reign and promoting the extension of English royal authority in Ireland would, furthermore, have made this barbarous image of existing Irish kingship an obvious choice. Someone must have told Gerald a particularly colourful tale on this occasion, or he may have received, through the remarkably developed medium of Celtic oral tradition, a garbled version of ancient pagan Celtic kingship rituals concerning the symbolic mating of the king with nature, in the form of a mare, for which there is some authority. Whatever its basis, the ceremony was certainly defunct in twelfth-century Ireland, but credulity suited the author's purposes, as well as presenting a 'ripping yarn'.

Most significantly of all, it contrasted the alleged barbarity of Irish kingship with civilized Angevin rule – after all, King Henry II would surely only ever have bathed in a stew composed of his own immediate family, if their volatile relationships are anything to go by!

Other illustrations of Irish life, such as the men of Connaught in their curragh, the musicians and the axe-wielding warriors, are a novel adjunct to Gerald's innovative contribution to ethnographical writing. Gerald's work in this area differs from most related literary endeavours, such as those of Adam of Bremen concerning the Scandinavians and Helmold of Bosau on the Slavs, in that it included illustrations, rather in the manner of more modern anthropological and travel writing.

Another prominent element in the visual themes is that of bestiality. The woman of Connaught is shown embracing a goat, and Johanna of Paris a lion, and the pathetic ox-man of Wicklow who became a household pet of the invaders, leading to his murder at the hands of the locals, is depicted. The bearded woman of Limerick – who, according to Gerald, was despite a flowing beard and a crested hairy spine in other respects 'sufficiently feminine' – sits naked upon a hillock spinning. Is she just gainfully occupying her time, or is there an implication of retribution for the sinful nature of this 'daughter of Eve', whose toil (after Adam and Eve were ejected from Eden) she emulates?

Gerald, like many contemporary churchmen, was decidedly misogynistic. Moral issues of this sort and the pastoral response were a major preoccupation of churchmen of the period; the thirteenth-century scribe known as the Tremulous Hand of Worcester, for example, displays a similar concern in his scholarly activities. An element of voyeurism also ensured that such episodes would capture the interest of lay and clerical audiences alike.

However, there is also the possibility of a darker political agenda, and it is worth bearing in mind that immorality was an essential factor in obtaining papal support for the Anglo-Norman invasion of Ireland. In a letter of 1172 from Pope Alexander III to Henry II, the spiritual head of western Christendom recounted bestiality among the sexual vices of the Irish and looked to Henry for the imposition of Christian discipline, as an adjunct of military and political conquest. Including such salacious details in the *Topography* thereby supported Gerald's agenda of persuading the English king to legitimize the activities of the Norman mercenary knights in Ireland by annexing it.

Gerald was determined to stimulate flagging royal interest in the conquest and colonization of Ireland, which was begun by his marcher kin. He saw their achievements as marginalized by the English court and lamented the laggardly nature of royal interest and backing. For Gerald's prime motive was not just to bring the Celtic regions, with their wonders and warts, to the attention of a mainstream European audience. He aimed at their integration, culturally, spiritually and politically. The perceived vehicle

Top: *Fictitious pagan Irish kingship ritual of the white mare's stew, marginal miniature from Giraldus Cambrensis,* Topography of Ireland, c. *1196–1223 (BL, Royal MS 13 B VIII, f. 28v). Such scenes played to Gerald's agenda of encouraging Angevin annexation of Ireland.* Bottom: *The naked bearded woman of Limerick and the naked ox-man of Wicklow, marginal miniature from Giraldus Cambrensis,* Topography of Ireland, c. *1196–1223 (BL, Royal MS 13 B VIII, f. 19r).*

for this worldwide Christian community was, for Gerald, the Angevin Empire. In 1188 he was to preach the crusading ideal throughout Wales, even taking the Cross himself. The East was to be wrested from the infidel and integrated into an Angevin Christendom, although here again Henry II's efforts were, to Gerald, half-hearted and in need of his encouragement. In the far west, urged Gerald, were a 'nominally' Christian people teetering on the edge of barbarity and paganism, who were equally in need of the 'good offices' of the Angevin Church and State. The *Topography* was, at a fundamental level, designed to capture the imaginations of king, Church and public and engage them in this project of integration.

King Henry II died in 1189, embittered and dispossessed, and five years later Gerald was to retire from court and subsequently embark upon a self-destructive bid for advancement through his claims to the bishopric of St David's and for its independence as an archbishopric, leading him to run aground upon the rocks of nationalism. The cracks were already opening while Gerald was composing the *Topography*, but in the first edition he was still able to include a dedication to Henry II and to write, in the epilogue,

> Your victories vie with the whole round of the world. Our western Alexander, you have stretched your arm from the Pyrenean mountains even to these far western bounds of the northern ocean . . . I shall attempt to describe the manner in which the Irish world has been added to your titles and triumphs; with what great and laudable valour you have penetrated the secrets of the ocean and the hidden things of nature; how you were recalled from a most noble enterprise too soon and inopportunely, too quickly and too criminally, because of an internal conspiracy (although your victory had been won, but the conquest had not yet been put in order) . . . postponed your eastern victories in Asia and Spain (which you had already decided in your noble mind to add to those of the West and so extend in a signal way the Faith of Christ).

What better way of capturing publicity for agenda and author alike than to adopt and extend a genre that had already helped to direct the attention of European society eastwards, namely that of the 'Marvels of the East'. For, in Gerald's own words,

> just as the marvels of the East have through the work of certain authors come to the light of public notice, so the marvels of the West which, so far, have remained hidden away and almost unknown, may eventually find in me one to make them known even in these later days.

In thereby claiming the authoritative basis of tradition, Gerald was, in established medieval fashion, empowered to embark upon his voyage into the choppy waters of innovation. En route he was able to establish a convention of authorial 'illustration' using new compositions, be it in a hands on or a supervisory capacity (rather like some of the work of later artists such as Van Dyck and Damien Hirst, much of whose work is fabricated by their teams).

7

THE THIRTEENTH CENTURY: MATTHEW PARIS'S CHRONICLE

CHRONICA MAIORA (CORPUS CHRISTI COLLEGE, CAMBRIDGE, MSS 16 AND 26, AND BRITISH LIBRARY, ROYAL MS 14 C VII)

England began the century under the rule of King John (r. 1199–1216), a younger son of Henry II and brother of Richard the Lionheart, for whom he acted as quasi-regent during Richard's protracted absence on crusade. We are used to portrayals of John as a weak, scheming, oppressive figure in versions of the Robin Hood legend. Other than John and Richard, the only verifiably historical figure therein is Friar Tuck, who had his own robber band in Sussex, far from Nottingham Forest. The myth that developed drew upon tales from other regions and upon ancient traditions concerning Herne the Hunter (ultimately based upon the Celtic Iron Age god of Nature and hunting, Cernunnos) and the Green Man, a mythical wild forest-dwelling figure. Tuck emerges as a rebellious mendicant, one of the new orders of friars that arose in the early thirteenth century in response to popular unrest at the abuses, injustices and wealth of princes of the Church and State. 'Mendicant' derives from the latin *mendicare*, 'to beg', and its brothers/friars, sisters/nuns and lay tertiaries did not form closed orders, restricted to the cloister, but were out and about in the world, travelling as preachers, feeding and nursing the poor and vulnerable, teaching and serving as spiritual advisors. The Franciscans were founded by St Francis in 1209 and the Dominicans by St Dominic in 1216. And these were followed by others, such as the Austin (Augustinian) friars. Robbing the rich to give to the poor might be seen as a popular extension of some of these precepts – or, rather, educating the rich spiritually to give, literally, to the poor and to espouse social justice. For a while these early orders and their founders teetered on the precipice of heresy, but Pope Innocent III had the wisdom to legitimize them and use them to turn the ship of the Roman Catholic Church aside from the rocks of Reformation (or at least postpone the impact for another three hundred years or so).

King John is, perhaps, best remembered for having to acquiesce, in the face of the barons' revolt, to signing Magna Carta, the 'Great Charter'. This was drafted by the Archbishop of Canterbury, Cardinal Stephen Langton, and was sealed by John at Runnymede on the River Thames on 15 June 1215 and is seen as a significant landmark in the development of civil liberties. Most of the clauses favoured the barons and enabled them to play a greater role in central government at Westminster, but some had wider relevance, such as the right not to be executed without trial by jury and the limiting of the ability to apply and increase taxes arbitrarily, without the consent of the barons. This is taken, also, to mark an important step in the evolution of Parliament, as it was to be implemented through a council of 25 barons. The failure of either of the parties to adhere to the agreement led Pope Innocent III to annul it, leading to the First Barons' War. A revised version, along with the 'Forest Charter' (which also made major concessions, diluting the exclusivity of royal hunting rights), was issued as part of the treaty ending this conflict in 1217, during the minority of John's son and heir, Henry III (r. 1216–72). John had lost most of the Angevin dynasty's continental possessions and from the time of Henry III until the advent of the Tudors in 1485 the English monarchs were known as the Plantagenets – a title that stems from the time of Geoffrey of Anjou and the practice of the Angevins and their supporters of wearing sprigs of broom (*planta genista*) to identify them on the battlefield – and their attention became focused more on Britain and Ireland, although they continued to pursue their territorial claim to Gascony in France. The Houses of Lancaster and York, the rivalry between which is known as the Wars of the Roses, are both cadet branches of the House of Plantagenet.

A little-known episode in English history should be mentioned here, namely England's temporary rule by a king of France. In 1216, at the conclusion of the First Barons' War, the future Louis VIII of France landed on the Isle of Thanet in Kent and marched to London, where he was met by cheering crowds. He was proclaimed King Louis of England at St Paul's Cathedral on 2 June 1216 (though not crowned). Within a month he controlled over half of the country and two-thirds of the barons but suffered defeat by the English fleet. He signed the Treaty of Lambeth in September 1217 and gained 10,000 marks in return for agreeing that he had not legitimately been the king of England.

Henry III enjoyed a long reign of just over 56 years and married Eleanor of Provence in 1236. Competition with the French court, which led European stylistic and artistic aspirations at this time, led to major building works at the Palace of Westminster and adjacent Abbey, which had been begun by Edward the Confessor. King Louis IX's construction of the magnificent Sainte Chapelle in the royal Palais de la Cité in Paris in 1241–8 to house his collection of relics, including the Crown of Thorns worn by Christ during his Passion, inspired much competition and emulation by his peers. This was a great age of cathedral building, producing masterpieces such as at Salisbury and Lincoln, replete with stained glass, sculpture, wall paintings and metalwork, woodwork and textiles – and, of course, illuminated manuscripts and choir-books for the theatre of the liturgy and for personal devotions, witnessing the introduction of books of hours. The Gothic age had arrived in Britain.

Westminster had emerged as the main seat of government, where the king and his barons discussed strategy. But Henry's reliance upon the counsel of his favourites, his high taxation and rising levels of famine led to unrest among the barons at large, which erupted into another mini civil war known as the Second Barons' War (1264–7), led by Henry's brother-in-law Simon de Montfort, Earl of Leicester, who sought to broaden the base of Parliament beyond the grandees to include representation from the Commons (essentially the lesser gentry and the mercantile class). The royal forces were led initially by the king and later by his son, the future Edward I. Henry and Edward were captured at the Battle of Lewes by Simon, who exercised a Protectorate until 1265.

During this time there were baronial attacks on the Jews in several towns and stirrings of popular unrest. In Lincoln, for example, the murder in 1255 of a boy who became known as Little St Hugh of Lincoln was blamed upon the Jews, nineteen of whom were hanged with a view to cancelling debts to Jewish moneylenders. This was upheld by the Crown (which in 1290, under Edward I, would scandalously expel the Jews from England as a means of cancelling the national debt owed to them). Papal and French royal interventions occurred and de Montfort was eventually defeated at the Battle of Evesham in 1265. In 1267 the last rebel forces surrendered at the Isle of Ely.

Those seeking to consolidate and extend their power in Wales also took advantage of any weakening of the English monarchy and were caught up in its fortunes. Gruffudd ap Llywelyn ap Iorwerth (*c.* 1196–1244), son of Llywelyn the Great ('Llywelyn Fawr'), was taken hostage by King John of England as a pledge for his father's continued good faith, until a clause in Magna Carta in 1215 compelled his release. Following a successful invasion of the Welsh borders by Henry III in 1241, Gruffudd was once again taken hostage and imprisoned in the Tower of London. It has often been said that a picture tells a thousand words and a good example of this is a drawing by Matthew Paris in the outer margin of a page in his *Chronica maiora*, which relates that Gruffudd met his death in 1244 falling from an upper window of the Tower, while detained at His Majesty's pleasure. Rumours were rife – did he jump or was he pushed? Matthew adds a simple, but highly politically charged, visual comment showing that the sheets that he had tied together to make an escape-rope had given way, leaving him to plummet to his death. The implicit verdict of history – or at least, this historian – is 'death by misadventure'. Matthew Paris became the great chronicler of England and Europe during the mid-thirteenth century.

Henry's son Edward I (r. 1272–1307), also known as Longshanks or 'the Hammer of the Scots', succeeded him and was famed for his hard-line tactics and the strength of his rule. Protracted military campaigns against the Scots, Welsh and French, along with castle building as part of this, characterized his reign. In 1254 he married his beloved Eleanor of Castile, who bore him sixteen children. When she died in the East Midlands, during a royal progress in 1290, Edward had twelve fine sculptural monuments known as the Eleanor Crosses erected at the places where her body rested on its way back to Westminster Abbey. Fine examples survive at Geddington, Hardingstone and Waltham Cross, while a Victorian version of one (erected in 1865) stands outside Charing Cross Station in London.

Returning to Matthew Paris – whose writing and elegant tinted drawings characterized so much of English history and culture during Henry III's reign – while Gerald of Wales may have effectively overseen the publication of his own works Matthew was perhaps the first 'desktop publisher'. He was a habitual frequenter of the Westminster court and was a Benedictine monk of St Albans Abbey (Hertfordshire), which lay within a day's journey north of London along the Roman road of Watling Street. He was a historian, cartographer, artist and scribe. Although known as Matthew 'of Paris', we know of no immediate connection, although perhaps his family came from there; some believe, however, he was of the Paris family of Hildersham, Cambridgeshire. He has left us a fine portrait of himself, kneeling humbly before the Virgin and Child, in his *Historia Anglorum* of 1250–59 (British Library, Royal MS 14 C VII, f. 6r). Some of Matthew Paris's works were written in Latin, others in Anglo-Norman or French verse. Like Bede, he was his own 'notary' and wrote many of them in his own hand (several of these autograph copies still survive) and also illuminated some of them in elegant yet lively ink drawings

washed with colour in a technique known as 'tinted drawing', reviving a technique that the Anglo-Saxons had popularized. An interim example of this is the Guthlac Roll (British Library, Harley Roll Y.6), probably made at Crowland Abbey (Lincolnshire) around 1200, which consists of roundels containing tinted drawing scenes illustrating the Life of St Guthlac, an Anglo-Saxon warrior-prince turned hermit, who was tormented by demons on his island fastness in the fens. This takes the form of a vellum scroll, rather than a codex, and the roundels may have been intended as models for stained glass.

Matthew also embraced the idea of using the marginal space of the page as an opportunity to comment on the text through images, in the way that textual commentaries had come to form wrap-round texts in the books used in the cathedral schools and early universities in the late twelfth century and the thirteenth. His lively little tinted drawings recount a lot of additional information to the text, as well as illustrating parts of it.

Matthew recalled that he had entered the monastery around the age of seventeen. He must have been of good family and naturally personable, affable and gregarious, for he became a regular frequenter of the court of Henry III at Westminster and was even entrusted with a diplomatic mission to Norway in 1248, taking a letter from Louis IX to King Haakon IV, who entrusted him with the reformation of the Benedictine Nidarholm Abbey near Trondheim.

Matthew included interviews with Haakon, Henry III and Richard of Cornwall, as well as sundry bishops and other worthies, in his works and was not sparing with his own opinions. He both praised and denigrated Frederick II, the Holy Roman Emperor, and was not enthusiastic about the papacy, advocating greater local autonomy in the Church, although he also seems to have painted at least one of the Becket Leaves and was well aware that Becket had withstood royal hijacking of such independence for political purposes.

Henry III, during a week-long visit to St Albans, kept Matthew beside him night and day, 'and guided my pen', says Paris, 'with much goodwill and diligence'. That did not stop Matthew from being critical, however, and he was certainly no official historiographer. He even wrote the note 'offendiculum' (offensive/sensitive) beside some passages of his work, indicating that he

Matthew Paris's marginal drawing of Prince Gruffudd ap Llywelyn ap Iorwerth of Wales's fatal attempted escape from the Tower of London in 1244, from the original manuscript of his Historia Anglorum, *1250–59 (BL, Royal MS 14 C VII, f. 136r).*

O felicia oscula lactentis labiis impressa
MATHIAS : PARISIENSIS

knew he was skating on thin ice, but these nonetheless made it into some subsequent copies.

Most of his time was spent at St Albans Abbey, however, where he completed and carried forward the work of his forebear as historian there, Roger of Wendover (d. 1236), extending his *Flores historiarum* (Flowers of History), which stretched from the Creation to 1235, to his own death in 1259 to form the *Chronica maiora*. This has become his most famed work, but near-contemporaries preferred the two abridgements that he made, the *Historia Anglorum* and his own *Flores historiarum*. An abbreviation, the *Abbreviatio chronicorum* (or *Historia minor*), remained unfinished at his death.

Matthew also wrote hagiography and showed an interest in natural history and cartography. Outstanding among his maps were four versions of a pilgrim itinerary from London to Rome, with stylized little depictions of towns (like the symbols in the key to a modern map) that marked the destination of each day's travel. These itineraries are unparalleled in their technique.

The English cartographic tradition that the Anglo-Saxon world map Giraldus and Matthew had helped to carry forward would culminate at the end of the century in the Hereford *mappa mundi*, the most famous medieval map of all. This is a large 'single sheet' document – almost as large as the sheet for a single bed – which likely served as an altar reredos at Hereford Cathedral (a wooden frame for it was discovered in a barn in the late twentieth century). This presents a visual compendium, in diagrammatic cartographic form, of Creation – with Christ in Majesty depicted at the top, presiding over it – with key places and moments from biblical history, the mythical peoples and animals of Africa and Asia and other towns

Opposite: *Self-portrait of Matthew Paris before the Virgin and Child, from the original manuscript of his* Historia Anglorum, *1250–59 (BL, Royal* MS *14* C VII, *f. 6r).* Above: *Roundel of St Bartholomew giving a scourge to St Guthlac so he can repel the demons who have carried him to the gates of hell, from the Guthlac Roll (BL, Harley Roll Y 6, roundel 8). Perhaps made as an artist's model book in scroll form, possibly for stained-glass windows, Crowland Abbey, Lincolnshire,* c. *1200.*

and features of note depicted upon it, as well as images referring to the ages of Man, which echo the passage of human history. Another large map, now lost but probably resembling this, had been painted a few decades earlier in Henry III's royal chamber in the Palace of Westminster.

On the Hereford map, the texts of works such as the Anglo-Saxon Scientific Miscellany have migrated from the pages of books onto an encyclopaedic map for public devotional display and edification. English and German map-making had led to this in recent times, drawing upon classical cartography and geographical writings (and from the fourteenth century would absorb the influence of modern portolan charts, accurately depicting coastlines, made by Italian and Iberian navigators for practical sailing purposes). The badly charred fragments of the Aslake *mappa mundi* (British Library, Add. MS 63841), made at Creake Abbey in Norfolk around 1350 and which served as an altar retable there until damaged by fire, shortly after it was made, shows us the dilemma faced by its artist. Confronted by a convincing early portolan chart (perhaps while having a beer with a sailor from southern Europe who had landed on the coast nearby), he resorted to depicting two sets of Canary Islands, one in the traditional location and the other in the correct position copied from the evidently well-observed chart – a judicious solution in the absence of corroborative evidence.

Many of Matthew's works were given to St Albans, with inscriptions indicating that they were regarded as his property to dispose of at will (whereas monastic property was generally held in common). The principal surviving copies are as follows.

The *Chronica maiora* (Cambridge, Corpus Christi College, MSS 26 and 16), composed 1240–53. His major historical work, containing annals (records of yearly events, which originated many centuries earlier in the practice of making notes on liturgical calendars and tables for the calculation of Easter) from the Creation to 1253. It is written in Matthew's own hand from the entry for 1213 onwards and, although not the most copiously illustrated of his works, contains one hundred marginal drawings, some fragmentary maps and an itinerary, and full-page drawings of King William I.

An unillustrated copy of the material from 1189 to 1250, with criticism of Henry III modified or removed under Matthew's supervision, now forms

The most developed of Matthew Paris's four maps of Britain (BL, Cotton MS Claudius D VI/1, formerly f. 12v of Cotton MS Claudius D VI), depicting a central south–north itinerary from Dover to Newcastle, with the crenellations representing Hadrian's Wall and the Antonine Wall clearly drawn.

SCOCIA : VLTRAMARINA
hec et albania dicta est
Suthernelande
Orkade Insule
WALLIA
Richemund
Dunestap
London
Chanet
NORTHFOLK
SVFOLK
DORSET
ORIES
OCCIDES
AVSTER

part of British Library, Cotton MS Nero D V, ff. 162–393. A continuation of the *Chronica*, from 1254 until Matthew's death in 1259, is bound with the *Historia Anglorum* in British Library, Royal MS 14 C VII, ff. 8v–156v. A history of England, begun in 1250 and perhaps completed around 1255, it covers the period 1070 to 1253. It is an abridgement of the *Chronica*, also drawing on Roger of Wendover's *Flores historiarum* and Matthew's earlier edited version of the *Chronica*. It also contains the final part of his *Chronica maiora*, covering the years 1254–9 and prefatory material including an itinerary from London to Jerusalem and tinted drawings of England's monarchs. Everything is in Matthew's own hand, apart from ff. 210–18 and 154v–156v, which are in the hand of a scribe who also added a note of Matthew's death (f. 218v). The *Chronica* ends with a portrait of Paris on his deathbed. By the fifteenth century the manuscript volume was in the possession of Humphrey, Duke of Gloucester, son of Henry IV, who inscribed it 'Ceste livre est a moy Homffrey Duc de Gloucestre'. It was later in the hands of the Bishop of Lincoln, who added a note that if St Albans could prove the book was a loan, he would return it.

Matthew is ascribed the authorship of the *Flores historiarum* (Manchester, Chetham's Hospital and Library, MS 6712), but only the section from 1241 to 1249 is written by his hand. It is an abridgement of the *Chronica* with additions from the annals of Reading and Southwark. Textual interpolations indicate that the volume was made for Westminster Abbey, where it had been started, copying another manuscript of Matthew's text that went up to 1240. It was sent back to him later to update, probably in 1251–2. The illustrations resemble his style but are not by him. Later additions extended the chronicle to 1327.

Another shortened history by Matthew, mainly covering 1067 to 1253, is known as the *Abbreviatio chronicorum* (or *Historia minor*; British Library, Cotton MS Claudius D VI, ff. 5–100). Commenced around 1255, it remained unfinished at Matthew's death. He illustrated it with a royal genealogy depicting 33 seated figures of English kings and the most developed of his four maps of Britain.

The *Chronica excerpta a magnis cronicis* (British Library, Cotton MS Vitellius A XX, ff. 77r–108v) covers the period 1066–1246 and was written sometime between 1246 and 1259, probably under Matthew's supervision, with some of the text in his own hand.

The Hereford mappa mundi, *c. 1300, vellum. One of the greatest medieval world maps, this may have functioned as an altar reredos at Hereford.*

The *Liber additamentorum* (British Library, Cotton MS Nero D I) contains maps, the illustrated *Vitae duorum Offarum* ('Lives of the two Offas' – Anglo-Saxon kings of the Angles and Mercians, who were said to have played their parts in the foundation of St Albans Abbey), the *Gesta abbatum* (the lives of the first 23 abbots of St Albans with a little image of each), coats of arms and numerous copies of original documents including letters. It contains a large image of Christ, not by Matthew, and his famous drawing of an elephant that was given to Henry III's royal zoo in the Tower of London, which must have been as incongruous as William Randolph Hearst keeping polar bears at Hearst Castle overlooking San Simeon in sultry California. It is a charming drawing from life and Matthew also affectionately depicts the poor creature's keeper, who loved it so much that he slept alongside it at night, until its premature death. This image also gives an insight into Matthew's response, as an artist and historian, to the age-old dilemma of the relationship between *traditio* and *innovatio*. Innovation could be considered borderline heresy during parts of the Middle Ages, unless achieved by standing on the shoulders of the intellectual giants of the past (tradition/received wisdom) in order to see further, a bit like legal law of precedence informing judgments. His earlier depictions of elephants, such as the practice of fighting atop an elephant (an 'elephant and castle') adhered to the convention of showing them without kneecaps, for, as Pliny the Elder had related in Antiquity and as preserved in the medieval Marvels of the East and the bestiaries, you should not fight on them, because if they toppled they could not arise as they did not have kneecaps. Faced with an actual elephant, Matthew could not but defy convention and depicted the knobbly kneecaps he saw with his own eyes. This was, after all, still the age of scholasticism, when experimental science and observation from Nature was being balanced with the wisdom of ages in the universities, under the stimulus of interaction with the learning preserved and developed in the Near East and other areas of cross-cultural interaction (an approach also embraced by Bede and some other early Christian scholars).

Another good example of this intersection of *traditio* and *innovatio* is to be found in an illustrated herbal made in Durham Cathedral (or perhaps northern France) at the end of the twelfth century (British Library, Sloane MS 1975). This contains fully illuminated cycles of images, some of them stemming from Late Antiquity and the early Middle Ages, illustrating the medical and medicinal works of Graeco-Roman authors such as the *Herbarius* of Pseudo-Apuleius, the *De herbis feminis* of Pseudo-Dioscorides and the *De medicina ex animalibus* of Sextus Placitus. At the end of the book are a few leaves bearing a series of illuminated scenes in registers, together forming larger miniatures, fully painted by the same artist as the rest of the book, illustrating new treatments learnt in the East during the Crusades, such as treating an anal fistula, conducting a lobotomy, removing cataracts and showing cautery points. There is no accompanying text. The new experimental, innovative knowledge is integrated into an age-old corpus of traditional knowledge by means of images extending the illustrative cycle.

Matthew's *Life of St Alban*, written about 1230–50, survives in Trinity College Dublin, MS 177, containing 54 miniatures, mostly half-page, bound in with a 'Life of St Amphibalus' and sundry other works relating to the history of St Albans Abbey, both also illustrated. The *Life of St Alban* is in French verse, adapted from a Latin *Life of St Alban* by William of St Albans (*c.* 1178). The book contains notes in Matthew's hand, showing that his manuscripts were lent to various aristocratic ladies for periods, and that he probably also mediated between commissioners of manuscripts and the other artists (some of them likely to have been lay people) who adorned them.

A *Life of King Edward the Confessor* (based on an earlier Latin *Life of Edward the Confessor* by Aelred of Rievaulx, written around 1162) was composed by Matthew in the 1230s or 1240s. The only surviving copy of this

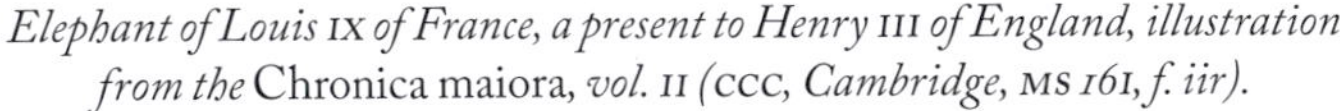

Elephant of Louis IX *of France, a present to Henry* III *of England, illustration from the* Chronica maiora, *vol.* II *(*CCC*, Cambridge,* MS *16I, f. iir).*

work (Cambridge University Library, MS Ee.3.59) is thought to be a slightly later London copy, probably illustrated by court artists.

The *Life of St Thomas of Canterbury* (British Library, Loan MS 88), comprising four leaves now known as the Becket Leaves, survive from a French-verse history of the life of Thomas Becket with large images. This was based on the Latin *Quadrilogus* compiled by Elias of Evesham at Crowland Abbey in 1198. The illuminations are attributed to Matthew Paris by Janet Backhouse, but Nigel Morgan disagrees. The style of the tinted drawings is very similar, but none of the several scribal hands is Matthew's. It may be that he was involved in designing the manuscript, or that it was based upon work by him.

The 'Life of St Edmund', a French-verse history of the life of Edmund Rich, Archbishop of Canterbury from 1233 to 1240, was based on Matthew's own Latin prose life of Rich, composed in the late 1240s, a fourteenth-century copy of which survives as British Library, Cotton MS Julius D VI, ff. 123–156v.

The *Liber experimentarius* of Bernardus Silvestris and other fortune-telling tracts (Bodleian Library, Oxford, MS Ashmole 304) contains author portraits, including Plato, Socrates, Pythagoras and Euclid, depictions of birds and diagrams thought to be by Matthew.

Miscellaneous writings by John of Wallingford (the Younger; British Library, MS Cotton Julius D VII), written and illustrated about 1247–58 by John, who was also a monk of St Albans, contains a portrait of him by Matthew, along with a map of Britain and an image of Christ in Majesty by him.

Other works thought to be by Matthew are fragments of a Latin biography of Archbishop Stephen Langton and various other works, including maps. A panel painting on oak of St Peter, part of a tabernacle shrine now in the Museum of Oslo University, has been attributed to Matthew and was probably brought by him as a gift during his visit in 1248, for it is not on the usual Norwegian pine used there for such purposes.

Like Eadui Basan two centuries earlier, Matthew got about a bit and defies the stereotypical image of cloistered monks and nuns, working away in the communal monastic scriptorium in relative anonymity. Nor was he working as a spiritually charged hermit, alone in the desert of the book, like

Opposite: *New medical procedures learnt in the Near East for removing an anal fistula, nose fungus and cataracts, incorporated as a visual extension of the programme of illumination in a compendium of classical herbal medicine, probably made at Durham Cathedral,* c. *1200 (*BL, *Sloane* MS *1975, f. 93r).*
Below: *King Offa and his master-mason oversee the building of St Albans Abbey, miniature from Matthew Paris, 'Book of St Albans', 1240–50 (*TCD, MS *177, f. 59v).*

Bishop Eadfrith of Lindisfarne and the early church fathers of the East, if only seasonally as a dynamic prayerful retreat from the world and from the busy responsibilities of his office. Matthew Paris was simultaneously monk, scholar, historian, scribe, artist, publisher, courtier and diplomat. He was also, effectively, a scholarly desktop publisher, capable of both penning and illuminating his own works.

This was a counter-trajectory to the development of the urban book trade, which evolved apace alongside the growth in towns and universities throughout the thirteenth century and beyond. This is, perhaps, the time for an overview of this phenomenon, which greatly increased the consumption of books and enhanced rates of literacy.

The rise of the university book trade in centres such as Bologna, Paris and Oxford hastened the spread of certain trends in bookmaking, in which the Latin Bible featured prominently. The Parisian book trade was dominated in the late twelfth century by the making of copies of biblical commentaries by Peter Lombard and others, arranged in complex wraparound formats that enabled text and commentary to be compared and further glosses and annotations to be made in the generous margins. The size of script, with the use of decorated initials, coloured paragraph marks, running titles and the like, helped the reader to navigate the text. Hugh of St Victor advocated the cultivation of mnemonic skills, such as using the shape of the text and the layout of decorated initials as a means of keying its content into the reader's memory, which was especially valuable to students and those who had to consult texts in volumes that could not be removed from their institutional libraries and which might even be chained to their presses in chained libraries (of which fine, if later, examples survive at Lincoln and Hereford Cathedrals, Wimborne Minster and Grantham parish church).

During the thirteenth century Paris went on to develop compact single-volume study Bibles, with tiny script, decorated or historiated initials, and decorative apparatus. These resemble the modern printed 'Gideon Bibles' in format and were readily portable, being issued to each friar upon graduation to aid their preaching. The book trade was also dominated at this time by the resplendent *Bibles moralisées*. Several copies of these survive, which were made for members of the French royal house and their Spanish relatives. Each of these elegant tomes contains some 13,000 images, arranged in roundels like contemporary stained-glass windows, which convey moralistic didactic typology designed to foster royal piety and good government. Copies of biblical history (the *Bible historiale*), often imbued with moral interpretation (such as the *Speculum humanae salvationis* or 'Mirror of Human Salvation') were also made in the later Middle Ages. These were heavily illustrated, in a range of styles and costs.

Visitors attracted to Paris by its intellectual reputation in the twelfth to thirteenth centuries included Peter of Capua, Lothar of Segni (who became Pope Innocent III), Guala Bicchieri (the son of a governing family of Vercelli, later cardinal and legate to England, who bought around fifty books in Paris, some second hand), Alexander Nequam, Herbert of Bosham, Stephen Langton (later Archbishop of Canterbury), Walter Map and Gerald of Wales, all of whom also probably bought books while there (deluxe glossed psalters, epistles and decretals, not just the cheaper university books). What made Paris such a premier focus was that it combined the functions of royal court, ecclesiastical focus, financial hub and university. The collective efforts of the Crown, the Church and the university authorities to control trade, including book production, led to the rise of university-approved booksellers who effectively became publishers and, eventually, printers.

These middlemen and middlewomen, entrepreneurs known as stationers, *stacionarii*, libraires or *cartolai*, would accept commissions from customers or have books made to sell off the peg themselves, and would subcontract out the various strands of work associated with producing manuscripts by hand to craft specialists: scribes (who also established the layout, pricking and ruling the writing lines and framing lines of the text and leaving appropriate spaces for the decorated initials and any other illuminated components), illuminators/limners, gilders and pen-flourishers (who decorated initials, borders and other parts of the page layout with fine ink flourishes). The same pages would be passed from street to street, hand to hand until all the elements were provided and the sheets of membrane were all returned to the stationer who arranged for them to be bound. The stationer also provided the parchment (sheep or goatskin) or vellum (calf-skin) for the project. The involvement of so many people in the production line meant that graphic mark-up devices were developed to allow the work to be assembled together easily: quire numeration was usually written on the last page of the gatherings/quires to indicate which order they were to be bound in; quire signatures were written on the front bottom left of each double-width sheet of membrane (bifolium, plural bifolia) to show their order within the quire; from around the year 1300 catchwords were written in the lower margin at the end of the quires, giving the opening words of the next quire, thereby catching/linking the two quires in sequence; running heads telling the reader which part of the text they were in were written decoratively at the top of each opening. The scribe would often leave guide-letters telling the illuminators painting the initials which letters to paint; instructions might be written discreetly in the margins, telling the artists which iconographies/subjects to paint or instructing the binder. By the end of the thirteenth century in Paris an Italian system of making multiple copies of the same text for university use – effectively syllabus books – was introduced known as the *pecia* system. This was essentially piecework, in which scribes would hire quires of an approved text and copy them faithfully, so that their pieces of work would tie in seamlessly with those hired out and copied by other scribes. A *pecia* mark (usually a little 'p' with a superscript 'a' for *pecia* followed by a number) would be written in the margin, indicating where that quire of the approved exemplar began. Rental prices were also set by the university. By 1342 a closed-shop monopoly had emerged, with 28 libraires, of whom four were *libraires principaux* and the others *petits libraires*. This effectively gave the university authorities greater control over production and ensured accurately copied approved texts. They also insisted that parchmenters sell the best-quality membrane for use in university books and that parchment should be bought in rather than manufactured in Paris.

From the mid-thirteenth century there was a growth in the publication of vernacular texts and in control by Paris University authorities. Jean de Meun/Meung, who completed the writing of the *Roman de la Rose* in the late 1270s, wrote that this tightening of control was provoked around 1254 by the case of the *esvangile pardurable* or 'eternal gospel'. This was an interpretative commentary on work by Joachim of Fiore by the Joachite Franciscan friar Gerard of Borgo San Donnino, who asserted that Joachim's works effectively constituted a third gospel that superseded the Old and New Testaments. This raised the question of whether the Bible/*biblios*/library of Scripture should have its doors closed to new acquisitions. The anti-mendicant party in Paris University had Gerard and his work, which was widely available for purchase on the Rue Neuve, condemned as heretical in 1255. The university authorities wished to stamp out such unorthodox publication, especially by mendicants, and took measures to limit this in future.

Paris was the only university to exercise such control, however ineffectual at times, and accordingly the book trade there never developed guilds, unlike London or Bruges and the other trades in Paris. University regulations applied rather than guild regulations. This established the hierarchy of the trade and the rights and obligations of membership.

From the time of an ordinance of Philip the Fair in 1307, university control was upheld by royal authority. In return, the sworn libraires of the university gained tax and watch duty exemption.

Those lecturers and students who could not afford to buy copies from approved university stationers might hire public notaries to attend lectures and take notes for them, or they might even make such notes themselves.

The family was the core unit of urban book production. Then the street on which you lived (such as the Rue des Ecrivains in Paris) and the neighbourhood guided working relationships, with neighbours often collaborating as colleagues and frequently intermarrying and thereby expanding the business. Some, such as Maître Honoré, are still famous; others, such as Raoul Joseph, were famous in their day but are now little known. Around 1267 the Franciscan friar Roger Bacon wrote of his time as a student in Paris in the 1220s and '30s, when the Paris study Bible was issued and the trade was run, so he said, by unlettered married men (clerics in minor orders – a technicality to facilitate relationships with the university and to avoid taxes and duties such as turning out of your bed to take your turn at the night watch). Bacon complained of resulting corrupt texts and that the mendicants often had to correct volumes they had purchased. This is essentially an observation upon the gradual secularization of the business of making books, but it also serves as a reminder that many of those involved in book production from around 1200 were still clerics. We cannot tell to what extent religious devotion played a part in the work of those paid to undertake it professionally, but we certainly cannot preclude faith inspiring some if not all of them. Certainly John Fifhide, the artist-maker of the Holkham Bible, discussed in the next chapter, gives us an insight into his faith.

From about 1250, when a 'Rogerus stacionarius' (Roger of Addington) and his wife are recorded owning property along the street known as St Giles, there is the first mention of a *stacionarius librorum* (bookshop proprietor) in Oxford documents. One of the best known of those involved in book production in Oxford was William de Brailes, who, with his wife Selina, owned an illuminator's workshop in Catte Street (on which also lies Duke Humfrey's Library, part of the older Bodleian Library buildings), along with other properties in town from around 1238 to 1252.

The de Brailes Hours (British Library, Add. MS 49999), illuminated by them around 1240, contains a marginal self-portrait of William on f. 43r. It is captioned 'W. de Brailes qui me depeint', in the courtly French of the day rather than everyday Middle English, and God's hand lovingly reaches down to stroke the cheek of his beloved William, who is shown with a tonsure, which indicates that he was a married clerk in minor orders. This is considered to be the earliest surviving fully formed book of hours, a newly evolved form of private devotional manual that enabled lay people to participate in the corporate life of the Church by following an abbreviated form of the prayers, psalms and readings followed by professional religious in the Divine Office, followed eight times each day and night at the intervals of Matins (around 2 a.m.), Lauds (dawn), Prime (around 6 a.m.), Terce (around 9 a.m.), Sext (around noon), None (around 3 p.m.), Vespers (around 6 p.m.) and Compline (around 7 p.m.). The number of times the whole book was recited in the course of a year or a lifetime depended upon the devotional fervour of its owner(s). The style and opulence of the illumination of such volumes depended upon the location, taste and purse of said owner(s). Part of the stationer's role was to gauge the depth of the latter and tailor to the customer's wishes the choices that could be made concerning what optional elements of the contents, both written and painted, were to be included.

Thus, a book of hours commissioned by a noble would look rather different to that ordered by a merchant and his family, probably the only book they would own, which catered for their spiritual, didactic and entertainment needs. Confessors in wealthy households and the matriarch of other households might use them to teach their children to read. Different liturgical variants, known as 'uses', were available, for example, 'Rome use', 'Paris use', 'Sarum use' (the Salisbury rite, which became that generally used in England from the fifteenth century until the Reformation), 'Dominican use' and so on. Their devotions focused upon one or more offices, which might include the Hours of the Virgin, the Hours of the Compassion of the Virgin, the Hours of the Cross, the Hours of the Passion and the Office of the Dead. The imagery of these focused upon scenes from the life and Passion of Christ, on King David, the Virgin Mary and on the obsequies of the Office of the Dead, along with the Gradual and Penitential Psalms and liturgical calendars featuring the late Roman iconographic cycles of the labours of the months, the zodiac signs and images of the saints. The feasts celebrated in the prefatory liturgical calendar might, like the use, litany and suffrages of the saints included, indicate the whereabouts and concerns of the patron, with 'red letter days' being those accorded particular honour by the use of red ink. St Frideswide, for example, would indicate an Oxford connection or origins, Genevieve for Paris, Erkenwald for London, and the choice of saints invoked in the Litany, and perhaps even depicted in illustrations, might indicate particular concerns such as protection during childbirth (St Margaret of Egypt and St Catherine), which might indicate a female owner or a wedding gift.

Sometimes the patrons themselves were depicted, in modest attitudes of prayer or, in the case of Jean, Duc de Berry, ostentatiously enacting the various labours of the months in their calendars by having themselves depicted at the feast, the hunt or in scenes of courtship, depending on the season. Owners might also, over the years, enter important events such as births and deaths (obits) into the calendar of their book of hours. Psalters, the traditional resource for public and private prayer, also continued to be made, as did Psalter-Hours, combining both. Wealthy patrons, such as John, Duke of Bedford, regent of France on behalf of Henry VI from 1422 to 1435, might own more than one of these options, as we can see from his household accounts.

Another book that was popular among wealthy patrons in late thirteenth- and early fourteenth-century England and France was the illustrated Apocalypse, in either Latin or French. This seems to have been generated by an increasing lay audience for romances and vernacular literature, for although the Apocalypse/Book of Revelation was a biblical text, sometimes accompanied by the commentary of Berengaudus, the illustrations were spectacular and exciting in their iconographies and often elegant in style. There was also a sense of impending doom as the turn of the century approached in view of declining political and economic stability. The Tartar invasions of eastern Europe in the 1230s and the fall of Jerusalem to the Muslims in 1244 gave rise to fears of the End Times and some perceived the ambitious Holy Roman Emperor as something of an antichrist figure.

Particularly fine examples include the Getty Apocalypse (J. Paul Getty Museum, MS Ludwig III 1 (83.MC.72)) of about 1255–60 and the Lambeth Apocalypse (Lambeth Palace Library, MS 209), also made in London in the 1260s for Eleanor De Quincy, Countess of Winchester (d. 1274), who is pictured kneeling in prayer. The Abingdon Apocalypse (British Library, Add. MS 42555), made for Abingdon Abbey and later owned by a queen of Scotland, even though it was only half finished, provides a rare opportunity to observe a manuscript in various stages of completion and to examine techniques and sequences of different elements of the work.

Female religious had traditionally played a significant, if underplayed, role in making manuscripts from the early Christian period onwards and this may have had some bearing upon the interesting fact that, during the Middle Ages, it was only in the various craft skills associated with book manufacture that women could trade in their own right, often after inheriting the family

business from their fathers or husbands, or as part of an extended family enterprise. One of the most famous female publishers, Christine de Pizan/Pisan (1364–1430), came to her profession through personal loss. She was the daughter of Tommaso di Benvenuto da Pizzano, astrologer, alchemist and physician to Charles v of France. She married in circa 1379, at the age of fifteen, Etienne du Castel, a royal secretary to the court. Ten years later she lost both father and husband to disease and was faced with supporting her mother, a niece and her two surviving children by making an unwanted second marriage or entering a nunnery. She chose instead to take the unprecedented step of earning her living by her pen. Her initial poems lamenting her loss gave way to instructions to her son on how to survive in politics and high places and to classical allegories, such as the 'City of Ladies' (*Cité des dames*), parodying misogynistic male society. She wrote entirely in her adopted language, Middle French, and served as a court writer for several dukes (Louis of Orléans, Philip the Bold of Burgundy and John the Fearless of Burgundy) and King Charles vi. She composed 41 works during her career of more than 30 years, and although she was not active in England, she was working in the latter years of her life in a Paris occupied by the English under Henry vi's regent, John, Duke of Bedford.

Christine even took on, and won against, the Paris University authorities in her attacks upon the bestselling *Roman de la Rose*, which she saw as objectifying women. Having attracted the patronage of the French queen, to whom she presented a copy of her collected works, largely written and illuminated by herself, she was able to employ others and set up her own publishing house. The cellar storerooms of her premises, along with those of many others and various other successful merchants, can still be wandered among in the archaeological site that lies beneath the present square in front of Notre Dame de Paris.

Self-portrait of the artist William de Brailes being blessed by the hand of God, from the de Brailes Hours, the earliest fully fledged book of hours, made in Oxford, c. *1240 (*BL*, Add.* MS *49999, f. 43r).*

Another successful female illuminator, who illustrated a number of the vernacular romances of the day, was Jeanne de Montbaston, who worked alongside her husband, Richard (*fl. c.* 1325–53). They illuminated a fine copy of the *Roman de la Rose* but expressed their scorn for some of the allegedly virtuous allegories its authors, Guillaume de Lorris and Jean de Meun/Meung, purported that it contained, by exposing its sexual nuances, depicting in its margins nuns plucking male organs from a penis tree, as a warning of its morally corrupting propensities (Bibliothèque nationale de France, Fr. 25526, f. 106v).

Book production had changed considerably since around 1200, with the growth of towns and the universities in Europe, which stimulated a wider readership and market for books and became the centres of the trade, although ecclesiastical centres did not cease the labours of the scriptorium, and royal courts and noble households might have their own secretaries and chaplains who wrote. Increasingly books were made by a variety of urban-based craft specialists (scribes, illuminators, gilders, pen-flourishers, binders and parchmenters), whose labours – along with the attraction of commissions and marketing – were coordinated by professional entrepreneurs known as stationers, the forerunners of publishers. Only in these book arts could women trade independently in their own right, sometimes inheriting businesses from fathers or husbands or working in partnership with them. This was perhaps an acknowledgement of the key role that women had played in the production of the book over previous centuries. Not all of these men and women were lay people, with the mendicant friars taking part and also clerks in minor orders, who could marry and who gained certain civic perks such as not having to turn out of bed to take part in the night watch. Between 1200 and 1500 there were around 1,200 named and dated men and women involved in book production in Paris, while London had 499 stationers recorded for the period 1300–1499, a number that may be distorted by the fact that the conjunction of royal court, bishopric, trading centre and university in Paris, its royal and university control and the degree of record keeping and private litigation (which those engaged in producing books seem to have been particularly prone to) means that there was more evidence for book historians to extract such data from. Richard and Mary Rouse rose nobly to this task, excavating the archives for evidence of the Parisian book trade, as did C. Paul Christianson for London, which was not a university town per se, despite its important specialist schools clustered around St Paul's Cathedral and production around the royal court at Westminster, and which did not keep the same high volume of records yielding evidence for book producers as Paris. What follows is largely distilled from their academic works.

In Paris tax records were kept from 1292; before that there were the rent books and *censiers* of the Abbey of Ste Geneviève (1243–66, with some as early as 1239) and local property records such as the cartularies of the Hôtel Dieu, of Notre Dame and of the Collège de Sorbonne.

Private acts – written agreements between individuals – grew rapidly in number during the thirteenth century and extended from nobles to the bourgeoisie. 'Gracious jurisdiction' was granted when contracts were drawn up before the bishop's *officialis* or the king's *prevot* at the Châtelet: these were sealed and authenticated and are a valuable source of named individuals and their trades. It seems to have been particularly popular to have written agreements drawn up in litigation or business deals among bookmen and bookwomen. During the years 1292–1300 there was also a witnessed street by street royal *taille* (tax) on commerce, which was recorded like a census.

Wills were also a valuable source of information, for example, that of Emery d'Orléans, *venditor librorum parisius* ('bookseller of Paris'). Emery travelled for his trade and dictated his will in Lyon in 1246. This shows that he was wealthy and left generous charitable bequests. He lived (according to a document of 1230) on Rue Neuve, at the heart of the book trade, next to Richard the scribe, with his mother and his older brother Nicholas. His will also mentions his sister, her daughter Sapience and her son Emery. He was an unmarried clerk in minor orders and owned two granges (farms), rural land and vineyards. Book traders were becoming investors. Adverts soon began to appear, with some of those from the Netherlands giving great detail concerning the prices of different sorts of script, decorated initials and so on.

Perhaps the most successful of all was the artist Maître Honoré d'Amiens, who was living in Paris by 1289, sharing his residence and business with his daughter and son-in-law Richard of Verdun (*c.* 1250–1313), an illuminator who had trained in his atelier; there was also a paid live-in assistant. They resided on the fashionable Rue Erembourg de Brie (now known as Rue Boutebrie). An illuminated copy of Gratian's *Decretum*, a legal text, was purchased from Honoré in 1289 for 40 louis d'or and by 1296 he was on a crown retainer, regularly illuminating for the king. This included publishing a text instructing monarchs in the virtues of good government, *La Somme le Roi* (The Dream of the King) by Fr. Laurent, including the presentation copy for King Philip the Fair (British Library, Add. MS 54180). Evidently, the calibre of the illumination meant that the artist could lead the publication process, rather than a stationer. As the king's painter he was paid £20 per year, which he invested in a clothing business and other property on the court and financial district of the Right Bank. Richard was paid £120 for a Bible (perhaps Bibliothèque nationale de France, fr 157), a royal commission, when he was in his sixties and had been illuminating for over forty years.

Others were less commercially successful and had to undertake two trades. Records show that parchmenters such as Robert le Fanier and binders such as Jehan de Sevre could also be tavern keepers; Thomasse, a female illuminator, was a tavern keeper on the Left Bank in the early fourteenth century.

By the early fifteenth century, amid the demands of the Hundred Years War with England, control of the Parisian book trade was breaking down. Andry le Musnier (d. 1475), a libraire on the Rue Neuve, was involved in litigation with Peter Schoeffer, who had worked as a scribe in Paris as a student and who subsequently became a prominent Mainz printer (having served as an apprentice to Johannes Gutenberg), and other early printers in Paris who were importing printed works. Musnier was probably selling printed books himself and objected to foreign competition, rather than to printing per se. By the end of the fifteenth century printers were also living on the Rue Neuve, such as Jean Guymier and his family who made the transition from libraires to printers, and Geneviève Pelletier, the daughter of a bookbinder, who inherited her father's shop on Rue Neuve and married the libraire-printer-binder Simon Vostre. Businesses were consolidating and expanding. The successful female printer Yolande Bonhomme printed some two hundred titles in Paris between 1525 and 1557. Books printed during the early phase of printing during the second half of the fifteenth century are known as *incunables*, from the Latin *incunabulum* ('in the cradle/swaddling', that is, in the early stages).

The changes to society stimulated by the growth of towns, trade and culture were immense and the lure of court and urban life and the diversity of work opportunities contributed to a drift from the land and a gradual erosion of the feudal order. The bourgeoisie slowly became a force to be reckoned with. The next chapter will turn to the very personal story of an independent artist making a book of his own devising in the heart of the book trade in the City of London – on the eve of the Black Death.

8

THE FOURTEENTH CENTURY I: JOHN FIFHIDE'S 'POOR MAN'S BIBLE' PICTURE BOOK

THE HOLKHAM BIBLE (BRITISH LIBRARY, ADD. MS 47682)

Our next book is very unusual and gives us a unique insight into the mind of its maker. This was, I have suggested, one John Fifhide, a citizen and merchant of the City of London during the fourteenth century. He was a skilled artist making *opus anglicanum* or English work – a form of embroidery in which Englishwomen had been deemed highly proficient since at least the time of the Bayeux Tapestry – in the form of embroidered vestments and altar hangings, a craft for which England was famed and in which he excelled, accepting important commissions even from the papacy. In the 1320s and '30s he took it upon himself to make a book in which the Creation, Christ's Life and the Apocalypse were all brought together and conveyed in pictures, with captions composed in a curious hybrid of Church Latin, Court French and everyday Middle English. He depicted himself as a witness to and recipient of the process of salvation portrayed.

This, the Holkham Bible Picture Book, was the first of the 'Poor Man's Bibles'. By the fifteenth century these were being produced in opulent illuminated copies for noble patrons (such as the British Library *Biblia pauperum*, King's MS 5, made for Count Albrecht of Holland or his wife, Margaret of Cleves, in The Hague around 1405) and in cheap versions illustrated by woodblock prints. Images were the prime means of conveying the biblical narrative and message of redemption, complementing the imagery encountered on church walls, in liturgical drama and mystery plays and in the often heavily visual language of preachers. Examination of the records of property rentals at that time reveals that he lived above the shop in a prime property next to St Paul's Cathedral, which, with its theological, musical and legal schools, also formed a proto-university of London. His premises were cheek by jowl with those of garment makers, the rosary bead makers of 'Pater Noster' Row and the makers of manuscripts. Nearby were the butchers' shambles and execution ground of Smithfield and the great Dominican preaching centre of Blackfriars. This was a buzzy, connected place to be where, later in the century, important civil servants-cum-gifted authors such as Chaucer and Gower would work and play.

Fifhide made what is now known as the Holkham Bible Picture Book (owing to its later provenance at Holkham Hall in Norfolk) during the late 1320s to 1330s, a time of great political and social instability during which Edward II was murdered in 1327 by the insertion of a red-hot poker where such was never meant to go; some have speculated that this was at the behest of his French queen, Isabella, and her lover Mortimer (who were subsequently imprisoned and executed, respectively). Although he was a highly gifted artist, Fifhide was not used to illuminating books. The manuscript's codicology (how hand-made books were prepared and put together, physically) indicates that he was not used to making them either. He has not left enough room in the inner margins to take account of the curvature of the pages when the book was bound and was opened, for example. His artwork is bang up to date and very fashionable, but the script of the text was written by a rather old-fashioned hand, more in keeping with the previous generation, so perhaps he was not employing a professional contemporary scribe or notary, but an older acquaintance or relative.

In 1327 Edward III granted the Great Charter of the City of London and trades really took off. Books were produced in London before this, though, focusing upon the court and abbey at Westminster and St Paul's Cathedral in the City of London. Old London Bridge, built in stone in 1176–1209 (begun under chaplain Peter de Colechurch), replaced the old wooden bridges that had served since Roman times and acted as a ceremonial and symbolic entrance to the City. Its maintenance and embellishment was a matter of civic duty and pride. The Bridge House Trust, administered by its Warden and clerks, owned extensive properties in the City and the region south of the Thames, for example in Southwark, Rotherhithe, Peckham, Sydenham, Lewisham and Deptford, rents from which paid for the bulk of its maintenance. The bridge was only 6 metres (20 ft) wide but its road was lined on each side by 139 overhanging retail premises. There was also a chapel dedicated to Thomas Becket, born on Cheapside, for which records were kept charting its purchases and refurbishment of books. Bridge House Estates records (which were begun in 1381 and extend to the present and which have been kept in the Guildhall Library) provide invaluable evidence of daily London life, of its own patronage of books and artworks, and the rental of premises in the City (on land donated by King John), many associated with the book trade. Other trading and university towns also made books from around 1200, including Oxford, Cambridge, York and Norwich, and ecclesiastical foundations and colleges also carried on producing or commissioning books.

The records for the London book trade comprise Calendars of the Plea and Memoranda Rolls (CPMR 1323–1482) and the City Letter-books (LB 1275–1498), held in the London Metropolitan Archives, which record transactions with the mayor's court or civic administration. These reveal that there were three stationers active there in 1300–1309 and 41 by 1490–99.

There are also records of book people's wills, legal transactions, transfer of apprentices, standing surety for one another and so on.

The Bridge House rentals reveal that the focus of the trade was Paternoster Row, by St Paul's Churchyard, with outlying premises on Old Chaunge and some outliers on the bridge itself and in the parish of St Nicholas at the Shambles, in the butchers' precinct.

In 1358 there were rents from 28 shops in Old Chaunge totalling £30 6*s* 8*d*. In Paternoster Row 32 shops yielded £40 8*s* at the following rates: 1 at £10; 2–19 at 26*s* 8*d* each; 20 at 12*s*; 21–3 at 8*s* each; 24–5 at 16*s* each; 26 at 12*s*; 27–8 at 4*s* each; 29 at 12*s*; 30–31 at 8*s* each; and 32 at 16*s*. In 1404 rental records read, 'In Paternosterrowe est unum magnum mesuagium et triginta shopa cum solars que locantur ut patet' (a large tenement block, and thirty shops with solars, rooms lit by windows in which to live above the job).

Payments for books were also sometimes recorded. The Bridge House chapel required the frequent repair, rebinding, furbishing and replacement of books. For example, an entry in its register for 1510 reads: 'To Thomas Symondes Stacyoner for byndeng gluyng, pastyng and coveryng of two antyphoners w'yn the sayd chapel fyndeng to the same stuff and workmanship xvjs xd' (The London Archives, BHA 1509–25. 30). Sometimes work continued on a volume over time, as cash flow or need dictated: in 1407, for example, Warden John Whatele purchased a new book of legends for the chapel for £5 14*s*, and seven years later limner John Walcote was paid 2*s* 4*d* for illuminating it.

Books could be much cheaper though. In 1423, for example, a collectar (containing collects, the specific prayer for each day) was acquired for 33*s* 4*d*, probably from a stationer. Sometimes the Bridge House clerks would themselves copy books to save money.

In 1530–31 £4 20*d* was paid to the stationer Lewes Sutton for 'lj antiphoners in pauper pryntid conteyning iij bookes, oon legend in pauper pryntid and oon masse boke in paper pryntid'. Printing on paper was much cheaper than the £24 5*s* 2*d* spent on two vellum antiphoners 135 years earlier.

A two-volume portiforium (containing directions instructing clergy on the performance of divine office and the administration of the sacraments) commissioned for royal use from one Frampton, clerk, in 1408–10 for £35 14*s* 6*d*, was recorded in the accounts of the Duchy of Lancaster and was mentioned by Henry V in his will in 1415 as 'pulchrum portiphorium in duobus voluminibus, scriptum per Johannem Frampton' (a beautiful portiforium in two volumes, written by John Frampton). Scribal reputation might endure, evidently.

The trades noted were scriveners (notaries), text-writers, limners, parchment sellers, booksellers, binders, stationers and, from the 1470s, printers. Some of them undertook more than one role – for example, in 1404 Thomas Bowland and Thomas Fysshe were each both limner and stationer; Peter Bylton, bookbinder and stationer; Roger Ybott, limner and/or text-writer; and Thomas Marleburgh, stationer and perhaps text-writer. Of the seventeen shop-holders mentioned, most only occupied one shop, but Peter Bylton, the bookbinder/stationer, rented four shops and Thomas Marleburgh, stationer/text-writer, rented two shops. So, there was some variation in scale and wealth of businesses. The tenement was probably sublet. Living alongside one another forged fraternal bonds and collaborations. Often more than one person had the same name and these were probably relatives, with some properties being passed down in the family. Women often rented with their husbands and could inherit businesses themselves.

Some had to engage in other trades alongside the book arts, serving as haberdashers, tavern keepers and letting rooms. Some may have been high-quality illuminators, such as John Hun (the 'Johannes' responsible for some illuminations, and who signed one, in Bodleian Library, MS Bodley 264, Part B, around 1400), who may conceivably have been John Siferwas, principal artist of the Sherborne Missal (British Library, Add. MS 74236), and Herman Skereueyn/Scheere, the illuminator of the 'reconstructed' Carmelite Missal (British Library, Add. MSS 29704–5, 44892); Hun and Skereueyn rented the same shop successively. Both were probably German International Gothic artists, presaging the immigration of German printers, many of whom began in the Paris manuscript trades.

In 1403 the misteries (mysteries/masteries) of limners and text-writers came together in one bookcraft guild, which by the 1440s was known as the Mistery of Stationers, and other book trades were incorporated; it was awarded its royal charter in 1557.

It may be that, seeing his book-trade neighbours' work and considering himself to be their equal as an artist, Fifhide decided to experiment by making his own book. Or it may be that he initially made a model-book containing designs for his embroideries, for part of the book seems to have been made first and contains images relating the life of Christ, themes which also feature on his vestments and altar retables, some of which survive still. This parchment pamphlet was not finished and was expanded into a book by adding further gatherings (or quires, as they are often known) that supplied the prequel and sequel, from Creation to Apocalypse. This was related primarily by images, rather like a film storyboard, with text captions that appear to have been composed to fit the pictures and which, although mainly in the Latin used for religious texts and legal documents, lapse periodically into upper-class Anglo-Norman French or the sort of everyday Middle English used in the home and on the street.

The artwork is executed in a technique known as tinted drawing, with fluent drawings in ink given washes of colour (a thinned-down version of the tempera pigments used in fully painted miniatures) to model forms and draperies. The colour combinations, such as green and an acidic lemon and blue and white, and the way in which they are used for modelling drapery, parallels that used in the threads of *opus anglicanum*. The earth is also treated the same way in both art forms, as are the architectural surrounds and the backgrounds with their geometric diaperwork of leaves and acorns drawn in outline, as if sewn. It is astounding how deftly Fifhide's needle emulates the surety of penwork.

This was the first example of what is known as the 'Poor Man's Bible', although over time they came to be made for very wealthy patrons too. This is because of the phenomenon of using images to tell the Bible stories, which was considered by scholars to be aimed primarily at the illiterate. Some of the assumptions about medieval literacy are perhaps too stereotypical, however. Acquisition of the skills of reading and writing (the latter did not necessarily accompany the former) was not determined solely by socio-economic status or gender. If you were the son or daughter of a grandee whose interests

The Bologna Cope, London, c. *1310–20, a high-class liturgical vestment depicting the life of Christ, embroidered in* opus anglicanum, *perhaps by John Fifhide, maker of the Holkham Bible Picture Book.*

lay primarily in warfare and hunting, you might not receive much of an education. But if you were the daughter or son of a merchant you might gain as much literacy, numeracy and linguistic skill as was required to help the family business to prosper. Yet Fifhide is evidently aware of the misconception, even then, and turns it to his advantage.

The prefatory full-page miniature depicts a handsome young artist, his blond curls protruding from beneath his layman's working cap. He is on the job, drawing full-page heads of a king and queen on the parchment bifolium. He turns to answer a Dominican friar, holding a string of prayer beads probably made nearby in Paternoster Row. Scrolls issue from their mouths, the forerunners of speech bubbles in graphic novels and cartoons. The friar tells the artist to be sure to make a good job of it, as his images will be shown to important people. The artist, whom I suggest is a self-portrait of Fifhide (precociously pre-dating the growth of portraiture from the end of the century onwards), replies that it will be the best work he's ever seen, if he the artist is spared to complete it. This is a subtle subterfuge, for by claiming that the book was commissioned by a Dominican to instruct wealthy, or even royal, patrons it in fact provides cover for Fifhide's own temerity in composing and illustrating a new form of book on his own initiative. For, brave attempt though it is, there are theological and factual errors that a learned Dominican preacher (of the sort that Fifhide would have heard at Blackfriars, relating and commenting upon Scripture in sermons, which is how most folk got their biblical knowledge) would never have condoned.

On the contrary, Fifhide would appear to have composed both text and images himself, no doubt considering himself sufficiently learned from his familiarity with his ecclesiastical neighbours all around him and from his designs for liturgical embroideries, 'by appointment' to the pope. He has left us a number of pictorial colophons, I have suggested, to identify himself. His cap, curls and brow appear several times, the rest of his body concealed by a group of five doctors of the Law who cluster around him, while his eyebrows react to the action, registering concern, amazement or joy. The five other figures consistently hide the artist, partially concealing him from view. This seems to me to be a game that the artist is playing with us: spot me if you can and try to work out who I am. The placename Fifhid, which occurs at the period in the

Detail of a piece of opus anglicanum *embroidery (depicting Christ's Charge to St Peter), London,* c. *1300–1350, perhaps by John Fifhide, showing the similarity of his style, whether executed by needle or by pen and brush.*

parish of Leigh in Reigate hundred in Surrey and which takes other forms elsewhere, such as Fyfield and Fifehead, means 'five hides' and it may be that, his surname having derived from the family's place of origin, our artist devised his own punning pictorial colophon as his signature or brand. The group appears whenever John the Baptist is in view, perhaps indicating that this was Fifhide's name-saint, for whom he had been christened John. When it comes to Salome's lascivious lap dance for King Herod, our artist emerges in full-figural form, holding his quill pen to his lips as he looks up at the text above, while Salome performs her seductive acrobatic antics, as if to say 'this is going to end badly!' It does indeed, and he is depicted on the next page gazing in wide-eyed disbelief as the severed head of his beloved patron-saint is borne upon a platter to Queen Herodias, Salome's mother, whom he had offended.

The Fifhide who rented premises near Paternoster Row later in the century was also named John: might he have been our artist, or was he the father with the premises and business passing through the family line to his son, as was often the case? The conceit of depicting the artist, identifiable from the opening self-portrait, surrounded by five other figures could form the pictorial colophon (signature) Fifhide: he who hides amid five. Another manuscript that had its marginal illumination added in Paternoster Row around this time employs a similar conceit for its colophons: John de Bataille, a canon of nearby St Bartholomew the Great in Smithfield, signalled his ownership by depictions of battle skirmishes in the Smithfield Decretals, a legal manuscript from the law university in Bologna, intended for use in the University of Paris, but soon completed in London.

Fifhide's depictions of the biblical scenes take place in his own city, for example the depiction of the Temptation of Christ, in which he is goaded by the Devil to throw himself off the Temple roof in the form of the spire of St Paul's Cathedral, then the tallest structure in Europe. A windmill on the hill nearby might be that owned by the St Paul's community on Hampstead Heath, the highest point visible from the City of London and to which they retreated during times of pestilence on account of its cleaner air.

*The Holkham Bible Picture Book, the first 'Poor Man's Bible' (*BL, *Add.* MS *47682, f. 1r), worn frontispiece, perhaps indicating that the book lacked a binding and may have been a model book for commissions or a personal devotional book for its maker John Fifhide, an* opus anglicanum *artist working in London in the 1330s. This frontispiece depicts him as a handsome young artist, engaged in a fictitious commission from a Dominican friar to make a fine book to be shown to important patrons. This provided Fifhide's cover for his audacity in making a book that told his version of the Bible story in captioned images.*

Comeint Heroudes seet a sa table a une feste ovekes tut pleyn de genz. E la fille Heroudie se meist devaunt li, ceo est a savoir de tumbler e de autre abitement. Dount Heroudes en out graunt joie. E disoit: Fille, demaunde ceo qe tu voiz coveiter e deuhaitest qe la te dounrie. E ele allat a sa mere Heroudie pur la cunseiler quoi ele devoit demander. E ele la disoit la teste seyn Jan en une esquele qe estoit en prison. E ele allat demander la teste seyn Jan le Baptist qe estoit en sa prison. E Heroudes la ottriet.

Comeint seyn Jan le Baptist estoit decole de un turmentour. E la teste mise dedeinz une esquele. E la fille Heroudie la aportat devaunt Heroudes e Heroudie sa mere qe en out graunt joie.

In one image depicting Noah's Ark and the great flood, the upper levels of the ark's walls are constructed in wattle-work, rather than the clinker-built planking of its lower structure, a graphic illustration of the point that Noah did not obey the Lord's command with sufficient alacrity and the build turned into a rushed job! The bodies of humans and other creatures drowned for their disobedience float suspended in the transparent waters beneath. A beautiful, realistically observed horse is among them, as are the naked bodies of a young man and woman. Their anatomies are veristically depicted in astoundingly frank detail for the period, with their pubic areas exposed. His toe brushes against her pert nipple. Her long blonde hair streams in the water, as do his blond curls. Might this be a depiction, from the life, of John Fifhide and his wife – a *memento mori* of their own sinfulness and mortality, however beautiful their bodies were now and however pleasurable their sexual congress? These are among the most explicit and best-observed nudes in medieval art and anticipate an aspect of the Renaissance.

Their home-working premises may also be depicted in a scene where an irate father berates the Virgin Mary as she tends the shop, complaining that his son, who was playing with the Christ-child and their pals in the solar dwelling upstairs, has fallen out of the window and broken his neck as the play was so raucous. Christ duly heals him. Below, Christ surfs on a rainbow, while his playmates topple off – for they are not the Christ-dude.

Christ would, of course, come again as Judge and Saviour at the Apocalypse. At many times people have felt that the world may be approaching the end times, although the New Testament tells us not to look for them as they will be too horrendous to wish upon your own generation. Fifhide's was one of them. The breakdown of royal and governmental behaviour and authority was causing widespread concern and unrest. Harvests were failing, cattle were dying and the Black Death would soon be on its way. Dissension was rife. Fifhide depicts this, illustrating environmental disasters, such as the seas burning and whales being cast up on the beaches, and both nobles and commoners fighting among themselves – the end times, presaging the Second Coming. What might he visualize now? Might he be a prominent film director?

In other images our artist displays an unparalleled interest in and knowledge of Jewish dress and religious practices, some forty years after they

Salome dances for King Herod and receives John the Baptist's head on a platter as a reward, while John Fifhide, the artist and conceiver of the Holkham Bible Picture Book, looks up at the text and then down in horror at the martyrdom of his beloved name-saint (BL, Add. MS 47682, f. 21v).

were expelled from England in 1290 to allow its government to renege on the national debt owed to them as moneylenders and bankers. In the scene of the circumcision of Christ, prayer shawls and head coverings are worn by those conducting and assisting in the procedure. Elsewhere, Jews are shown wearing *tifilin* (phylacteries) on their foreheads to keep Yahweh and the Law ever on their mind, which became an official visual label of faith for England's Jews.

How did a hip young artist such as Fifhide gain such knowledge? Might it have been through his trading contacts abroad? Later in the century, a textile dealer named John Fifhide was made an aldorman and a sheriff of London in recognition of what must have been a significant civic profile. Might this have been our enterprising artist? If he made the Holkham Bible Picture Book as a young man in his twenties, in the 1330s, it is not inconceivable that he might have achieved high office in later life, in his sixties, in which case we may just be witnessing the work and records relating to a single, long-lived person. That illuminators could have a long working life, despite the strain their profession placed upon their eyesight, is corroborated by the case of fashionable Flemish illuminator Simon Bening (*c.* 1483–1561) who had a working life of some sixty years.

This John Fifhide, who is most likely the one who is recorded renting the premises in Paternoster Row, also appears in records listing the mayors and sheriffs of London and in other of its official records, his name taking the forms Fifhide, Fyfhide, Fyfhyde or Fysshyde. Spelling was not standardized at this time and it may also be that at some point a double 'ff' was mis-transcribed as a double tall 's'. Two sheriffs (a word derived from the Anglo-Saxon office of shire reeve) were appointed by the City of London each year, to assist the mayor, collect taxes and undertake certain judicial duties in London and Middlesex. The career trajectory for such prominent citizens was usually aldorman, sheriff and then, perhaps, Lord Mayor. Here are some of the records that I have found relating to him in the archives (a fuller set of references with sources is given at the end of the Bibliography for this chapter):

In 1370–71 John Fyfhide appears in a list of citizens who lent money to the king, recorded in the City of London letter-books. John lent £100, a significant sum (about five times the annual value of Sir Geoffrey Luttrell's manor of Irnham).

The great flood and Noah's Ark, a rushed job made partly of pre-fabricated wickerwork, in the Holkham Bible (BL, Add. MS 47682, f. 8r). The surprisingly graphic anatomical detail of the bodies and genitalia of the drowned young man and woman may have been drawn from life by Fifhide, that is, of his wife and himself, and served as a memento mori *of their sin and mortality.*

Achunt Noe son vessel de tout auoyt charge. E son linage q' deux luy di
syt: e yl estoyt entre. Adunk le ewe comencoyt: fortement de ceel descendre.
E la fluuie haute cresoyt: le pecheours gerdun rendre. Carante iours e xl nuy[t]s
ne finat de pluuer. Ke nuyl poeit conustre la tere de la meer. E tut estoyt
mort neie: q' deu ne plesat de fere. Ke uiuant nuyl estoyt troue: par tut en nule
tere. le cent e cinkauntime iur apres: q' tant auoyt plu. Noe a la fenestre: tot estoyt
cunu. E la uuerit e hors gardoyt. si il veeyt poynt de tere. E par tut yl se pensoyt.
queys fu meuz a fere. Vn corbeu hors yl mist: p' porter enseine. Sure caroine yl seas
syt e ne vint plus la semeine. Vn colu[m]b apres enueya: q' branche de oliue aporta: E q' le ewe fu retrete.

Alors Noe ioye auoyt: e a ses ens ben tot disoyt: a deux fesums feste.

Coment Elyzabet fẽme Zacarie esveske de la ley gisoyt en gisine de son fuyz Jhoan le Bap
tist. Et coment Zacarie out perdu son parler e estoyt tut muet de loure ke le aungel ly out dyt
ke yl engendroyt un enfaunt sure Elyzabet. Et yl ne esperoyt mye pur ceo ke ele estoyt baraine e ne con
ceuoyt unkemes enfaunt. e ke yl le nomeroyt Jhoan geskes lenfaunt estoyt circumcise. Et comẽt le pouple
le vousist nomer Zacarie apres son pere. Et coment Zacarie pryst une greffe e escrisoyt sure deus
Tables ke le enfaunt nomeroyt Jhoan. Et tot apres yl cõmenceoyt
aparler e dire. Benedictus dñs deus isrl: qr uisitauit e c.
Et comẽt seyn Jhoan le Baptist quaunt yl estoyt de age allat en deserd et demoroyt entre bestes
sauages geskes alage de trente aunz. Et adunc yl allat a le flum Jordan e cõmencoyt a sarmuner
de la bapteme. Et mult de genz de enuiroun veneyent oyer son
sarmoun. E entreyent dedenz le flum. Et seyn Jhoan pryst de
leuue e disoyt. Ego baptizo
vos in aq̃ in noĩe dei Ame.

John Aubrey and John Fifhide were sheriffs of London between Michaelmas 1373 and Michaelmas 1374. Adam de Bury served his second term as Mayor of London in this year. Their election is recorded as follows: 'Wednesday the Feast of St. Matthew [21 Sept.], 47 Edward III. [AD 1373], John Aubrey and John Fyfhide elected Sheriffs for the year ensuing, viz., John Aubrey by the Mayor and John Fyfhide by the Commonalty.' John Fifhide and John Aubrey/Awbry appear as the sheriffs for the years 1373 and 1374 in the list of sheriffs of London. On 5 July 1374 the former is listed as Aldorman of Bassishaw Ward in the City of London, a small but significant ward, in which lay the Guildhall. After this, in 1375, he once again appears as an aldorman of the City of London, enforcing the settlement of a dispute in the City:

> 606. Adam Fraunceys and Margaret his wife complain that Thomas, parson of St Michael de Bassyeshawe, William Willesdon and John Sandon, parishioners, have built a stile (*scaleram*) across the path (*viam*) leading from the street to their tenement in the churchyard, by which they and all the tenants of their same tenement have had free passage, time out of mind, for themselves, their servants, horses, carts and all manner of transport (*cariagio*), with every kind of merchandise (*mercandizus*) and goods (*rebus*). John Haddele and William Neuport, sheriffs, have testified elsewhere that the defs. have been summoned by John Hoke and Robert Cog, but they make default. The mayor and aldermen view the premises, and because the nuisance caused to the pls. by the stile is manifest, it is adjudged that within 40 days etc. the defs. remove it. The sheriffs are ordered to warn them accordingly.
>
> [m. 36d.] Fri. 29 June (after the feast of St. Leo, pope) 1375. William Waleworth, mayor, William Halden, recorder, John Mitford, John Tornegold, Adam Stable, John Fyfhide and John Hadele, aldermen.

In 1377 he was once again an aldorman, engaged in similar dispute resolution cases:

The Holkham Bible (BL, Add. MS 47682, f. 18v): detailed observations of Jewish dress and rituals are made in this image of the circumcision of Christ, some forty years after the Jews had been expelled from England to allow the government to renege on the national debt. Fifhide probably traded with Jews on the Continent. In the lower image depicting people being baptized by John the Baptist, Fifhide depicts himself hidden amid a group of five doctors of the law, with only the top of his head visible. This forms one among several such pictorial colophons in which he identifies himself as John who hides in five.

> 612. On 8 May 1377 John Coraunt, goldsmith, and Thomas Farndon appear before Nicholas Brembre, mayor, in a dispute concerning two stone walls in the pars. of St Michael and St Peter de Wodestrete in which both claim a share. They agree to submit the matter to the arbitration and judgment of the masons and carpenters, who thereupon, by order of the mayor, view the walls in question, and, that same day, certify upon oath that the wall in the par. of St Michael, which extends as far as Wodestrete and of which Thomas claims half, belongs wholly to John Coraunt; but the stone wall in the par. of St Peter, in which John claims to have corbels, belongs wholly to Thomas Farndon, and John ought not to have any corbels in it unless he can show a specialty. The parties agree to abide by this judgment from now on.
>
> [m. 38] Fri. 5 Dec. 1376. Adam Stable, mayor, William Cheyne, recorder, John Pyel, William Waleworth, John Tornegold, John Aubrey, John Fyfide, John Haddele, John Organ, Adam de St. Ives (Sancto Ivone), John Norhampton and Robert Launde, aldermen.

As sheriff, he also became involved in dispute resolution, but a recorded example shows that the cases might be more complex, involving foreign merchants and the Crown, and Fifhide is mentioned as sheriff in the following:

> Petition by Peter de Bromous (Brumes) and William Mege, merchants, to the King and council.
>
> The petitioners, speaking for themselves and their companions, burgesses and merchants of Bordeaux and Libourne, request restitution of wines taken from them for the use of the King and others. An order was given in the last parliament that the King and others who received these wines were to pay for them and for two years' suit, but still received very little of this payment. They ask the King to order the Treasurer to pay the remainder of what he owes, and to order the Mayor of London to pay his share, and to make execution against the other defaulters. They also request restitution of the equipment and boat belonging to one of their cogs, which are currently at Rye and Hythe.

The endorsement seems to be 1379, which may be when the case was finally settled:

> The persons named within are to be compelled by all reasonable means, both by writ of the great seal and otherwise, to make due and swift restitution to the complainants for their wines or the value thereof. And with regard to what is due to them from the King, they are to sue to the said King's Treasurer.

This document was in court French, but the local disputes are often in Middle English. This facility for moving between languages, depending on context, along with legal and church Latin, is seen in the curious mixed-language text of the Holkham Bible, made in his youth some thirty to forty years earlier by this John Fifhide, who was still trading in textiles and who had achieved high civic office and responsibility, or by his father of the same name. Either way, his case gives us an indication of the varied career to which a gifted and ambitious urban artisan might aspire.

A mercer (dealer in fine textiles) named John Fyfhyde, who is probably the same person, or his son, is recorded as having a claim upon rents in Fenchurch Street in 1384–93:

> *In the parish of St Dionis Bacchurch*
>
> 117. Grant by Richard Estbrok, brewer, and Agnes his wife to John Fifhyde, mercer, William Creswyk, John Wakefeld, citizens, Peter Wysbech, chaplain, of 40*s*. of quit rent from their lands and tenements in Fanchurchstrete in the parish of St Dionis de Bakchurch which they had as a gift and feoffment of William Bullok, citizen and tapicer; grantees to distrain if the rent is unpaid for a full year; [f. 26v] if insufficient distress taken then the grantees to take the tenements as if they were their own and hold them and occupy them and lease until the full payment is made; sealed; dated 1 Oct. 1384 . . .
>
> 119. Release by John Fyfhyde and Peter Wysebech of 40s. quit rent to William Cresewyk; dated 1 June 1393.

These entries taken together give us a snapshot of the career enjoyed by Fifhide and the place he and his family occupied within London mercantile society.

We cannot know why Fifhide dared make his own version of 'The Greatest Story Ever Told', whether to show potential clients, to try to move into a new part of the market with a new product or, which given

After the which t
And ther fore s
And lat me tellen

Explic

Heere bigy

his wyf and eek
the sores weren
And gotten laddr
been oynted and
Thyne mortal wo
his feet. in his h
And leften his f
tormented was in
was man pertyn
e his wyf as fe
fer to styrte bu
the moore The

his temerity may be likely, as a form of moral biblical instruction for the edification of his own family. His humour, as well as his artistry and personal quest for salvation, certainly shine from its pages, not least in the final one, where excitable demons convey armfuls of naked figures of kings, bishops and alewives (the barmaids and landladies of the taverns of the day) to be cast into a cauldron bubbling away in the fireplace of just such a tavern. The caption concludes, 'and you think you've got it bad, in hell they don't even get Sundays off!' We can almost hear the apprentice lads of London chortle.

The latter part of the fourteenth century witnessed a flowering of Middle English literature and of other literary endeavours in which civil servants who wrote all day for their administrative work and drank together in city taverns in the evening found time to write important masterpieces. Some won fame in their day that endures still: Chaucer, Gower, Hoccleve, Langland.

Chaucer was a celebrity in his own day. Born into an Ipswich family of vintners and merchants, he was the son of a London wine merchant by royal appointment. In 1357 the lad became page to Elizabeth de Burgh, Countess of Ulster, wife of Lionel, Duke of Clarence, the second son of Edward III. For the rest of his life he was a courtier, diplomat and civil servant and performed several royal and public offices. He was widely travelled, accompanying Lionel and his troops to France, where Chaucer was captured at the siege of Reims in 1360 and was ransomed back by the king for £16. He may have undertaken pilgrimage to Santiago de Compostela and also visited Italy, where he encountered Petrarch, Jean Froissart and perhaps Boccaccio and their works, which helped to inspire his own ventures into vernacular poetry.

Around 1366 Chaucer married Philippa (de) Roet, a lady-in-waiting to Edward III's queen, Philippa of Hainault, and a sister of Katherine Swynford, who around 1396 became the third wife of her long-term lover John of Gaunt. Chaucer's *The Book of the Duchess* (also known as the *Death of Blaunche the Duchesse*) was written in commemoration of Blanche of Lancaster, John of Gaunt's first wife. Chaucer's children all did well and his great-great-grandson, John de la Pole, Earl of Lincoln, was designated heir to the throne by Richard III before his deposition. Chaucer wrote his scientific *Treatise on the Astrolabe*, the first piece of technical writing in Middle English, for one of their sons, Lewis.

Geoffrey Chaucer as a pilgrim, miniature from the Ellesmere manuscript (Huntington Library, Los Angeles, EL 26 C 9, *f.153v) of Chaucer's* Canterbury Tales, *London,* c. *1400–1410, which seems to have been owned by John de Vere, 12th Earl of Oxford (1408–1462).*

Geoffrey is said to have studied law in the Inner Temple and became a member of Edward III's inner court circle as a *valet de chambre* in 1367. In 1374 the king granted him a gallon of wine per day for life and Chaucer took up the important role of comptroller of the customs for the port of London for the next twelve years, a period during which he wrote some of his best literary work and also relocated to Kent as a commissioner for peace, in the face of a feared French invasion. There he is thought to have started work on the *Canterbury Tales* in 1387–40, his home lying close to the Pilgrim's Way, linking Becket's birthplace in Cheapside, London, to his shrine in Canterbury Cathedral. In 1386 Chaucer became an MP for Kent and from 1389 to 1391 served as Clerk of the King's Works. He became a royal pensioner in 1394 and disappears from the record after Richard II's deposition in 1399. Upon his death in 1400 Chaucer was interred in Westminster Abbey and in 1556 was moved to become the first occupant of Poets' Corner there.

Chaucer's London was a trilingual society at its core, employing Latin, Court French and Middle English. In his use of the last of these for his verse he helped to standardize the dialect used and there are some 2,000 words in the *Oxford English Dictionary* that are ascribed to him for their first known use. He wrote in the accentual-syllabic metre, used on the Continent and then in English literature from the twelfth century as an alternative to alliterative Anglo-Saxon metre. He also engaged in metrical innovation, inventing the rhyme royal, and was one of the first English poets to use the five-stress line, arranging them into rhyming couplets. His influence can be traced in the work of John Lydgate (monk and poet of Bury, who wrote the continuation of the *Canterbury Tales*, the *Troy Book*, the *Fall of Princes* and the *Life of St Edmund*, among others), John Barbour in Scotland (the first major named writer in Scots, who wrote the verse romance *The Brus*, 'The Bruce') and the Pearl Poet, working in the north of England (Chester, Staffordshire or York), whose poems *Pearl*, *Patience*, *Cleanness* and *Sir Gawain and the Green Knight* occur together in the Pearl Manuscript (British Library, Cotton MS Nero A x/2), one of England's most famous literary manuscripts of this period. This contains twelve full-page illustrations in a provincial but robust fashion, including the Green Knight with his gruesome severed head before the king,

Sir Gawain and the Green Knight *in the Pearl Manuscript, one of England's most famous literary manuscripts of this period (*BL*, Cotton* MS *Nero* A *x/2, f. 94v). This contains illustrations in a provincial but robust fashion, including the Green Knight with his gruesome severed head before the king, and is thought perhaps to be a commission by a merchant or a civic group such as a guild, or to have been intended for regional gentry. Made in northern or central England in the late 14th century.*

and is thought perhaps to be a commission by a merchant or perhaps a civic group such as a guild, or to have been intended for regional gentry.

Among his friends Chaucer counted John Gower, author of the *Confessio amantis*, whom Geoffrey called 'moral Gower', and Thomas Hoccleve, a poet whose works included the *Regement of Princes* (designed to instruct Henry V on the virtues and vices and on good government). Hoccleve was a clerk of the Office of the Privy Seal and promoted Chaucer as 'the father of English literature': he had a posthumous portrait of him painted in a copy of his *Regement* (British Library, Harley MS 4866, f. 88).

Other such figures were and are little known but laboured diligently, such as James le Palmer (before 1327–*c.* 1375), Treasurer's scribe in the Exchequer (mentioned in documents from 1357 to 1375), who had a grace and favour apartment above Moorgate, one of the entry gates to the City of London, and who spent his nights from 1360 to 1375 writing a massive four-volume encyclopaedia of his own composition, the *Omne bonum*, or *All Good Things* (British Library, Royal MSS 6 E VI and VII). It employs 1,100 leaves of membrane, with 1,350 entries and over 650 little miniatures illustrating topics as varied as dentistry, arson and James himself scribbling away. It was left unfinished at James's death and 23 further pictures were added around 1380, painted by an artist for whom someone left marginal instruction notes. The illustrations give a vivid and often amusing insight into everyday life. Its text ranges across natural history, theology, history and geography, drawing upon sources (which he lists) as varied as the Vulgate Bible, the patristics, Cicero, Averroes and Avicenna, canon law, the *De proprietatibus rerum* (On the Properties of Things) of Bartholomaeus Anglicus, Thomas of Ireland's *Manipulus florum* and the *Secreta secretorum* of Pseudo-Aristotle. It is the first encyclopaedia to be arranged alphabetically. He never completed it, with the letters N–Z receiving only one entry each, but his great work nonetheless made it onto the shelves of the Royal Library in the mid-sixteenth century or the seventeenth, with the shelf mark 1226. James recommended his work to those seeking learning and as an inspiration towards all good things worth thinking upon. He wrote of it, 'In this work [can be found] all good things heretofore scattered widely both in canon law and in various other books or authoritative volumes ... [and] without difficulty or tedium all those things that lead to the well-being of every person.'

Another who deserves to be better known is Cornishman John Trevisa (1342–1402), a native of Trevessa in St Enoder parish, near Newquay, who gained his early education at Glasney College, an important religious establishment in Penryn. Glasney College had been founded in 1265 by Walter Branscombe, Bishop of Exeter, perhaps as part of his dispute with Edmund, Earl of Cornwall, who was attempting to take over ecclesiastical rights. Edmund had used the early history of Cornwall, especially its Arthurian links, in his bid to establish a separate power base of his own. As part of this contest between secular political and Church agendas, Glasney may have formulated a dual agenda of making Cornwall feel a valued part of England and of promoting and celebrating its own cultural traditions. Manned by secular canons rather than monks, and with an educational remit that prefigured the Tudor grammar schools, Glasney equipped Cornishmen and boys for study at Exeter College, Oxford, regardless of status, enabling them to contribute as clerics, lawyers, physicians, churchmen, academics and authors. Trevisa made an extremely significant contribution to the written Cornish vernacular when around 1375 he created the *Ordinalia*, the mystery plays from Creation to Doomsday in Middle Cornish.

Dentistry, from an early encyclopaedia, the Omne bonum *(All Things Good), authored and made by civil servant James le Palmer, London, 1360–75 (*BL*, Royal* MS 6 E VI, *f. 503v).*

Trevisa was educated at Exeter College and became vicar of Berkeley, Gloucestershire, chaplain to the 5th Lord Berkeley, and Canon of Westbury on Trym. He translated into English for his patron the Latin *Polychronicon* of Ranulf Higden, adding remarks of his own, and prefacing it with a 'Dialogue on Translation between a Lord and a Clerk'. He likewise made various other translations, including Bartholomaeus Anglicus's *On the Properties of Things*, a medieval forerunner of the encyclopaedia.

A fellow of Queen's College, Oxford, from 1372 to 1376 (at the same time as John Wycliffe and Nicholas of Hereford), Trevisa may well have been one of the contributors to the 'Early Version' of Wycliffe's Bible. The preface to the King James Version of 1611 singles him out as a translator among others at that time: 'even in our King Richard the second's days, John Trevisa translated them [the Gospels] into English, and many English Bibles in written hand are yet to be seen that divers translated, as it is very probable, in that age'. Subsequently he translated a number of books of the Bible into French for Lord Berkeley, including a version of the Book of Revelation, which his patron had inscribed on the ceiling of the chapel at Berkeley Castle. Trevisa and Berkeley together are credited with a continuous programme of enlightenment for the laity, through the provision of translations of key works of Scripture and general knowledge.

Trevisa is the eighteenth most frequently cited author in the *Oxford English Dictionary* and the third most frequently cited source for the first evidence of a word (after Geoffrey Chaucer and the *Philosophical Transactions of the Royal Society*).

Cornish expertise and scholarship thus evidently helped to develop the English language as well as Cornish and opened up the Bible to ordinary folk in their own languages, in written and aural forms, using the multimedia vehicle of increasingly popular drama.

The *Ordinalia* is a suite of plays in Cornish in the manner of the well-known medieval miracle or mystery (mastery/craft guild) plays performed on the Continent and at York, Chester, Wakefield (the Towneley Cycle) and Clerkenwell in London, and by travelling players using the so-called N-Town Cycle of plays from East Anglia (*c.* 1500; British Library, Cotton MS Vespasian D VIII). These were composed in Middle English with Latin instructions, designed to be performed by a band of travelling players in 'N' town (N for *nomen*/name, or N as in 'A N other'). It has extensive stage directions and the names of the cast members are accompanied by their relationships in the lower part of the page. The other English mystery plays were performed by guilds of tradesmen in specific towns over several days, telling the biblical story from Creation to Last Judgement. The cycles were performed during the feast of Corpus Christi, a moveable feast that fell between late May and late June. The York Cycle (first recorded as being performed in York in 1376) was the longest and contained 48 episodes/ pageants, performed and staged by different guilds.

There are signs that Fifhide was familiar with the performance of mystery plays at nearby Clerkenwell. Such visual narratives as his illustrations of biblical and apocryphal scenes, with their speech scrolls (some numbered like play parts), their emphasis upon the mystery/trade of textile workers (mercers), who would have been responsible for staging some of the plays, just as the butchers were in charge of the Crucifixion, and the way in which Fifhide dons a costume over his usual garb when asked to make the nails for the Crucifixion and offloads the dirty work onto his wife (an episode echoed in a comic tale in the Cornish *Ordinalia*), may have influenced the staging of tableaux in plays, including those in Cornwall.

This was a time of political and economic meltdown, compounded by the Black Death, which by 1349 had extinguished a third of the population of Europe, and the Peasants' Revolt in 1381. The natives were getting restless, workers were fewer on the ground and many were leaving the land and old feudal ties to work in towns. New settlements founded around the start of the century had largely become deserted villages, inhabited only by ghosts. The traces of their streets, homes and fields can still be seen as echoes in the landscape. Food production was becoming key, with new markets such as Penzance being developed (in its case by Lady Alice de Lisle) to support agricultural trade as well as the traditional fishing and mining export centres.

The rural and urban populaces, then as now, wished to be distracted and entertained and needed to be educated. Such plays offered diversion, provided a context for the instruction and affirmation of faith that extended the experience gained in church services. They also sought to foster a sense of local community in which people played as well as worked together, and to explain the relationship between past, present and future, which was embedded within the concept of the communion of saints – the community of all people across time and space (those already in heaven, those doing the work in the world and those awaiting liberation from hell) that was interpreted by some theologians as extending beyond people to a cosmic harmony and union of all things.

9

THE FOURTEENTH CENTURY II:
SIR GEOFFREY LUTTRELL'S PYRAMID

THE LUTTRELL PSALTER (BRITISH LIBRARY, ADD. MS 42130)

Commissioned manuscripts often provide unique windows into the lives of their patrons. Among the most highly customized is the Luttrell Psalter, created in the 1330s–40s for the lord of the manor of Irnham in Lincolnshire, Sir Geoffrey Luttrell. At the centre of the House of Lords in Parliament sits the Woolsack, symbolizing the source of the wealth and power of the nobles. The wealth of wool barons such as Sir Geoffrey ornamented the country, especially the rich farming country of East Anglia, with churches, sculpture and paintings, including a large number of illuminated manuscripts for them and their families and favourite religious foundations, as did the monarchs and their courts. Richard II was deposed in 1399 by the first of the Lancastrian dynasty's kings, Henry IV, because of his authoritarianism and lavish lifestyle.

Elegant, courtly works such as the Queen Mary Psalter (British Library, Royal MS 2 B VII), thought to have been made around 1310–20 for Edward II or his queen, Isabella, is one of the most beautiful, in both its fully painted illuminations and its tinted drawing *bas-de-page* scenes in its lower margins. Its drapery and elegant figures announce its aspirations to French fashion and to high court culture and couture, but its programme of illumination sets up a threefold layer of reading throughout, with fully painted historiated initials opening each psalm depicting Old Testament scenes and prophesies which prefigure the New Testament scenes in the accompanying half-page miniatures. The tinted drawings in the lower margin (the '*bas de page*') include episodes from saints' lives and the bestiary, as well as grotesques, which extend the message of the salvific mission of Christ and his ethical teaching into ongoing human history. The team of artists that produced it take their name – the Queen Mary Psalter artists – from this, their masterwork. They illuminated for the Westminster court and also for the great wool barons and towns of East Anglia, upon which the wealth of the nation rested – as symbolized by the wool sacks that still occupy the central space of the parliamentary House of Lords.

The Ormesby Psalter (Bodleian Library, MS Douce 366), also of early fourteenth-century date but begun a little earlier, aspired to such high taste, emulated efficiently by Norwich craftspeople over several decades for a marriage that never took place, leaving the manuscript unfinished. Another important manuscript from this period and area is the Gorleston Psalter (British Library, Add. MS 49622), notable for containing early music instruction and for its lively and amusing marginalia, which was made for a patron associated with the church of St Andrew's, Gorleston, in Norfolk.

d dominū cum tri
bularer clamaui:
et exaudiuit me.
Domine libera a
nimā

The Peterborough Psalter (Brussels, Royal Library, MS 9961–62) was produced for Abbot Godfrey of Croyland around 1300, but around 1317–18 it was presented as a gift to the papal nuncio, Gaucelin d'Eux, who gave it to Pope John XXII. It then passed to Clementia of Hungary, the widow of Louis X of France, and after her death was bought by Philip VI, so prized was it for its beauty. The Luttrell Psalter, by contrast, is a more robust, earthy beast in its style, but displays even greater imagination, daring and innovation in its highly individual and often extremely personal imagery.

The identification of the owners and makers of medieval manuscripts usually involves a fair bit of detective work to determine their origins and provenance. Not so the Luttrell Psalter (British Library, Add. MS 42130), which proudly proclaims in its colophon 'To the glory of God. Sir Geoffrey Luttrell caused me to be made.' It was intended as his 'pyramid', the lasting memorial of the lord of the manor of Irnham and his family. Sir Geoffrey was a player in unsettled times; his hopes and fears for eternity are manifest in the programme of marginalia in which his achievements and faults, and those of his society, are held up for scrutiny (if often obliquely portrayed) against the age-old backdrop of the cry *de Profundis* and the shouts of joy of the Psalms. The rigorous spiritual programme of self-examination and of exhortation to good works, and much of the intimate coded iconography, was probably the work of his confessor, the Dominican William of Fotheringay, who was probably also the artist of some of its most personal and revealing scenes.

The Psalter was made in the 1330s and '40s, during what has been dubbed 'the worst century ever' on the eve of the devastation caused by the Black Death in 1348–9. In 1381 the Peasants' Revolt would mark the culmination of this turbulent century of social, political and economic unrest, which began to transform the feudal order, escalating migration from the land to the towns, and which was marked by heightened personal piety and preoccupation with mortality. Wat Tyler would assemble his force of ordinary folk, forced to breaking point by poor, self-serving government and the imposition of a poll tax to pay for warfare and court excesses, on

The Queen Mary Psalter (BL, Royal MS 2 B VII, f. 256v), made at Westminster in 1310–20 by a group of artists who also worked in East Anglia and who take their name from this masterwork (the Queen Mary Group). It was perhaps made for King Edward II or his queen, Isabella. In the initial A, the high priest and people of the Old Testament pray for salvation, which is achieved through Christ's crucifixion in the miniature. The tinted drawing in the bas de page *echoes this theme with an image of St Christina, whose prayers are answered when angels save her from the river into which a pagan royal would-be lover, whom she has resisted, has thrown her to drown. This is a complex threefold iconographic scheme, executed in the height of fashionable courtly style.*

pudore: ⁊ operiantur sicut diploide
confusione sua
Confitebor domino nimis in
ore meo: et in medio multorum
laudabo eum
Qui astitit a dextris pauperis:
ut saluam faceret a persequentib;
animam meam.
Gloria patri
Dñs Galfridus louterell me fieri
fecit

Blackheath in southeast London before marching on the City and Tower of London. The radical cleric John Ball would fire up the rebels, preaching 'When Adam dug and Eve span, who was then the Gentleman?' When Wat agreed to parlay with Richard II, he was cut down by the Mayor of London, William Walworth; he was publicly beheaded and his head displayed on London Bridge – the rebellion was quelled. The frenetic, gruesome scenes are depicted in the colourful, elegant miniatures of Flemish fifteenth-century copies of the *Chroniques* (Chronicles) of Jean Froissart. The Luttrell Psalter, like the Holkham Bible, serves as a window on to its age, helping us to penetrate something of the mindsets of representatives of diverse sectors of medieval English society, while the later illuminated chronicles have preserved the official, sanitized view of the victors.

The Luttrell Psalter can be dated, I have argued, to between 1330 and Sir Geoffrey's death in 1345 and is one of the supreme expressions of English Gothic. Remarkably, not only is the patron of the work, Sir Geoffrey

Opposite: *The Luttrell Psalter (BL, Add. MS 42130, f. 202v): 'To the glory of God. Sir Geoffrey Luttrell caused me to be made,' the colophon above the miniature proclaims. The old soldier is depicted on his war horse, which he left to the church at Irnham in his will as part of its war-levy, while his wife, Agnes Sutton, and daughter-in-law, Beatrice le Scrope, hand him his arms, the heraldic dress indicating which families they came from. He had served Edward I on the battlefield for much of his career and was now preparing his soul for its final joust – with humility and death.*
Below: *The Luttrell Psalter (BL, Add. MS 42130, f. 170r): ploughing scene, part of a cycle of labours on the land throughout the manorial year. The mould board plough and clothing are contemporary with the manuscript, but the scene takes on a symbolic meaning, as well as a narrative one, with the plough team. Visitations of the period show that even before the Black Death struck there were food and cattle shortages and that larger mixed bovine/equine teams were used. These four bullocks represent the four evangelists, ploughing the soil to receive the seeds of faith.*

(1276–1345), named in the book but he, his family, his retainers and the world they knew are depicted on many of its pages. Family members are seen at prayer, feasting and preparing for military service, accompanied by those alongside whom they lived in close proximity: the domestic staff who ran their affairs, dressed them and cooked their meals; the people who worked their land – men who ploughed and sowed, drank, gamed and trained as military levies, women whose backs strained with their burdens and spun wool for the famed Lincoln red cloth to support their families, boys who raided their fruit-trees and turned the spits in the lordly kitchens, and dogs that guarded their property and saw off peddlers. For once the memory of ordinary folk is preserved, alongside that of the wealthy. The things they owned and the places they inhabited are conveyed in graphic detail, but more importantly still, we are given a glimpse of the ways they may have thought and felt.

Yet these scenes are not there just to document manorial life – they are imbued with symbolic meaning and moralistic interpretations. The Luttrells' world is reinvented and reinterpreted in the light of biblical time

The Luttrell Psalter (BL, Add. MS 42130, f. 158r): life in the Luttrell household and estates is depicted in detail, as a mini-Domesday book of their achievements, such as the windmill, a technological advance that Sir Geoffrey was one of the first to adopt. Spiritual meanings are incorporated too. Here a well-off young farmer rides in comfort to bring a sack of grain to the mill (symbolizing Christ, the 'mystic mill', which converted the grain of the Old Testament Law into the life-giving flour of the Eucharist). A little dog growls at him (a pun on the Latin domini canes, *the hounds of the Lord, seeking out sin, and on the name of the Dominican order of friars). A poor older woman has struggled and brought an even fuller bag to the mill on her shoulders – the widow's mite is more acceptable than the offerings of those who can well afford them.*

and perpetual prayer, cohabited by the Trinity, the Virgin, angels, Old and New Testament figures and saints. Sir Geoffrey's Psalter celebrated the good old days and the social status quo but was made at a time of rapid change in society, when old age and the prospect of meeting his Maker were fast approaching. It was planned as his memorial and was probably used when prayers were said for his soul's repose in Irnham's church.

Geoffrey was baptized at Irnham, where he was to die and be interred. He inherited the estate in 1297 on the death of his father and between then and 1322 he participated in thirteen campaigns of military service (on average every other year) including the Scots Wars. His father had been summoned to attend Parliament in 1295, and so the family technically enjoyed baronial status, if minor league. Its status must have been considerably enhanced by Sir Geoffrey's military service, property acquisitions and dynastic marriage contracts. Sometime between 1297 and 1300 he married Agnes Sutton, daughter of Sir Richard Sutton of Sutton-on-Trent and Warsop, Nottinghamshire, great-great niece of Oliver Sutton, Bishop of Lincoln. They had at least four sons and two daughters (Robert, Andrew, Geoffrey, Robert II, Elizabeth and Isabella).

Sir Geoffrey sailed close to the wind, in legal terms, when furthering the interests of the family and its allies. In 1312 and 1320 he was accused of collaborating in the seizure of the goods of two neighbours: the Gilbertine Priory at Sempringham and Ralph de Sancto Laudo. Joyce Coleman has shown that these events were part of a bigger picture of dispute in which Sir Geoffrey was supporting other of his neighbours, as part of a web of relationships and events revolving around the wider interests of the Lancastrian party. Such legal spats, and dabbling in dynastic politics, would have made a match with the Le Scrope family of Masham, the leading 'legal eagles' of the day, doubly attractive to Sir Geoffrey. (The Le Scrope arms appear on the pennant of a trumpet held by a hybrid creature in the outer margin of f. 161r.) In 1320 he married off his son Andrew, only seven years old, to Beatrice Le Scrope, in the year that his eldest son, Robert, died. His youngest son, Geoffrey, was also married to Constance Le Scrope – Sir Geoffrey was not taking any chances in securing this family merger – but the young couple seem not to have lived to maturity. In 1324 the girls' father, Geoffrey Le Scrope (d. 1340), a second son who became a distinguished diplomat and soldier and a political survivor, became Chief Justice of the King's Bench (fulfilling Luttrell's hopes for the alliance), and in 1327 was the legal enforcer of King Edward II's deposition. The Luttrells and their in-laws evidently enjoyed a dangerous proximity to royal affairs. That same year Sir Geoffrey was one of forty knights summoned to attend the Great Council of Westminster and the following year received the office of Commissioner of Array for Kesteven, in which Irnham lay, but he pleaded that he was unable to assume this role as he was already too old and in poor health.

The Luttrells' support for the house of Lancaster, whose political fortunes were erratic, also left them potentially exposed. On f. 56r of the Psalter is a depiction of the beheading of an anonymous saint. A fourteenth-century reader has inscribed him 'lancastres' and it is thought that this was intended as a covert commemoration of the 'modern martyrdom' of Thomas, Earl of Lancaster, executed at his castle of Pontefract, some 14 kilometres (9 mi.) from the Luttrells' Hooton Pagnell estate, in March 1322 for a rising against King Edward II. Thomas was popularly considered a saint, the commemorations devised for his cult linking it with that of Thomas Becket of Canterbury (whose martyrdom is illustrated on f. 51r). Both were martyrs to affairs of state and pilgrimages to sites associated with him would have passed the Luttrell's northern properties. Sir Geoffrey may even have visited them. Attempts were made to secure Thomas's canonization soon after the accession of Edward III in 1327 and commemoration of the earl in the Psalter would have been acceptable after this date.

To emphasize the Luttrells' fidelity to the crown, the Psalter's imagery stressed Sir Geoffrey's service under Edward I, and the family's continued allegiance to his grandson, Edward III, after the unfortunate interlude of the reign of Edward II. This was marked by civil war and economic decline, by Edward's deposition in 1327, the usurpation of power by his wife, Queen Isabella, and her lover Mortimer (who was accused of having Edward killed) and their subsequent seizure in 1330.

Isabella and Mortimer's adulterous relationship may be parodied on f. 68r where a young male acrobat, one leg raised, balances upon his shoulders the sinuous, swaying figure of a young woman. She is viewed from behind: her delicately shaded purple gown is beautifully draped, her head is coquettishly tilted and fashionably veiled and her raised arms, with their long loose sleeves, the height of contemporary courtly fashion, are carefully posed to frame her head. The man's glance sweeps sideways to engage the upturned gaze of a beautiful young queen whose head is contained within a historiated minor initial D. This opens Psalm 35/36, 'An oracle is within my heart concerning the sinfulness of the wicked. There is no fear of God before his eyes. For in his own eyes he flatters himself too much to detect or hate his sin' (Psalms 36:1–2). The queen wears a slender gold crown and her head and throat are veiled in white, like those of the female acrobat opposite. Her hair is arranged in two fashionable 'cornette' coils over her ears (resembling Princess Leia's 'cinnamon buns' hairstyle in the original *Star Wars* film), which are also echoed in the coiffure of the female acrobat. This may be an allusion to the scandalous conduct of Queen Isabella who, with her lover Mortimer, is believed to have ordered the murder of her homosexual husband, Edward II. The balancing act of the lovers and Mortimer's need to support Isabella may be being emulated by the entertainers, and the behaviour of those in the highest places compared to that of the lowest and most morally lax – the wandering troubadours and jongleurs.

The pose of the acrobat resembles that of another male figure on ff. 159v–160r in which a young man holds aloft above his head a stone monument. A smaller figure dressed in the same garb sits on its lower steps. The form of the edifice is close to that of the surviving Eleanor Crosses, the monuments erected to mark the places where the body of Queen Eleanor of Castile, wife of King Edward I, lay on its return from Lincoln, where she died in 1290, to Westminster. Sir Geoffrey would certainly have seen such crosses at Lincoln and Stamford. The supporter may be the mason, the smaller figure representing him finishing his work, for they both grasp either end of a metal implement and the little man appears to be chiselling the base of the sculpture. There may be some relationship to the adjacent text, which reads 'For who in the skies above can compare with the Lord? Who is like the Lord among the heavenly beings?' (Psalms 89:6), for Eleanor was a much-loved queen, greatly mourned by her husband and his people. In the lower margin is a bull, perhaps the symbol of St Luke, who represented Christ as the sacrificial

Overleaf: *The Luttrell Psalter gives an insight into Sir Geoffrey's deep concern for his immortal soul. He was a philanthropist to the poor and to places of pilgrimage and evidently heeded his confessor, who was probably the artist of this opening of the manuscript. His marginal images here (*BL, *Add. MS 42130, ff. 159v–160r) form a meditation upon Sir Geoffrey's spiritual and worldly journey: he can be seen wearing his 'cosy hat' in a boat rowed backwards by howling oarsmen (his sins) but is compelled by truth and mercy (mentioned in the adjacent text – a kind of medieval hypertext link), who pull the boat towards humility and awareness of mortality, symbolized by the snail, which the bestiary said pulled in its horns before righteous authority. What greater authority than the bull, symbol of Christ the sacrificial victim of the Crucifixion (and the nickname, 'taurus', of his beloved late master, King Edward I)? The apotheosis of the latter's royal house, and Sir Geoffrey with it, is represented by an Eleanor Cross, of which there were two near Luttrell estates, the memorials to Edward's much-loved saintly queen. This is raised heavenward by its mason, as, he trusts, will be the loyal royal servant, Sir Geoffrey.*

Quoniam quis in nubibus equabi
tur domino: similis erit domino in
filiis dei.
Deus qui glorificatur in consilio
sanctorum: magnus ⁊ terribilis su
per omnes qui in circuitu eius sunt.
Domine deus uirtutum quis simi
lis tibi: potens es domine ⁊ ueritas
tua in circuitu tuo.
Tu dominaris potestatis maris:
motum autem fluctuum eius tu mi
tigas.
Tu humiliasti sicut uulneratum su
perbum: in brachio uirtutis tue dis

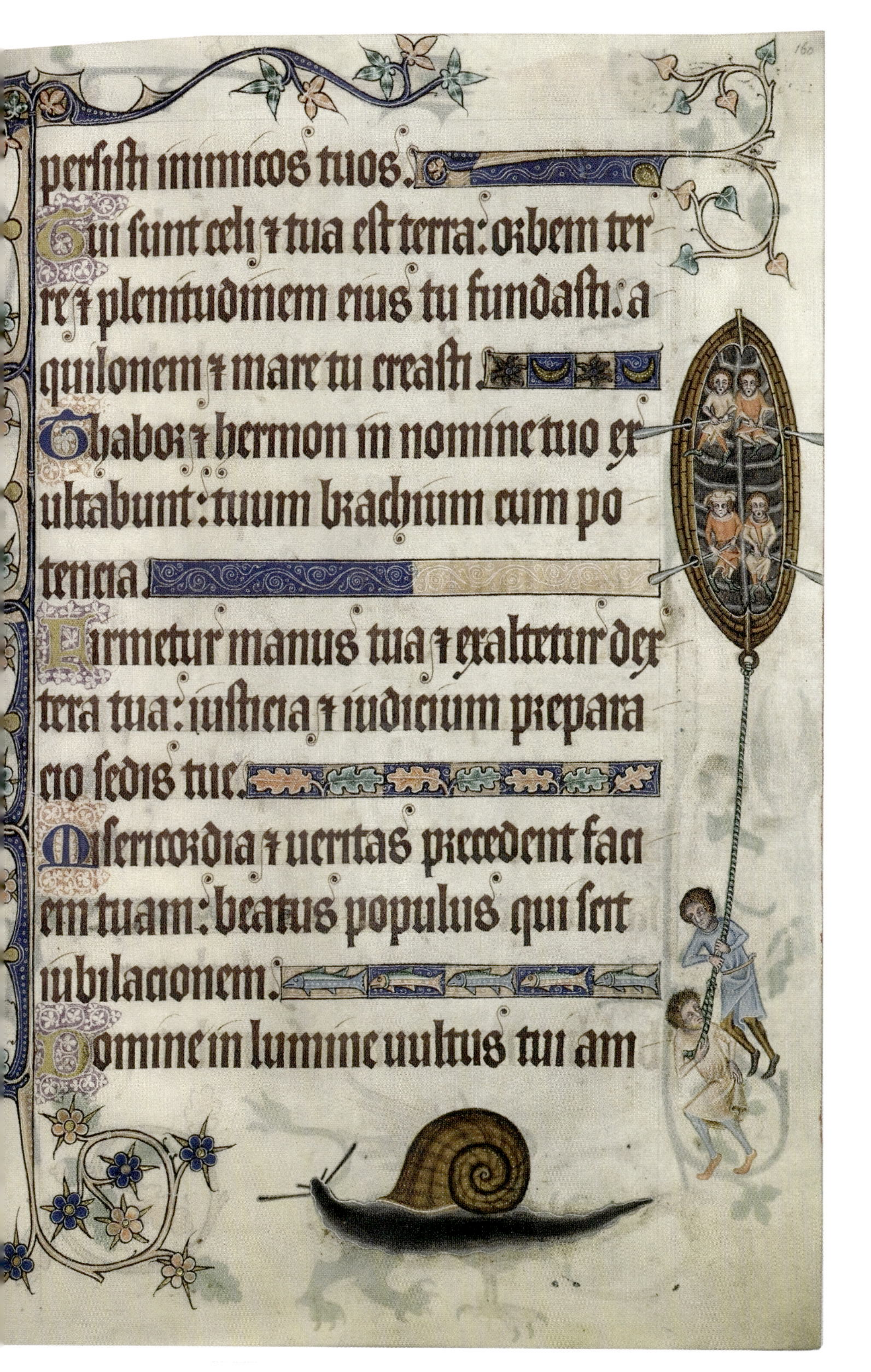

160

persisti inimicos tuos.
Tui sunt celi ⁊ tua est terra: orbem ter
re ⁊ plenitudinem eius tu fundasti. a
quilonem ⁊ mare tu creasti.
Thabor ⁊ hermon in nomine tuo ex
ultabunt: tuum brachium cum po
tencia.
Firmetur manus tua ⁊ exaltetur dex
tera tua: iusticia ⁊ iudicium prepara
cio sedis tue.
Misericordia ⁊ ueritas precedent faci
em tuam: beatus populus qui scit
iubilacionem.
Domine in lumine uultus tui am

victim, or a sign of strength in reference to the verse above 'with your strong arm you scattered your enemies' (Psalms 89:10). That strength is also displayed by the mason who holds the Eleanor Cross aloft, his pose recalling that of the acrobat on f. 68r who holds the swaying lady on his shoulders, perhaps parodying Queen Isabella who stands on the shoulders of her lover, Mortimer. The immorality of that couple might be intended to contrast with the virtue of Queen Eleanor and her commemoration by Edward I, whom Sir Geoffrey served.

I have proposed a reading that unifies the marginal imagery across the entire opening as follows: Sir Geoffrey is depicted as one of four men rowing a boat backwards and identified by the same distinctive headgear that he wears at the feast (f. 208r). He is pulled backwards by his sins (his fellow oarsmen), while Truth and Mercy (who go before the face of the Lord in the accompanying Psalm), in the form of two men hauling ropes and pulling the boat onwards, impel him towards humility. This is symbolized by the snail in the lower margin, which was read as a signal of humility for it pulled in its horns when touched by proper authority. Such righteous authority is signified on the opposite page by the figure of a bull that symbolized both Christ's sacrifice and royal strength, the name 'Taurus' sometimes having been applied to King Edward I. The proper use of such authority leads to elevation, commemoration and good fame, signified by the memorial to the saintly Queen Eleanor elevated heavenward.

It may have been the onset of an awareness of personal mortality, already signalled by his having to decline office in 1327, which led Sir Geoffrey to begin to set his affairs in order to ensure the dynastic succession. In 1331 he petitioned the pope for a dispensation to remain in his marriage, for it had come to Agnes's attention (and her concerns are also likely to be voiced within the Psalter's imagery) that, as second cousins, they had married within the third and fourth degrees of consanguinity. This may not have been a serious obstacle in the eyes of those other than canon law jurists, but it may have added a note of emotional tension to their marriage of over thirty years' standing and now presented an impediment to the inheritance of their surviving son, Andrew, who had now reached eighteen years of age but who would only reach legal maturity at the age of 21 in 1334. The petition for legitimization of Sir Geoffrey's marriage was granted, however, and Andrew duly inherited on Sir Geoffrey's death in 1345.

The folio on which his distinctive patronage colophon occurs also bears a grand portrait of Sir Geoffrey, arming for warfare and for his own final battle, as an old soldier who had spent half his life in the field in the service of King Edward I, with his own humility and with death. Sir Geoffrey could no longer climb upon his mighty warhorse, caparisoned in heraldic finery like the womenfolk, Sir Geoffrey's wife Agnes Sutton and his prized (but sadly barren) daughter-in-law Beatrice Le Scrope, who pass him his arms and are thereby associated with his great endeavours, earthly and eternal, including the commissioning of the Psalter that was to serve as their monument. Sir Geoffery bequeathed his horse to the parish priest as part of an extravagant will, which provided for twenty chaplains to recite masses for his soul for five years, and for clerks to recite the Psalms, probably from this very book. The Irnham branch of the family died out in battle in 1419, but Sir Geoffrey's book has ensured that its fame lives on.

The body of the work was commissioned from a team of specialist scribes and artists (some of this team may also have gone on to work on the Macclesfield Psalter, Cambridge, Fitzwilliam Museum, MS 1-2005), probably based in Norwich, a city in which the Luttrells would have conducted much commerce. The portion containing the most intimate marginal scenes of manorial life, however, was enlivened by a rather different artist, perhaps himself a friar, who pulled no punches when encouraging the Luttrells to confront the spiritual speculum of their own lives and who was greatly preoccupied with salvation and social justice.

This was the age of spiritual teachers of the magnitude of Robert Mannyng of Bourne and Richard Rolle (who served as confessor to Luttrell womenfolk turned nuns at Hampole), whose thoughts pervade the Psalter's imagery. Comely young women defend the castle of love (their honour) and play courtly board games with their wooers in the enclosed garden (*hortus conclusus*) of chastity, but their fashionable veils billow in recollection of Mannyng's 'devil's sails', the vanities which carry all to perdition.

The forces of chaos that lurked on the margins of society, and of the book, threatening to overturn the divine, natural and social orders are symbolized by a bold and bizarre array of grotesques – a motley assembly of human, mammal, reptile, fish and bird body parts rearranged to parody or praise Creation. Some are benign or instructive, others threaten the divine and governmental stability of which Sir Geoffrey saw himself as the local guardian. The fens of Lincolnshire and East Anglia had long harboured the imagery of the grotesque since the visions of the Irish St Fursey (d. 650) and the Anglo-Saxon warrior turned hermit St Guthlac (d. 714). These would inspire, in turn, Dante, Bosch and 'Monty Python'.

Some of these grotesques, or babywyns (baboons) as they were known, might make pleasant household pets, however. Not all were threatening. Their use in manuscripts was encouraged by the spread into northern Europe of early legal books from the orbit of the University of Bologna from the late twelfth century onwards. In these, the combination of animal components might relate to the crimes and sins referred to in the texts they accompanied or refer to the moralistic virtues and vices symbolized by the creatures in the *Physiologus* or Marvels of the East that led to the medieval bestiary. During the thirteenth century some came into popular artistic and social currency. Among the commonest were monkeys (*similes* in Latin), which were similar to mankind and aped its ways, parodying its follies, and rabbits that represented sex and lust, owing to their prolific breeding habits.

Below: *The Luttrell Psalter (*BL, *Add.* MS *42130, f. 63r): a young lady admires herself, her jewel box at her side, a dragon of evil vomits, a young man with a clerical tonsure (growing out, betokening lack of commitment to his vocation) catches a bird in a net in the margin above. This may be a coded parody of the elopement of Sir Geoffrey's daughter, Elizabeth Luttrell, with an ambitious young clerk, a scandal that the artist, who was probably the family's Dominican confessor, was urging the Luttrells to learn from and repent of vanity, lust and ambition for power.* Opposite: *The Luttrell Psalter (*BL, *Add.* MS *42130, f. 208r): the Luttrell family at the New Year feast. Sir Geoffrey is at the centre, his wife, Agnes, to his right. His heir, Andrew, is on the left, then his brother Guy or son Robert and Andrew's fashionably clad wife, Beatrice. At the other end of the table are two Dominican or Austin friars; the younger looks longingly at the kitchen scene on the opposite page, rather than at the vegetarian fare he is allowed, before him. The older Dominican looks straight at the viewer, engaging with them, and is probably the artist of this part of the book, Brother William of Fotheringay, the family confessor. The steward who carries in the plates received the tableware and tapestry depicted here in Sir Geoffrey's will. But there is also a deeper symbolic meaning to this image, which urges the family to confront its spiritual shortcomings.*

The Luttrell Psalter went way beyond this, personalizing its marginalia to a remarkable extent. The most personal scenes of all were painted by one very distinctive artist. His figures are often a little squat and can have an almost deathly pallor, as if anticipating the grave. He depicted not only the Luttrell family but those who worked in their kitchens and their fields, those who formed the military levies they had to supply to the Crown. He parodied those who held power but abused it, and he painted complex little scenes containing many layers of meaning, which commented upon society and eternity and both praised and encouraged the Luttrells, but pulled no punches in shaming them when their behaviour necessitated some spiritual tough love.

One such marginal scene depicts a fashionable girl having her long hair braided by her maid, whose own hair is modestly covered. Her drapery resembles the tail of a mermaid on a nearby leaf of the manuscript; mermaids were the medieval trade sign of prostitutes. A locked jewel casket sits between them and a little dragon, symbol of evil, vomits nearby. In the adjacent margin, a young man with a clerical tonsure on his head catches a bird in a net. His tonsure, the sign of his religious vocation, sprouts stubble and is growing out – he obviously lacks commitment. I have suggested that this alludes to a famous family scandal. When she was twelve years old, Sir Geoffrey's daughter Elizabeth was sent to the household of Walter de Gloucester to become engaged to his son. While there, she was seduced by an ambitious young cleric on the make, Thomas of Ellerker. They eloped and a group of high-ranking nobles set off in pursuit – the Mr Darcys of their day – for there was a lot riding on the political match between the house of Worcester and the Luttrells and their friends, as the seeds of the Wars of the

Roses were being sown and Sir Geoffrey was of the Lancastrian persuasion. A king's ransom of £1,000 (the Psalter likely cost around £20, the annual value of Sir Geoffrey's main estate) was paid to get Elizabeth restored to the bosom of her family, with her virginity declared intact. Ellerker went on to enjoy a successful career in politics and high places.

What artist would be brave enough to depict this in their employer's big book? I have posited that it was his confessor, Brother William of Fotheringay, a Dominican friar whose job was to get Sir Geoffrey's soul and those of his family to heaven to participate in the eternal feast. He shows them seated at the table at their own New Year's feast (f. 208r), which includes two Dominican friars at the high table, presumably two of the five clerics Sir Geoffrey kept on payroll at Irnham, so that he did not have to share his affairs with those who might then reveal his confessions and business to others.

In the feast scene the steward, his importance within the household emphasized by the purse he wears at his belt, places dishes on the table while the butler, wearing an exotic eastern-style striped scarf reminiscent of those worn by Jewish rabbis, proffers the feast to his master, Sir Geoffrey, who presides at the centre of the high table. To his right sits his wife, Agnes Sutton, flanked by two friars in white cassocks and black cloaks. These are Austin or Dominican friars, possibly serving as the Luttrell chaplain and confessor and/or perhaps those who planned and even undertook the main work on the Psalter and who would have been given board and lodging as part of their payment (the dish of eggs before them signalling the austerity of their mendicant diet). The friar next to Lady Luttrell has particularly well-defined features and is the larger and more important of the two: he may conceivably have been the mastermind behind the planning of Sir Geoffrey's Psalter. At Sir Geoffrey's left hand sit two young men and a young woman. One of these is his son and heir, Andrew (probably the one who sits at his left hand and who mirrors his posture), and the woman is his wife, Beatrice Le Scrope, wearing long sleeves in the height of fashion. The other may represent one of his other sons (although two were already deceased – Robert, who died in 1320, and Geoffrey, who, with his Le Scrope wife, Constance, died before achieving maturity). This would probably be a second Robert, who was a Knight of the Hospital of St John of Jerusalem, or Sir Geoffrey's brother, Guy. Four of the figures, Sir Geoffrey, his heir and the two friars, stare frontally at the viewer, while the other gazes sideways at their lord. On the table is a plethora of luxury tableware in pewter or silver and gold, including knives and spoons, and behind it is a hanging decorated with the Luttrell martlets. By contrast the foods are relatively restrained, perhaps indicating an awareness of the need of some modesty and restraint in consumption in the face of times of wider social instability and deprivation (rather as the Anglo-Irish gentry during the late eighteenth and early nineteenth centuries favoured an external architectural severity for their country estates, belying the wealth and opulence within and serving as a social signal of sympathy with comparative rural poverty). The tableware and kitchenware depicted were bequeathed in Sir Geoffrey's will to several of the leading staff represented. The inclusion of such a distinctive depiction of the patron and his family, servants and chattels is extremely rare. Its placing within the volume, as with that of Sir Geoffrey on his warhorse, is significant. The feast and cooking scenes run throughout and illustrate Psalm 114/115, which includes the verses:

> They have mouths but cannot speak, eyes, but they cannot see; they have ears, but cannot hear; noses, but they cannot smell; they have hands, but cannot feel; feet, but they cannot walk; nor can they utter a sound with their throats. Those who make them will be like them, and so will all who trust in them. O house of Israel, trust in the Lord – he is their help and their shield. O house of Aaron, trust in the Lord – he is their help and shield. You who fear him, trust in the Lord – he is their help and shield. The Lord remembers us and will bless us. He will bless the house of Israel, he will bless the house of Aaron, he will bless those who fear the Lord – small and great alike. May the Lord make you increase, both you and your children. May you be blessed by the Lord, the maker of heaven and earth. The highest heavens belong to the Lord, but the earth he has given to man. It is not the dead who praise the Lord, those who go down to silence; it is we who extol the Lord, both now and for evermore (Psalms 115:5–18).

The righteous Luttrells praise the Lord, in the present and for evermore, at a terrestrial and celestial feast. Sir Geoffrey and Beatrice raise chalices to their mouths and the two other Luttrell men consume pieces of food resembling wafers, the whole scene carrying overtones of the imagery of the Last Supper and the celebration of the Eucharist. The composition is highly reminiscent of that of the Last Supper on f. 90v, Sir Geoffrey occupying the position of Christ, the family and friars those of the Apostles, and a figure with a withered hand and prayer stole that of Judas. The earth has been given to them, and they enjoy its fruits, the latter-day equivalent of the house of Israel. Both 'great and small alike', master and servants, are included in this blessing and their senses, unlike the unrighteous lamented in the opening verses, are fully engaged and satisfied.

Another simultaneous allusion perhaps intended by the Luttrell feast scenes is to the Marriage at Cana, in which Christ turns water into wine, with which Mark commences his Gospel as the first public declaration of Christ's divine nature (as one of the Epiphany signs proclaiming Christ's divinity, along with the coming of the Magi and the baptism of Christ). In this Gospel passage the steward does not know where the wine has come from, but the servants do, which can be read at one level of biblical commentary as the high priesthood of the Temple not seeing what those following Christ do. This symbolism might also have extended to Sir Geoffrey's view that those currently leading his own nation were blind to the inadequacy of their own provision (that is, government), which the people themselves perceive and know that Christ has come to rectify, which would tie in with the Luttrells' aspirations for political regime change.

The Luttrell feast is not intended to depict one particular moment in time, but the symbolism of the celebration of Epiphany, the start of the medieval new year, would be appropriate and may be signalled by the figure of the 'Janus Bifrons' who heralds the Psalm on f. 206v and whose two faces looked back at the old year and forward to the new as the personification of January, the season of feasting. Such an allusion would accord with the symbolism outlined above, reinforcing Sir Geoffrey's role as Christ's representative on a local and domestic scale, and might also have served to commemorate the legitimacy of Sir Geoffrey's own marriage and that of his heir, Andrew.

The Luttrell Psalter gives an insight into Sir Geoffrey's deep concern for his immortal soul. He was a philanthropist to the poor and to places of pilgrimage and evidently heeded his confessor, who was probably the artist of this opening of the manuscript, the marginal images of which form a meditation upon Sir Geoffrey's spiritual and worldly journey.

The Luttrell family and the Church were not the only ones to benefit from Sir Geoffrey's will, or to be depicted in his great Psalter. He seems to have been inordinately generous to certain of his retainers, some of whom are probably also depicted in the margins of his book: Joan of Meaux, lady's maid; John of Colne, butler, who may lead the procession into the Luttrell feast and inherited the silver and pewter plate and tapestry depicted therein; John of Bridgeford, cook, who prepares the feast; William the Porter;

Matilda Mabson, the brewer; Thomas of Chaworth, squire and a relative of the Luttrells. He also left substantial gifts to his chaplains and his confessor, Brother William of Fotheringay, and to the Dominicans of Stamford, which he was helping campaign to become an alternative to Cambridge University.

The Luttrells are known to have had connections with religious foundations in York, Lincoln, Southwell and Stamford, in the last case with both Augustinian and Dominican houses, although these are not known to have been involved in book production. The stylistic context for Sir Geoffrey's initial act of commissioning lies within East Anglia and the Fenlands, especially books made during the 1320s in Norwich, whence some of the Luttrell Psalter's makers may have been drawn, especially the scribe, those responsible for the border and minor decoration and the more conventional First Luttrell Artist. Sir Geoffrey would have transacted much business through Norwich and he may have placed the project with a stationer there to subcontract out the work. Norwich is even depicted in one scene as Constantinople, although its walls contain not Hagia Sophia but Norwich Cathedral (as depicted on its seal) and the trade signs of pubs that can still be found there today. The book was written and decorated there in one campaign and the marginalia painted in the first third, while the central third may have been sent home to Irnham for the in-house Dominican confessor to illuminate with his spiritually and politically hard-hitting marginal scenes. The final third never received its marginalia. Perhaps the money or enthusiasm ran out, or the Dominican artist or his patron died (or wife, for Agnes Luttrell died in 1340 and Sir Geoffrey in 1345). If Sir Geoffrey coordinated the making of his book in this way this might account for the rather unusual nature of the book's colophon, which ascribes its making not to artists or scribe, as is sometimes the case, but to the patron. In this case Sir Geoffrey Luttrell did indeed 'cause me to be made'.

Other books in the central Middle Ages might well be the work of a group of craftspeople working in an identifiable town, frequently being subcontracted together, but occasionally a particularly talented artist might be brought in to contribute something outstanding. Housing the makers of a book, in order to obtain the desired customized results, is paralleled by later commissions by the Bohuns, who housed artistic Augustinian friars in their castle at Pleshey, Essex, to illuminate some of their works, and by Westminster and Sherborne Abbeys, who proffered bed and board during the production of the Litlyngton Missal and the Sherborne Missal during the late fourteenth and early fifteenth centuries. Abbot Litlyngton paid his scribe/project manager £4 of the overall cost of £34 14*s* 7*d* and housed and fed him at the abbey for the two years' duration of the work. As we shall see in the next chapter, the Sherborne Missal (British Library, Add. MS 74236) was written around 1400–1407 by a Benedictine monk of Sherborne, John Whas, but the illumination was the work of several artists, led by an itinerant master-artist, the Dominican John Siferwas, commissioned by the abbot of Sherborne Abbey, Robert Bruyning, as a statement of its – and his – importance.

Sir Geoffrey's heir, Andrew, seems not to have approved of his father's expenditure on the book or upon the extravagant funeral, with £100 to be spent on candles and generous alms and food for the poor (to be repeated annually) and prayers for his soul in perpetuity for which he made provision in his will. Andrew died on 6 September 1390, having stipulated that nobody should be invited to his funeral and that he would only pay for prayers for a week for him and his overlord, Henry Grosmont. He had lived to 77, surviving the ravages of the Black Death and the social instability that surrounded both that terrifying time and the furore of the Peasants' Revolt. Nonetheless, his own son survived him by only seven years and the male line of Luttrell of Irnham, which he and Sir Geoffrey strived to secure, was extinguished at his grandson's death at the Siege of Rouen in 1419, in pursuit of Henry V's claims to France. The dynastic and personal ambitions, hopes and fears expressed in the pages of the Luttrell Psalter had come to naught, in this world, within a century of its making.

The accession of Edward III in 1327 ushered in a longer, more stable reign of fifty years. In 1377 he was succeeded by his grandson Richard II, the son of his heir Edward the Black Prince (who had predeceased him). In 1399 this flamboyant ruler, famed for the extravagance of his parties and lavish spectacles, and for his mishandling of the Peasants' Revolt in 1381, was deposed and confined to the Tower of London by Henry Bolingbroke, a representative of the House of Lancaster (born of Edward III's third surviving son, John of Gaunt, and Blanche of Lancaster), who was crowned King Henry IV. He would reign until 1413. A French author, Jean Creton, was on the spot at the time of Richard's deposition and upon his return to Paris composed his *Histoire du roi d'Angleterre Richard* in 1401–2 and instructed an artist to paint his eyewitness report of the English Revolution, depicting a finely dressed Henry escorting a downcast, plainly robed Richard along Cheap Street to St Paul's Cathedral in London, with the crowds crying out in support of Lancaster. This survives as British Library, Harley MS

1319, f. 53v and is the closest the age came to predicting today's front-line photojournalism. The book was soon in the hands of the powerful Jean, Duc de Berry.

The fourteenth century had been dominated by a series of extreme political and social challenges: regnal instability; the Black Death; warfare with the Scots (with William Wallace – Braveheart – and Robert the Bruce, who died in 1329, successfully defending the independence of the Scottish throne); popular civil unrest at the high levels of taxation, inflation and food shortages that culminated in the Peasants' Revolt, which came to a head in an attack on London and the execution of its leader, Wat Tyler, and others; and two stages of what has become known as the Hundred Years War, which constituted the longest military conflict in European history, prompted by the historical claims to territory in France inherited from the Norman, Angevin and Plantagenet dynasties. This has been divided by historians into three phases, punctuated by truces: the Edwardian War (1337–60), the Caroline War (1369–89) and the Lancastrian War (1415–53). This would dominate the first half of the following century.

10

THE FIFTEENTH CENTURY I: ABBOT BRUYNING'S MEGA-MISSAL

THE SHERBORNE MISSAL (BRITISH LIBRARY, ADD. MS 74236)

The rise of urban book production during the thirteenth and fourteenth centuries did not mean the end of the ecclesiastical scriptorium. Books for use in religious establishments might be commissioned from urban sources by their patrons or their own members. There was also a trade in second-hand books and gift exchange between individuals and institutions is a feature across the centuries. Some monasteries, however, continued to pen their own library and liturgical books. The Sherborne Missal, made at the Benedictine abbey of St Mary in Sherborne, Dorset, is one such and is one of the greatest acts of corporate sponsorship of the late Middle Ages, with the in-house team supplemented by buying in a leading mendicant artist. Commissioned by Abbot Robert Bruyning, the book abounds with depictions of him, his overlord the Bishop of Salisbury, the itinerant Dominican artist John Siferwas and the monk John Whas, son of a local cottar, who would have lived in a humble cottage with a little garden in which to grow fruit and vegetables to support him and his family. The liturgy throughout the year is enlivened by an opulent programme of illumination in which the historical primacy of Sherborne is proclaimed by virtue of its post-Roman and Anglo-Saxon origins.

The International Gothic style of the Sherborne Missal reflects the confluence of the art of the late Middle Ages with that of the early Italian and Northern Renaissance. The humanist revival of classical texts and script styles was complemented by the reappearance of classical figural naturalism and neoclassical motifs.

Manuscript miniaturists might also be panel or fresco painters, such as Giovanni di Paolo (who illuminated Dante's *Paradiso* and *Inferno*) and Gerard David. Illuminators such as Gerard Horenbout and Simon Bening, working in the mercantile Netherlands, might achieve artistic fame for illuminating deluxe works (including books of hours) for leading patrons. Opulent illuminated service-books and music manuscripts continued to be made too, as did illustrated biblical and secular histories and romances.

Before acquisition for the nation in July 1998, the Sherborne Missal was the most valuable English illuminated manuscript in private hands. Made in Sherborne in the first years of the fifteenth century, the volume was still in England during the Reformation, when images of the pope and St Thomas Becket were defaced in compliance with Henry VIII's edicts in the 1530s. Probably owing its survival to the opulence and quality of its illumination, it travelled to the Continent and was in France by 1703, when it was given to the overjoyed antiquary Nicolas Foucault by the Bishop of

Lisieux. It subsequently belonged to French bibliophiles Charles d'Orléans (d. 1744) and Marcellin-François-Zacharie de Selle, treasurer-general of the French Navy, failing to reach its reserve at a sale in 1761 two years after his death.

It returned to England, sometime after a French note dated 1785 had been added, and in 1797 was purchased by George Galwey Mills, based at Slaughter-house, Gloucestershire, and St Kitts in the West Indies. He lived beyond his means, with a gambling and drink habit, and his library was dispersed long before his suicide, leading to the purchase of the Missal by the 2nd Duke of Northumberland in 1800, for £215. The missal remained at Alnwick Castle until placed on loan at the British Library in 1983. The 12th Duke's decision to offer the book for sale to meet the costs of inheriting the estate mobilized a collaborative operation involving the British Library, various government offices, granting bodies and representatives of the book trade to ensure that this medieval masterpiece remained in the country and passed into public ownership.

The duke assisted in limiting the sums involved, in the face of giddily escalating saleroom prices, but even after the government agreed to accept the volume in lieu of inheritance tax a hefty sum was still required to meet the agreed valuation. An extremely generous grant of the unprecedented sum of £4,125,000 from the National Heritage Memorial Fund went a long way towards meeting this, but even so in mid-2000 the British Library had to raise approximately £1 million more for the outstanding payments and in order to give the manuscript the exposure it deserved. The volume is now BL, Add. MS 74236.

If size were a criterion of value, the Sherborne Missal would automatically qualify. It weighs over 20 kilograms (44 lb), measures around 536 × 380 mm and contains 694 parchment pages of elaborate Gothic script, musical notation and a gallery of illuminated images, which if they were panel paintings (like the stylistically related Wilton Diptych in the National Gallery in London, depicting the young Richard II) would fill a wing of a major art gallery.

The Missal is the largest, most lavishly decorated late medieval service-book to have survived the Reformation intact – a remarkable survival in the face of perils that began some twenty years after it was made when the

The Crucifixion in the Sherborne Missal (BL, Add. MS 74236, p. 380), a masterpiece of International Gothic art, by John Siferwas, Sherborne, 1407.

townspeople of Sherborne burnt the abbey in a dispute over ecclesiastical authority, the parish priest allegedly firing the first flaming arrow at its roof. Much of its fabric survived and was rebuilt. At the Dissolution of the Monasteries the abbey became one of the grandest parish churches in the realm. The world that the Sherborne Missal opens up to us is one of colourful personalities with ambitious agendas for this world and the next, who reflect not only the devotional fervour of the age but its political and social realities.

A missal contains the texts and often, as in this case, the music needed to perform the Christian mass throughout the year, with the variants required for special points in the liturgical year and for saints' feast days. All churches needed them, but few possessed such elaborate examples. The key to understanding this lies in the spiritual and political aspirations of its sponsors.

The Sherborne Missal is unusual in revealing much concerning its circumstances of production. The key patron, Robert Bruyning, abbot of Sherborne (1385–1415) is depicted at least one hundred times, usually kneeling in prayer and sporting an impressive array of vestments (probably those actually owned by Sherborne). He is joined eight times by the figure of his spiritual overlord and possible fellow patron, Richard Mitford, Bishop of Salisbury (1396–1407), who had enjoyed a position close to the throne as Richard II's Clerk of the Signet and was rewarded, despite a temporary imprisonment, with the sees of Chichester and then Salisbury. The decoration abounds with heraldic detail and the arms of Mitford (d. 1407) and of Henry V as Prince of Wales, a title he assumed shortly after the accession of his father, Henry IV, in 1399, giving a production date of around 1400–1407.

The overt celebration of the sponsors extends to the usually anonymous craftspeople, or at least to the most important of them. The scribe, John Whas, is shown seven times and states in a colophon that he had to rise early each day to write the book and that his body was much wasted as a result ('Librum scribendo Ion Whas monachus laborat, Et mane surgendo corpus multum macerabat'; 'John Whas, the monk, this book's transcription undertaking, with early rising found his body sorely aching'). He wears a Benedictine habit and was presumably a member of the Sherborne community. Bishop Erghum's rental for the manor of Sherborne in 1377 mentions a cottage dweller, John Whas, who may well have been the scribe's father – one of the poorest of the locals, reliant on a small cottage garden to live from. His son may have found a better living and a vocation by joining the abbey and exhibiting an aptitude for scholarship and the scriptorium.

The major artist, John Siferwas, has left us six portraits here. His dress proclaims him a Dominican and we know from other sources that he was a one-time member of the Dominican house at Guildford. He was ordained acolyte at Farnham by the Bishop of Winchester in 1380 and is still mentioned in Somerset wills of the 1420s. He was therefore probably in middle age while working on the Missal. He was proud of his family, which had its roots in Hampshire, Dorset and Somerset, modestly depicting himself accompanied by the Siferwas arms immediately adjacent to those of Henry V as Prince of Wales. It is possible that this genealogy was a fiction, however, and that he was actually the Johann recorded as sharing a premises in London (Paternoster Row) for a while with fashionable German artist

Self-portrait of the master-artist, John Siferwas, in the Sherborne Missal (BL, Add. MS 74236, p. 81). Although he may have been German, he depicts himself with his family's alleged West Country English coat of arms, adjacent to those of Prince Henry V and the royal swan emblem.

Hermann Scheerre. Hermann's masterwork is the now sadly mutilated Carmelite Missal (British Library, Add. MSS 29704–5), a massive and beautiful book that survived the Reformation and the other holocausts of history only to be given as a toy to the children of its early nineteenth-century owner, Philip Hanrott. They spent a rainy afternoon or two cutting it up. Some of its historiated initials survive to indicate its splendour. The age of 'art for art's sake' was well under way and only in the latter half of the twentieth century would the integrity of entire books once more be appreciated and their study now assumes a more holistic form, except for those who still break books for commercial gain.

A larger full-page self-portrait depicts him in the Lovell Lectionary (British Library, Harley MS 7026), presenting it to John, Lord Lovell, who ordered it for Salisbury Cathedral. It is tempting to imagine Bishop Mitford being so impressed by Siferwas's work on that project that he involved him in the Sherborne commission and that the points Sherborne and its abbot were making concerning their relationship to Salisbury led them to employ a leading artist who had recently produced one of the cathedral's most prestigious books on an even grander tome, as a gesture of 'one-upmanship'.

Siferwas is the only named artist, but a closer examination reveals that at least four others participated in the illumination, perhaps other members of the community or lay artists from the area working under the supervision of the master. It is assumed that John Whas was responsible for all the script, but this remains to be verified. Certainly, having that side of the work done in-house would have been a financial saving. The great two-volume missal commissioned for Westminster Abbey by abbot Nicholas Litlyngton in 1384 took two years for the bought-in scribe cum project manager, Thomas Weston, who contracted out the other parts of the work, to complete for £4 of the overall cost of £34 14*s* 7*d*, plus bed and board for the

duration in the abbot's lodging and a new suit of velvet clothes to make him look presentable at the abbot's dining table.

The Sherborne Missal is a treasure house of information on the world in which it was made, containing a whole gallery of electrifyingly inventive imagery and is a masterpiece of the International Gothic style (its monumental Crucifixion page owing much to Italian panel and fresco painting), celebrating Britain's contribution to and participation in late medieval European culture.

Local details also abound, from the West Country and elsewhere in Britain. The Missal's remarkable naturalistic bird depictions, who sing along to the music of the mass, bring us echoes from a world that was producing vernacular masterpieces such as the *Canterbury Tales* and *Piers Plowman*.

Birds had a long history in art, and certain species featured in the 'aviary' (*aviarum*), an ornithological equivalent of the medieval bestiary in which animals were imbued with symbolic Christian meaning, such as the pelican in her piety, who pierced her breast to feed her young with her lifeblood – an analogy to Christ's sacrifice. From the late thirteenth century their depictions had become naturalistic rather than stylized

Opposite: *Detail of the robin in the Sherborne Missal (*BL*, Add.* MS *74236, p. 382), one of the well-observed native British birds depicted in the margins of the Canon of the Mass, which is accompanied by musical notation to which they sing along. The speech scroll identifying him reads 'Roddoke Robertus' – not the traditional Robin Redbreast, but Robert Redbreast, perhaps an allusion to the proud, puffed-up breast of Abbot Robert Bruyning.*
Above: *John, Lord Lovell, and the artist, John Siferwas, from the Lovell Lectionary, southern England (Glastonbury?),* c. *1400–1410 (*BL*, Harley* MS *7026/1, f. 4v). Siferwas had already worked on this volume, which Lovell presented to Salisbury Cathedral (this depiction shows him inside his own chantry chapel, where he would pay for clerics to sing psalms for his soul's repose). This may have led to Abbot Robert Bruyning wishing to have him work on Sherborne's great missal and thereby go one better than Salisbury.*

(an early example being the Alphonso Psalter made in Westminster in 1284 to celebrate the marriage of Prince Alphonso, who died before that could take place) and this trend reaches its height in the Missal, where the species are easily recognizable and reinforced by labelling with their names written for the first time in English. They derived from sketches made in the north of England, to judge from the prevalence of coastal species such as cormorants, although most of the species are native to the West Country too.

Other of the exemplars available to the team devising the Missal included a heraldic roll of arms, known as the Seger armorial, originally compiled in the thirteenth century, and the twelfth-century Sherborne Cartulary (British Library, Add. MS 46487), which is one of the few other surviving relics of the Sherborne library, and a volume of administrative material relating to Sherborne (Bishop Erghum's volume), compiled about 1377 probably to assist the abbot during Bruyning's time (British Library, Cotton MS Faust A II).

How is this veritable gallery of images and texts arranged? It falls into several parts, geared towards enabling the community to perform the Mass throughout the year. It opens with a Calendar (pp. 1–12), which gives, by month, the feast days of the year celebrated at Sherborne, graded by coloured inks (we still say 'red-letter days') and decorated with figures of Prophets and Apostles, the signs of the zodiac and the labours of the months. This is a simplified version of the programme found in the Breviary of Jeanne de Belleville (Bibliothèque nationale de France, lat. 10483–4), a Parisian work of the 1320s of Dominican use, which was in English royal ownership in the late fourteenth century. Many of the feasts in such calendars were universal, but some are of more local interest or specific to the owners.

p. 1 Calendar. January: Jeremiah and St Peter; man before fireside; Aquarius.
p. 2 Calendar. February: David and St Andrew; digging; Pisces.
p. 3 Calendar. March: Isaiah and St James the Greater; pruning; Aries.
p. 4 Calendar. April: Daniel and St John; sowing; Taurus.
p. 5 Calendar. May: Hosea and St Thomas; hawking; Gemini.
p. 6 Calendar. June: Amos and St James the Lesser; cutting grass; Cancer.
p. 7 Calendar. July: Sofonias and St Philip; man with scythe; Leo.
p. 8 Calendar. August: Joel and St Bartholomew; harvesting; Virgo.

p. 9 Calendar. September: Micheas and St Matthew; flailing; Libra.
p. 10 Calendar. October: Malachi and St Simon; pig panage; Scorpio.
p. 11 Calendar. November: Zechariah and St Jude; slaughtering a pig; Sagittarius.
p. 12 Calendar. December: Ezechiel and St Matthias; feasting; Capricorn.

This is followed by the *Temporale*, or Proper of Time (pp. 13–358), which gives the variable elements of the Mass, with its particular readings and collects for all the seasonal feast days of the liturgical year, arranged to commemorate the sequence of events in Jesus Christ's ministry recounted in the New Testament (Advent, Christmas, Epiphany, Lent, Easter, Ascension, Pentecost, Trinity Sunday and so on), each lavishly adorned with images redolent of the iconography (symbolic depictions) of each episode.

The most splendid of the decorated pages mark the most important days of all: Christmas Day, Easter Sunday and Trinity Sunday (which was of particular relevance to Abbot Bruyning, with his personal devotion to the Trinity shown in his motto, *laus sit trinitatis*, 'praise to the Trinity', which occurs several times in the book's illumination).

This section is succeeded by the Ordinary of the Mass (pp. 359–78) giving the fixed components of the Mass, which were used on each occasion including the prefaces with musical notation sung by the celebrant priest, and the Canon of the Mass (pp. 381–93), the core ceremonial of the consecration of the Eucharist (the preparation and blessing of the bread and wine), which did not vary; these are accompanied by the choir of birds, as if all Creation were singing out in praise of its Creator, alongside the musical notation of the chant sung by the monks. It is also in this section that the benefactors and properties of Sherborne and of its place in the history of the world and of the Church occur as a set of cartouches, of the sort that may have adorned the walls of Sherborne Abbey, as such are thought to have featured in the Worcester Chapter House.

The Canon of the Mass is preceded by the magnificent full-page painting of the Crucifixion (p. 380); Christ's sacrifice, which is commemorated by this central moment of the Mass, is placed opposite a blank page so that nothing would distract from the devotional impact of the image, which functions almost as an icon or altarpiece in its own right.

Finally comes the *Sanctorale*, or Proper of Saints (pp. 395–611), giving readings and prayers appropriate to the feasts of all the saints commemorated

in the Calendar, and the Common of Saints (pp. 613–62), giving the texts appropriate to the feast days of categories of saints, these being introduced by small images of the saints concerned.

There then follow special votive masses, such as those interceding for specific intentions, such as peace or rain, to honour the Virgin Mary to whom Sherborne Abbey was dedicated, and those for the sick and the dead.

The iconographic scheme is at pains to emphasize that the see of Salisbury was a Norman 'Johnny come lately' introduction into the English ecclesiastical scene and owed its origins to Sherborne, one of the most ancient Anglo-Saxon bishoprics, founded in 705 and with an even earlier history extending back into the British Church with mention of a post-Roman-period bishop named Probus. Initials in the Missal feature some early saints, such as Alban (Britain's protomartyr who may have been executed at Verulamium, a Roman town now known as St Albans, during the third or

Opposite: *Trinity Sunday in the Sherborne Missal (BL, Add. MS 74236, p. 276). In the sculptural edifice in the left-hand border the book's patron Abbot Bruyning (who had a personal devotion to the Trinity) and his spiritual overlord, Bishop Mitford of Salisbury, kneel facing one another in their vestments while the scribe – John Whas, a Benedictine monk of Sherborne Abbey – and the principal artist, Dominican John Siferwas, kneel below.* Below: *St Juthwara is martyred by her brother and presents her severed head to the altar, with praying figure of the scribe, detail from the Sherborne Missal (BL, Add. MS 74236, p. 489). The inclusion of this early post-Roman saint points to the antiquity and primacy of the monastery.*

fourth century). Particularly unusual inclusions are St Balthild of Chelles (*c.* 626–680), an Anglo-Saxon slave-girl who made good, catching the eye of King Clovis II of Neustria and Burgundy (r. 639–58) and becoming his queen of Merovingian Gaul. Siferwas was evidently in no doubt about how she pulled this off, depicting her with a squirrel: the medieval symbol of female sexuality. Another is St Juthwara, a sixth-century British lass from the southwest (and perhaps sister of Paul Aurelian, or alternatively, some would argue, sister of the eighth-century female Anglo-Saxon St Sidwell), whose wicked stepmother tricked her into putting cream cheeses on her nipples to cure a chest cold. She then promptly shopped the innocent girl to her stepbrother, who had her beheaded, concluding that she was lactating after having got pregnant out of wedlock. Her martyrdom is said to have occurred near Sherborne and actually to have been a punishment for her aiding Christian missionaries. Her relics were translated to Sherborne by King Edward the Confessor in the eleventh century.

By 1400 Sarum liturgy had supplanted the plethora of other liturgical formats (known as 'uses') in Britain – and even some parts of Europe. Tellingly, the text of this Missal does not correspond to Sarum use, as might be expected, but consciously preserves the Old Gregorian form allegedly introduced to England by St Augustine, thereby preserving aspects of the oldest liturgies of the English Church and, again, stressing the antiquity of the Sherborne foundation. Couple this with the programme of decoration of the Ordinary of the Mass, which in effect includes a potted history of the Church, of Sherborne's role in its history, and a summary of its property holdings and record of its benefactors, and any informed and interested party could be left in no doubt of the firm foundations upon which any claims of the house, and its authority, rested.

Sherborne had long-lived royal connections, being the resting place of the brothers of King Alfred the Great, and the images in the Missal promote continued royal interest. Stressing connections with former royals to those of an incoming dynasty was always a delicate process, given the vagaries of regime change. Its relationship with Salisbury and its bishop was also important. It was the source of Salisbury's authority, counting Aldhelm and Asser among its bishops before the see was transferred to Salisbury in 1075.

In 998 St Wulsin introduced the Benedictine Order to Sherborne as part of the reformation of the Anglo-Saxon Church, an event graphically depicted in the Missal. Sherborne was amalgamated with the see of

Ramsbury, Wiltshire, in the eleventh century and in 1075 the continental incumbent, Herman, in accordance with the conqueror's policy, moved the see to nearby Old Sarum (an Iron Age hillfort turned Norman castle outside Salisbury). In the early thirteenth century the cathedral moved to a lower-lying site 3 kilometres (2 mi.) away and became the focus of the carefully planned Salisbury new town. The bishop, however, continued to have an interest in Sherborne. In a successful attempt to assert its independence during the twelfth century, Sherborne invoked the assistance of the pope and the head of the Cistercian Order, whose second leader, Stephen Harding, had trained there.

Even after the abbot of St Mary's was secure in his authority, the Bishop of Salisbury remained his spiritual overlord; from the mid-fourteenth century he was also lord of the manor and castle of Sherborne and therefore the nearest neighbouring landholder. Such a relationship was bound to be delicate and sometimes strained, especially with considerations such as rents and hunting rights to be considered.

It is not surprising then that one of the foremost agendas of an extremely complex scheme of book production was to emphasize Sherborne's strengths. Abbot and bishop are shown together eight times, but the abbot occurs on a hundred occasions, fulfilling the key roles, kneeling in prayer, modelling the abbey's finest vestments, posing with his hunting hounds and the like, and is undoubtedly the star of the show.

11

THE FIFTEENTH CENTURY II:
ANTHONY WOODVILLE'S PRESENT FOR DOOMED ROYALS

THE DICTES AND SAYINGS OF THE PHILOSOPHERS (LAMBETH PALACE LIBRARY, MS 265)

The fifteenth century was another dominated by warfare, at home and abroad. Escalation of hostilities during the final phase of the Hundred Years War (the Lancastrian War of 1415–53) drew others into the conflicts (with the Scots at times supporting France and the Burgundians England). Although England initially prevailed, with Paris falling to John, Duke of Bedford (d. 1435; brother of Henry V), the regent of France from 1422 on behalf of the young Henry VI of England, the French House of Valois ultimately retained control over the French realm, following the intervention of peasant girl turned military leader and saint Joan of Arc (Jeanne d'Arc). She succeeded in getting Charles VII crowned as king of France in 1429, before she was captured by the Burgundians and burnt at the stake, aged only nineteen, in 1431. The backlash to this, the defection of England's Burgundian allies and lack of funds gradually led England to back down. Henceforth, the French and English monarchies remained staunchly separate.

Even in the midst of intrigue and turmoil there was time for more civilized preoccupations. The household accounts of John, Duke of Bedford, reveal that he owned a number of illuminated devotional books, distributed between his various residences and his travelling chest, of which the three most important ones to remain are the Bedford Hours and the Salisbury Breviary, both made in Paris by the atelier of a leading artist dubbed the Bedford Master, and the Bedford Psalter-Hours of about 1420–23, which are English. John was evidently spreading his patronage, even-handedly, between Paris, which he had recently occupied with English forces, and the home market in London.

Bedford had been Governor in Normandy between 1422 and 1432, where the University of Caen was founded under his auspices. He based himself at Rouen and directed the English forces with some success. After she was captured, he had Joan of Arc tried by French clergy who were thought to have been pro-English collaborators, and did not intervene to prevent her execution at Rouen in 1431. That same year he ensured that Henry VI was crowned king of France in Paris. Joan was soon being lauded as the patron saint of France, although not formally canonized until 1920. Henry's passivity, weakness, mental incapacities and overbearing French wife, Margaret of Anjou (Charles VII's niece, whom he married in 1445), led to his loss of France, the growth of internal factions, his deposition and ultimately his death in the Tower of London. Posthumous miracles attributed to Henry led to him being informally regarded as a saint and martyr until the Reformation. Perhaps his greatest legacies were his educational foundations of Eton College, King's College, Cambridge, and (with Henry Chichele) All Souls College, Oxford. He may have made a better academic or a cleric than a king.

The focus then shifted to domestic conflict and another period of civil war, known as the Wars of the Roses, a protracted competition for the throne between the houses of Lancaster and York, in which they adopted the red and white roses respectively as their badges. If what follows by way of summary seems complicated, that is because dynastic politics and machinations are.

King Henry IV of England was succeeded in 1413 by Henry V, his son by Mary de Bohun. Henry married Catherine of Valois and their son duly succeeded him as Henry VI in 1422 and reigned until 1461. He was renowned for his piety but also for his weak rule. In 1455 counter bids to the throne began to be advanced by the House of York, which claimed the right to the throne through Edward III's second son, Lionel of Antwerp, but it inherited its name from Edward's fourth son, Edmund of Langley, first Duke of York.

In 1461 Henry VI was deposed by Edward IV, son of Richard of York and Cecily Neville (and a great-great-grandson of Edward III). Henry VI was reinstalled by his supporters in 1470 and recommenced his reign until his death, under suspicious circumstances, in 1471. Edward IV returned from exile in the Netherlands and reigned until 1483. His young son by Elizabeth Woodville, Edward V, only reigned for 78 days before disappearing from the Tower, at the age of twelve, along with his younger brother, Richard of Shrewsbury, Duke of York. Edward was promptly replaced by his uncle, Edward IV's brother, Richard, Duke of Gloucester (b. 1452), who promptly became Richard III (r. 1483–5). The question of whether the young princes were dispatched by order of their uncle, or whether one or both of them survived incognito or were one of the pretenders who soon emerged, is still hotly contested. The most favoured of these theories is that Perkin Warbeck, a pretender to Henry VII's throne, was actually Richard, Duke of York, who had escaped to Flanders after his uncle Richard's defeat at Bosworth, where he was raised by his aunt, Margaret, Duchess of Burgundy, and schooled to launch his bid for power when he landed in Britain in 1497, only to end in his execution two years later. It remains possible, however, that uncle Richard was the villain of the piece, as he removed the young Edward V from the care of those to whom his father had entrusted their education and upbringing, notably his mother's brother, Anthony Woodville, and had them executed. He then encouraged claims that the marriage of Edward IV and Elizabeth Woodville was irregular and that the princes were illegitimate. Charles II sought to lay the rumours to rest and the threat of pretenders claiming descent from the young princes, when he had what were purported to be their remains, found concealed in the Tower, interred in Westminster Abbey nearly two centuries later.

Richard III had strengthened his claim through his marriage in 1472 to Anne Neville (daughter of Richard Neville, Earl of Warwick, known as 'Warwick the Kingmaker'), who was the widow of Edward of Westminster, the only son and heir of Henry VI. Richard reigned for only two years and 58 days, before falling at the Battle of Bosworth Field in 1485, at the age of 32. He was buried at Greyfriars Abbey, Leicester, and his grave was lost sight of amid the destruction at the Dissolution of the Monasteries. In 2012 his remains were discovered underneath a nearby car park and the DNA from a descendant used to verify their identity. Richard now lies interred in Leicester Cathedral.

Richard's vanquisher was the last of the Lancastrian claimants, a great-great-great-grandson of Edward III via John Beaufort, an illegitimate offspring through the union of John of Gaunt and his long-term mistress, Katherine Swynford. Their union was later sanctioned by marriage, a papal bull, an act of Parliament and a proclamation of legitimacy by Henry VI as John of Gaunt's legitimate son. These enabled a royal claim to be passed by the female line to Lady Margaret Beaufort (1443–1509), who married Edmund Tudor, son of a Welsh courtier and Catherine of Valois, widow of Henry V. Issues of legitimacy on their part were again set aside by Henry VI, but when he and the house of Lancaster fell from power, so did the expectations of the Tudors. It was the son of Edmund Tudor and Margaret Beaufort who triumphed at Bosworth and, through his coronation as King Henry VII and his subsequent marriage to Elizabeth of York, daughter of Edward IV, united the houses of Lancaster and York in the reign of the Tudor dynasty, thereby drawing the Wars of the Roses to an end, symbolized by their hybridization under the emblem of the red and white Tudor rose.

The century was not all about conflict and commerce, however. Personal piety was causing folk from all sorts of backgrounds around Europe to seek new ways of serving their God. The thirteenth century had seen the rise of the Franciscan and Dominican tertiary orders, which provided for the participation of laypeople in their work.

One such was St Catherine of Siena (1347–1380), a tertiary of the Dominican Order and a scholastic philosopher and theologian. She also worked to bring the papacy of Gregory XI back to Rome from its exile in France and to establish peace among the Italian city-states.

Catherine was the daughter of a Sienese cloth dyer, Giacomo di Benincasa, and his wife Lapa, the daughter of a poet, whose grand Renaissance-style home can be seen there still. She was their 23rd child (of 25). She began having visions of Christ as a child and declined marriage to her dead sister's husband, triumphing over parental opposition to become a tertiary. She initially lived as a solitary in the family home but then left to nurse the sick during the plague. Her visions continued, including her mystical marriage to Christ. She became a peace envoy, due to the respect

Dictes and Sayings of the Philosophers, *London, 1477 (Lambeth Palace Library, MS 265, ff. viv–1r), showing the presentation miniature depicting the royal family and one of the distinctive Italian humanist white vinescroll initials, combined with a northern European secretary script. It copied Caxton's first printed edition of the text, which appeared only a month before this illuminated dedication copy was made for the author/translator, Anthony Woodville, Earl Rivers, to present as a Christmas gift to the royal family, his relatives.*

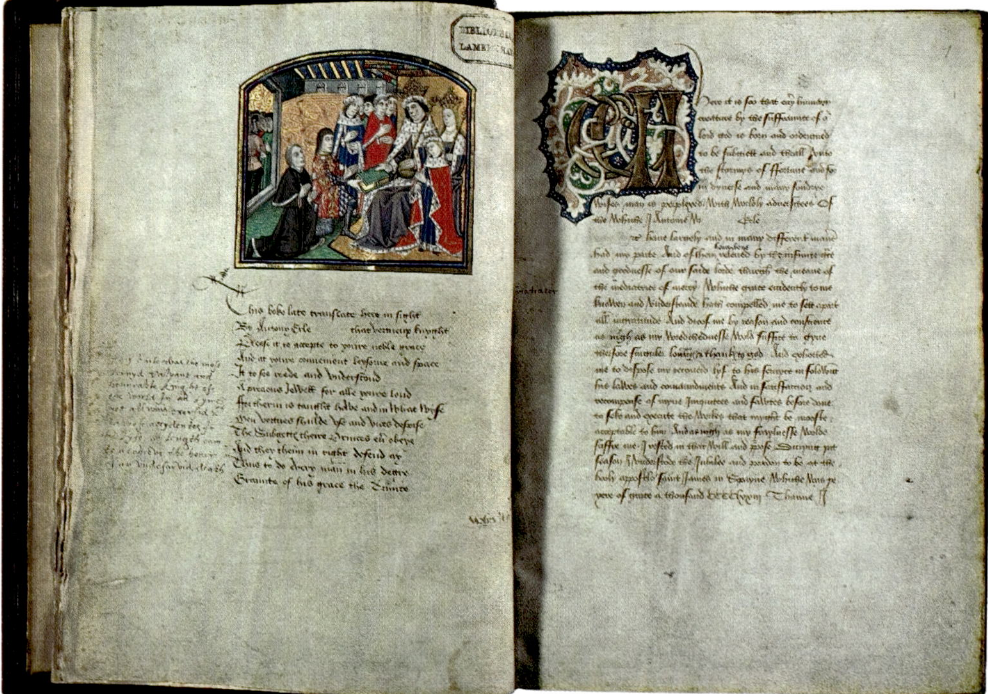

her life, visions and teaching inspired, and died in Rome aged 33 (the age at which Christ was crucified), probably of anorexia through excessive abstinence.

Other vocational responses included that of the Beguines, which offered an attractive model of living and serving in community to women who found themselves alone, perhaps as widows. One such was Marie of Oignies (1177–1213), who was born in Nivelles, which is now in Belgium. Marie chose to marry at fourteen and, having decided not to live a cloistered life as a nun, adopted a freer devout life characterized by strenuous asceticism, mysticism and manual labour in service of God. She convinced her husband to join her in prayer and charitable work ministering to lepers at Willambroux. Marie had visions, experienced ecstasy and wept when meditating on Christ's Passion. She adopted an austere lifestyle by becoming vegetarian, dressing in white and punishing her flesh in penance. Her work and faithful devotion inspired many other young women to join her community, which followed the rule of St Francis and, like the Poor Clares, emulated his example of service and living in poverty.

The examples of two English mystics during the early fifteenth century will give an insight into aspects of the motivation for this manifestation of faith. One is Mother Julian of Norwich (*c.* 1342–*c.* 1416), who was one of an age-old number of anchorites/anchoresses, who embraced the life of the solitary. She was one of the most significant English mystic theologians. Little is recorded of her life, even her name. She is named after the church of St Julian in Norwich where her anchoress's cell was built into a wall. Julian was a respected spiritual authority within her local community and even in high places, with many coming to seek her counsel through the window of her cell. She is still widely read.

Her *Revelations of Divine Love*, written around 1395, is the first book in the English language known to have been written by a woman. An early manuscript copy survives as British Library, Add. MS 37790, known as the Amherst MS, and is the shorter version of the text. It relates that Julian sought a deeper love of Christ and appealed to God for three things: a deeper understanding of Christ's Passion; a life-threatening illness during youth, that she might experience all that the body and soul experience in death (including fiendish assaults and receiving the last rites) but without actually dying, that she might live more mindful of God; and three 'wounds', namely absolute contrition, kindly compassion and steadfast longing for God. In 1373 her prayers were answered and she did indeed become perilously ill. Everyone, including Julian, despaired of her life and the last rites were administered by her priest.

Julian was granted her near-death experience, but at its crisis, between four in the afternoon and nine o'clock in the evening, she was given fifteen 'showings', or revelations. She later wrote that heaven opened to her and she beheld Christ in his glory and was able to comprehend the full extent, impact and significance of his sufferings. She was also able to see Mary, exalted beside her son.

In her thirteenth showing, Julian received a comforting answer to a troubling question:

> In my folly, before this time I often wondered why, by the great foreseeing wisdom of God, the onset of sin was not prevented: for then, I thought, all should have been well. This impulse [of thought] was much to be avoided, but nevertheless I mourned and sorrowed because of it, without reason and discretion.
>
> But Jesus, who in this vision informed me of all that is needed by me, answered with these words and said: 'It was necessary that there should be sin; but all shall be well, and all shall be well, and all manner of things shall be well.'
>
> These words were said most tenderly, showing no manner of blame to me nor to any who shall be saved.

She knew that the compassion she had prayed for had been granted and that she should be ever joyful, come what may, for all things will ultimately be healed and set right by Christ.

Julian wrote, 'And to me was shown no harder hell than sin. For a kind soul has no hell but sin.' However, she considered that sin brought self-knowledge and acknowledgement of the need for God's grace and forgiveness, explaining that God suffers with his Creation as it experiences evil.

The following night Julian received her final and sixteenth showing in her sleep. Satan and his hosts assailed her, but God gave her grace, and she fixed her eyes on the crucified Christ and trusted that because of his suffering and victory over sin he would protect her, and he delivered her from the demonic jeers and mutterings.

She survived for a further 33 years, the length of Jesus's earthly life. Soon after recovery Julian recorded a short account of her revelations,

'The Short Text'. Years later, in the 1390s, following lengthy meditation, she added additional thoughts on their meaning in 'The Long Text'.

Margery Kempe (*c.*1373–after 1438) mentions visiting her around 1414. The two women, both mystics, but of very different character and vocation, would have conversed through a window in Mother Julian's cell, where she dwelt with a cat for company and a maid to minister to her needs.

Margery Kempe was an English Christian mystic, known for dictating *The Book of Margery Kempe*, a work considered by some to be the first autobiography in the English language, of which the earliest extant copy is British Library, Add. MS 61823, made in King's Lynn about 1440. It chronicles her domestic tribulations, her extensive pilgrimages to holy sites in Europe and the Near East and her mystical conversations with God.

She was born Margery Burnham, or Brunham, around 1373 in Bishop's Lynn (now King's Lynn), Norfolk, an important trading centre, especially for the wool trade. Her father, John Brunham, was a merchant in Lynn, the town mayor and a Member of Parliament. When she was around twenty years old, Margery married John Kempe, who became a town official in 1394. They had at least fourteen children, some of whom probably died during infancy. After the birth of her first child, Margery went through a period of crisis for nearly eight months, which might now be viewed as post-natal depression. During this time, Margery experienced demons attacking and commanding her to 'forsake her faith, her family, and her friends', taunting her with thoughts of suicide. But, like other medieval mystics, she felt herself called into a closer relationship with Christ, who appeared to her and asked, 'Daughter, why have you forsaken me, and I never forsook you?' As her visions unfolded she claims that she had other divine encounters with other key Christian figures and participated at the birth and crucifixion of Christ. During these visions she would experience strange sounds and smells, with one melody leading her to seek chastity in her marriage, to wear a hair shirt in penance and to engage in very frequent confession and prayer.

She makes no mention of a formal education, simply saying that as an adult a priest read her 'works of religious devotion' in English; she evidently knew the Lord's Prayer, the Ave Maria, the Ten Commandments and other 'virtues, vices, and articles of faith'. This, and the fact that she tells how she dictated her memoir to various men (one perhaps her son and the other a local priest who may have been her confessor, Robert Springold), has led to assumptions that she was illiterate, but it should be remembered that classical and medieval authors usually dictated, rather than wielding the pen themselves.

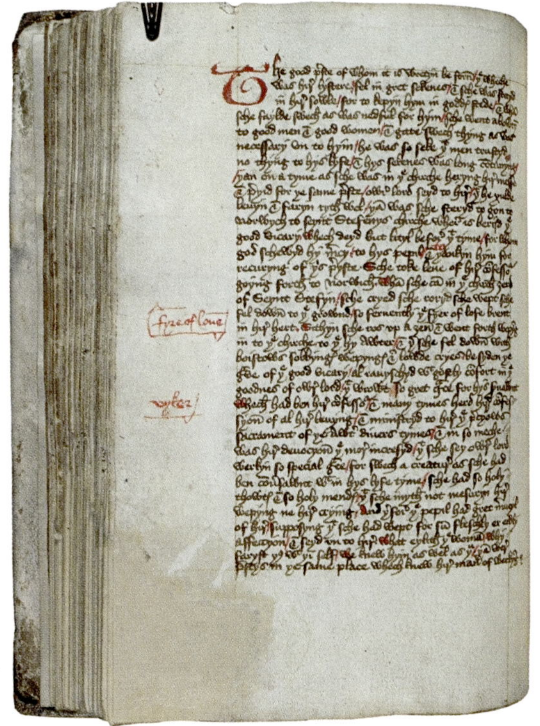

Margery was also known for her constant weeping as she begged Christ for mercy and forgiveness. In one vision even Christ had enough and Margery says that 'He gave her several commands: to call him her love, to stop wearing the hair shirt, to give up eating meat, to take the Eucharist every Sunday, to pray the rosary only until six o'clock, to be still and speak to him in thought.' He also promised her 'victory over her enemies, give her the ability to answer all clerks, and to be with her and never forsake her, and to help her and never be parted from her'. Margery did not join a religious order, but pursued 'her life of devotion, prayer, and tears in public', ignoring the derision that this brought her, for her public displays of wailing and writhing frightened and annoyed both the clergy and laypeople. At one point she was imprisoned by the clergy and town officials and threatened with the possibility of rape, which did not occur. Finally, during the 1430s Margery dictated *The Book of Margery Kempe*, which recounts her visions and experiences, including her 'temptations to lechery, her travels, and her trial for heresy'.

Nearly everything that is known of Kempe's life comes from her book. Kempe decided to record her spiritual autobiography, and in its preface she describes how she employed as scribe an Englishman who had lived in Germany, but he died before the work was completed and what he had written was unintelligible to others. A letter of 1431 discovered in Gdańsk suggests that this first scribe was John Kempe, her eldest son. She then persuaded a local priest, perhaps her confessor Robert Springold, to begin rewriting on 23 July 1436, and on 28 April 1438 he started work on an

Page from The Book of Margery Kempe, *with marginalia ('fyre of love', 'vyker'), probably copied from the original, which had been completed in 1436, c. 1440* (BL, *Add.* MS *61823, f. 71v).*

additional section covering the years 1431–4. The surviving manuscript is in a fittingly professional hand and is written in the sort of cursive script then deemed acceptable for non-biblical or liturgical texts, including literary compositions, as well as for legal documents such as wills and property transactions.

The narrative of Kempe's book begins just after her marriage and relates the experience of her difficult first pregnancy. After describing the demonic torment and Christ's apparition that followed, Margery relates that, following her difficult first encounter with childbirth and her initial visions, she embarked upon two domestic businesses: a brewery and a grain mill (both common home-based businesses for medieval women). Both failed after a short time. Despite her growing devotion, she was tempted by lust and social ambition and envy. Eventually she dedicated herself completely to her spiritual calling and in the summer of 1413 negotiated a chaste marriage with her husband and shortly after embarked on an adventurous pilgrimage to Jerusalem.

Although Chapter 15 of *The Book of Margery Kempe* describes her decision to lead a celibate life, Chapter 21 mentions that she is pregnant once again. It has been speculated that Kempe gave birth to her last child during her pilgrimage, for she later relates that she brought a child back with her to

Some salient extracts enable us to hear something of Margery's story in her own words, starting with the prologue in the original Middle English, as she dictated it:

A schort tretys of a creature sett in grett pompe and pride of the world, whech sythen was drawyn to ower Lord be gret poverté, sekenes, schamis, and gret reprevys in many divers contres and places, of whech tribulacyons sum schal ben schewed aftyr, not in ordyr as it fellyn but as the creatur cowd han mend of hem whan it wer wretyn, for it was twenty yer and mor fro tym this creatur had forsake the world and besyly clef onto ower Lord or this boke was wretyn, notwythstondyng this creatur had greet cownsel for to don wryten hir tribulacyons and hir felingys, and a Whyte Frer proferyd hir to wryten frely yf sche wold. And sche was warnyd in hyr spyrit that sche schuld not wryte so sone. And many yerys aftyr sche was bodyn in hyr spyrit for to wrytyn. And than yet it was wretyn fyrst be a man whech cowd neithyr wel wryten Englysch ne Duch. So it was unable for to be red but only be specyal grace, for ther was so mech obloquie and slawndyr of this creatur that ther wold fewe men beleve this creatur.

WHEN THIS CREATURE was twenty year of age and somedeal more, she was married to a worshipful burgess and was with child within short time, as kind would. And after that she had conceived she was laboured with great accesses till the child was born, and then, what for labour she had in childing and for sickness going before, she despaired of her life, weening she might not live. And then she sent for her ghostly father, for she had a thing in conscience which she had never showed before that time in all her life. For she was ever letted by her enemy, the Devil, evermore saying to her while she was in good heal her needed no confession but [to] do penance by herself alone, and all should be forgiven, for God is merciful enow. And therefore this creature oftentimes did great penance in fasting bread and water and other deeds of alms with devout prayers, save she would not show it in confession. And when she was any time sick or diseased, the Devil said in her mind that she should be damned for she was not shriven of that default . . .

And so they went forth into the Holy Land till they might see Jerusalem. And when this creature saw Jerusalem, riding on an ass, she thanked God with all her heart, praying him for his mercy that like as he had brought her to see this earthly city Jerusalem, he would grant her grace to see the blissful city Jerusalem above, the city of Heaven. Our Lord Jesu Christ, answering to her thought, granted her to have her desire. Then for joy that she had and the sweetness that s he felt in the dalliance of our Lord, she was in point to 'a fallen off her ass, for she might not bear the sweetness and grace that God wrought in her soul. The twain pilgrims of Dutchmen went to her and kept her from falling, of which the one was a priest. And he put spices in her mouth to comfort her, weening she had been sick. And so they helped her forth to Jerusalem.

And when she came there, she said, 'Sirs, I pray you be not displeased though I weep sore in this holy place where our Lord Jesu Christ was quick and dead'...

Then they went to the Temple in Jerusalem, and they were let in that one day at evensong time and they abide there till the next day at evensong time. Then the friars lifted up a cross and led the pilgrims about from one place to another where our Lord had suffered his pains and his passions, every man and woman bearing a wax candle in their hand. And the friars always as they went about told them what our Lord suffered in every place ... And when they came up onto the Mount of Calvary she fell down that she might not stand nor kneel but wallowed and wrested with her body, spreading her arms abroad, and cried with a loud voice as though her heart should 'a burst asunder, for in the city of her soul she saw verily and freshly how our Lord was crucified ...

And this was the first cry that ever she cried in any contemplation. And this manner of crying endured many years after this time for aught that any man might do, and therefore suffered she much despite and much reproof. The crying was so loud and so wonderful that it made people astonished unless that they had heard it before or else that they knew the cause of the crying ...

And as soon as she perceived that she should cry, she would keep it in as much as she might that people should not 'a heard it for noying of them. For some said it was a wicked spirit vexed her; some said it was a sickness; some said she had drunken too much wine; some banned her; some wished she had been in the haven; some would she had been in the sea in a bottomless boat; and so each man as him thought. Other ghostly men loved her and favored her the more. Some great clerks said our Lady cried never so, nor no saint in Heaven, but they knew full little what she felt, nor they would not believe but that she might 'a abstained her from crying if she had wished ...

And when this creature was thus graciously come again to her mind, she thought she was bound to God and that she would be his servant. Nevertheless, she would not leave her pride nor her pompous array that she had used beforetime, neither for her husband nor for none other man's counsel. And yet she wist full well that men said her full much villainy, for she wore gold pipes on her head and her hoods with the tippets were dagged [decoratively slashed fabric]. Her cloaks also were dagged and laid with divers colours between the dags that it should be the more staring to men's sight and herself the more worshipped.

And when her husband would speak to her for to leave her pride she answered shrewdly and shortly and said that she was come of worthy kindred – him seemed never for to 'a wedded her – for her father was sometime mayor of the town N and sithen he was alderman of the high Gild of the Trinity in N. And therefore she would save the worship of her kindred whatsoever any man said. She had full great envy at her neighbours that they should be arrayed as well as she. All her desire was for to be worshipped of the people. She would not beware by one's chastening nor be content with the good that God had sent her, as her husband was, but ever desired more and more.

And then, for pure covetise and for to maintain her pride, she gan to brew and was one of the greatest brewers in the town N a three year or four till she lost much good, for she had never ure thereto. For though she had never so good servants and cunning in brewing, yet it would never prove with them. For when the ale was as fair standing under barm as any man might see, suddenly the barm would fall down that all the ale was lost every brewing after other, that her servants were ashamed and would not dwell with her.

Then this creature thought how God had punished her beforetime and she could not beware, and now eftsoons by losing of her goods, and then she left and brewed no more. And then she asked her husband mercy for she would not follow his counsel aforetime, and she said that her pride was cause of all her punishing and she would amend that she had trespassed with good wil . . .

It befell upon a Friday on Midsummer Even in right hot weather, as this creature was coming from York-ward bearing a bottle with beer in her hand and her husband a cake in his bosom, he asked his wife this question: 'Margery, if there came a man with a sword and would smite off my head unless that I should commune kindly with you as I have done before, say me truth of your conscience – for ye say ye will not lie – whether would ye suffer my head to be smit off or else suffer me to meddle with you again as I did sometime?' 'Alas, sir,' she said, 'why move ye this matter and have we been chaste this eight weeks?' 'For I will wit the truth of your heart.' And then she said with great sorrow, 'Forsooth, I had liefer see you be slain than we should turn again to our uncleanness.' And he said again, 'Ye are no good wife'...

Then they went forth to-Bridlington-ward in right hot weather, the foresaid creature having great sorrow and great dread for her chastity. And as they came by a cross, her husband set him down under the cross, cleping his wife unto him and saying these words unto her, 'Margery, grant me my desire, and I shall grant you your desire. My first desire is that we shall lie still together in one bed as we have done before; the second that ye shall pay my debts ere ye go to Jerusalem; and the third that ye shall eat and drink with me on the Friday as ye were wont to do.' 'Nay sir,' she said, 'to break the Friday I will never grant you while I live.' 'Well,' he said, 'then shall I meddle with you again.'...

Then this creature thanked our Lord Jesu Christ of his grace and his goodness, sithen rose up and went to her husband saying unto him, 'Sir, if it like you, ye shall grant me my desire and ye shall have your desire. Granteth me that ye shall not come in my bed, and I grant you to quit your debts ere I go to Jerusalem. And maketh my body free to God so that ye never make no challenging in me to ask no debt of matrimony after this day while ye live, and I shall eat and drink on the Friday at your bidding.' Then said her husband again to her, 'As free may your body be to God as it hath been to me.' This creature thanked God greatly, enjoying that she had her desire, praying her husband that they should say three Pater Noster in the worship of the Trinity for the great grace that he had granted them. And so they did, kneeling under a cross, and sithen they ate and drank together in great gladness of spirit. This was on a Friday on Midsummer Even.

England. It is unclear whether the child was conceived before the Kempes began their celibacy, or in a momentary lapse after it.

Around 1413–14 Margery visited the female anchoress Julian of Norwich and stayed for several days, seeking Julian's approval for her visions and conversations with God. The text reports that Julian approved of Kempe's revelations and gave Kempe reassurance that her religiosity was genuine:

> And then she was told by our Lord, to go to an anchoress in the same city called Dame Julian. And so she did and showed her the grace that God put in her soul of compunction, contrition, sweetness and devotion, compassion with holy meditation and high contemplation. And many holy speeches and daliance that our Lord spoke to her soul, and many wonderful revelations which she showed to the anchoress to know if there were any deceit in them, for the anchoress was expert in such things and could give good counsel.

However, Julian did instruct and caution Kempe to calm down and to 'measure these experiences according to the worship they accrue to God and the profit to her fellow Christians'. Julian also confirmed that Kempe's tears were physical evidence of the Holy Spirit in the soul. In Chapter 62, Kempe also describes an encounter with a friar who criticized her incessant tears but admitted to having read of Marie of Oignies, who wept as a result of similarly authentic devotion.

In 1438, the year her book was completed, a 'Margueria Kempe' was admitted to the Trinity Guild of Lynn. It is not known whether this is the same woman, however, or when and where Margery died. Here is a synopsis of Margery's cv:

1373:	Margery Kempe was born around this time
1393:	First child born when Kempe was aged 20
1394:	Recovered from first breakdown and took up brewing and milling
1413:	Paid off husband's debts
Autumn 1413:	Began pilgrimage to Jerusalem
January–April 1414:	In Venice
May 1414:	Arrived in Jaffa
September 1414–early April 1415 (Easter):	In Rome

Mid-May 1415:	Reached the North Sea coast at Zealand and returned home to Lynn, England, two days later

Margery may well not have been able to write, but she could certainly talk and thanks to dictation we have this rare and full insight into the mind and heart of a late medieval townswoman who was wife, businesswoman, traveller, mystic and, it is thought, a Lollard seeking access to the Scriptures in her own vernacular language. This desire was answered by the work of Wycliffe, the Cornishman John Trevisa and others who worked on the Wycliffe Bible. At the heart of Lambeth Palace, the London residence of the Archbishop of Canterbury, lies the Lollard Tower, where several of them were imprisoned. It is pleasing to think of a little episode in which Margery gained an audience with the archbishop and kept him prisoner in the garden until she had related her spiritual and earthly adventures on pilgrimage to the Holy Land to him, while his retinue and her embarrassed husband waited until she had finished with him.

The Black Death in 1348 and the Peasants' Revolt of 1381 had impacted upon the growth of trade, but a steady upturn nonetheless, by the end of the fourteenth century, continued a population drift to the towns from the countryside as the workforce increasingly freed themselves from the ties of the feudal order ushered in by the Norman age.

Christianson's work on the records of the book trade in London shows that between 1460 and 1500 most of those recorded were stationers and perhaps also limners, text-writers or binders, which implies that they were handling their own commissions.

Records show that large stocks of paper were ordered between 1404 and 1460 as an alternative to parchment and vellum, as it was cheaper, and it became the main vehicle for printed matter, although extremely expensive editions, especially those intended to be illuminated by hand in colour, might still employ membrane. The crypt of St Paul's Cathedral contained a chapel dedicated to St Erkenwald, patron saint of London and the healer of eyesight – and therefore beloved of the book trades. Large paper stocks were housed there and were lost at the time of the Great Fire of London in 1666.

Around 1500 the urban craftspeople who had traditionally made medieval manuscripts morphed, seamlessly in some cases, into the publishers of early printed books. The previous century had seen a trend towards diversification, with specialist illuminators, scribes and binders increasing the ranges of skills available and moving in on the territory of the entrepreneurial stationers responsible for subcontracting out work or commissioning it themselves to sell off the peg. This variety of interconnected urban specialists gradually consolidated their operations to become the publishing houses of early modern Europe. John Rastell (*fl.* 1516–36), for example, ran a printing house known as 'The Mermaid', which subsequently passed to the stationer Lewis Sutton; John Redman (*fl.* 1530–42) owned a shop called 'Our Lady of Pity'. Such premises subsequently gave their names to publishing houses. Such trends helped increase access to books, but it would not be until the educational reform acts of the 1880s that real mass literacy would be achieved.

Early printed books, such as the Gutenberg Bibles, were generally distributed unbound, cutting transport costs and allowing their bindings to be customized as required. Colour, which had played a significant role not only in decorating medieval manuscripts but in helping to navigate their texts, was often added by hand to incunables. Where it was absent, some volumes were given even more extensive cycles of marginal engraved imagery in compensation, while in fifteenth- and sixteenth-century manuscripts woodblock prints of sets of miniatures painted elsewhere were sometimes pasted in. A high point in early biblical print history was Albrecht Dürer's *Apocalypse* series of 1498. That deluxe illuminated manuscripts were not immediately ousted by print is shown by the Prayer Book of King Henry VIII in which the 'Defender of the Faith' (and spoliator of monasteries and their libraries) had himself portrayed as King David composing the Psalms, with his jester as audience. We shall encounter Henry and his book in the next chapter.

Our present book, *The Dictes and Sayings of the Philosophers* (Lambeth Palace Library, MS 265), is significant in several ways. It contains the intellectual work of Anthony Rivers, who raised and educated the young Edward V and was himself 'disappeared' during his disposal. It fused medieval and early Renaissance humanist features in its script and decoration and was a special illuminated manuscript copy of a text that had already become one of the earliest English printed texts, commissioned by its author as a gift for the royal family, to which he was related. The regime that they represented was about to change forever, as the Wars of the Roses gave way to the 'modern' Tudor age.

The Dictes and Sayings of the Philosophers marks a tipping point in the transition from manuscript books to print. The text was one of the

Dictes and Sayings of the Philosophers, *London, 1477 (Lambeth Palace Library, MS 265, f. viv), detail of the miniature depicting Anthony Woodville, Earl Rivers, kneeling (with the scribe, Hayward) and presenting this actual manuscript to King Edward IV while Queen Elizabeth (Woodville's sister) and the Prince of Wales (later, very briefly, Edward V) look on. Another figure, wearing ermine and lurking in the wings amid a group of courtiers, may be the future Richard III, the uncle who some believe was responsible for ordering the murder of his nephew Edward (depicted here) and his brother – the 'princes in the Tower'.*

first books printed in England by William Caxton and was evidently a bestseller since he published it twice in 1477 (Short Title Catalogue 6826, 6827), again in 1480 (STC 6828) and, finally, in 1489 (STC 6829). Not all readers, however, chose this new-fangled form, preferring manuscript copies (Lambeth Palace Library, MS 265, British Library, Add. MS 22718, Chicago, Newberry Library, MS f. 36 (Ry 20), and Columbia University Library, Plimpton MS 259, were all copied from Caxton and excerpts also occur in the 'Winchester Anthology', British Library, Add. MS 60577). Rivers had met Caxton in Bruges while exiled there, which led Caxton to print two of the Earl's English translations of French works, the other being *Cordyale; or, Four Last Things*, published in 1475–6.

The Lambeth manuscript copy is the most handsome, featuring an illuminated dedication miniature, and is beautifully written with major text-divisions signalled by white-vine initials in the latest humanist fashion and blue and gold paraphs (paragraph marks) indicating minor divisions.

An inserted leaf bearing the miniature and dedicatory verse (f. vi verso) establishes that this was the presentation copy, in Middle English, of the translation from the French of Guillaume de Tignonville by Anthony Woodville, Earl Rivers, whose title has been erased in the verse, possibly after his execution in 1483. He is depicted, in armour and a surcoat bearing his arms, kneeling and presenting this actual manuscript (the gilt-edged leaves depicted remain, but the binding has been replaced) to King Edward IV while Queen Elizabeth (Woodville's sister) and the Prince of Wales (later very briefly Edward V, from April to June 1483) look on. Another figure, wearing ermine and lurking in the wings amid a group of courtiers, may be the future Richard III, the uncle whom some believe was responsible for ordering the murder of his nephew, Edward (depicted here), and his brother – the 'princes in the Tower'.

The tonsured figure in black may be the scribe, Hayward, who signed the book (f. 106r) at St James in the Fields, a hospital near Westminster Abbey where Caxton set up his press. Kathleen Scott suggests that this figure is the original author, but this is unlikely as Tignonville was a knight.

The manuscript, copied from Caxton's first edition, is dated 24 December 1477: STC 6827 is dated 18 November 1477. Could the manuscript have been produced so quickly? The specific date was, however, added to STC 6827, while STC 6826 is only dated 1477, as Lotte Hellinga has noted. Thus, Hayward may have had longer to copy the text than first appears. Another copy, British Library, Add. MS 22718, is dated 28 November.

Anthony Woodville obviously commissioned this luxury copy as a Christmas or New Year's gift for his sister and her family. Both she and her husband, Edward IV, are known to have owned other books.

Edward IV gave a tremendous boost to the royal library by adding more than forty books that he had purchased from Flanders, having become enamoured of its culture during his exile there in 1470–71 when Warwick the Kingmaker led a revolt against him along with Edward's brother George,

Poems of Charles, Duke of Orléans, who is shown here writing them while imprisoned in the Tower of London, from an Edward IV manuscript (BL, Royal MS 16 F II, f. 73r), commissioned in Bruges in 1483. The old London Bridge is shown in the background. The Bridge House Trust rented out premises to many of those employed in the book arts in the City of London, as recorded in their rentals.

Des nouvelles dalbyon
Sil vous en plaist escouter
Mon frere z mon cōpaignō
Sachiez qua mon retōner
Iay este deca la mer
Recu a ioyeuse chiere

Duke of Clarence. This briefly reinstalled Henry VI, the last Lancastrian king, who died in the Tower after the Yorkist Edward regained the throne. Both his brother, Richard, and his brother-in-law, Anthony Woodville, had shared his exile, where they encountered the culture of the early Northern Renaissance. This provides a context for Woodville undertaking a translation of the *Dictes and Sayings of the Philosophers* from the original French into English, demonstrating his own scholarship and proto-humanist tastes (with its Italianate *bianchi girari*, or white-vine initials, a badge of humanist taste) and alluding to their cosmopolitan time together in fashionable Flanders. Edward's court became renowned, during the stable latter part of his reign, for its stylishness, scholarly tastes and over-consumption. Edward himself is thought perhaps to have died of excessive consumption of food, drink . . . and women.

It is recorded that Edward transferred volumes from the Great Wardrobe to Eltham Palace and that he had a yeoman 'to kepe the king's bookes'. More than forty of his books survive intact, mostly on historical and religious themes, which suggests they were carefully stored and subsequently prized. They now form part of the Royal Collection of manuscripts in the British Library. Imported illuminated books feature in English book history of the period as much as those made by the domestic market. Those from the Netherlands were especially popular, as were those imported from France in Scotland as a result of the 'auld alliance'.

The finest illuminated manuscript to have survived from medieval Scotland is the Murthly Hours (National Library of Scotland, MS 21000), made in Paris in the 1280s and which also contains miniatures painted by English artists a little earlier (perhaps a prefatory cycle from a Psalter), and medieval additions including what may be the second oldest example of Gaelic written in Scotland, where it was owned from the fourteenth century. It was originally made, however, for an Englishwoman, Joan de Valence. Another book prized in Scotland, the Iona Psalter (National Library of Scotland, MS 10000), was probably made in Oxford between 1180 and 1220, for a woman in the Augustinian priory of Iona, perhaps Beatrix, its first prioress.

Manuscripts actually produced in medieval Scotland are rare – but then, it is estimated that only 1 per cent of religious books survived the Scottish Reformation. Among those extant is the Culross Psalter, made at the abbey there around 1470 (National Library of Scotland, Adv. MS 18.8.11) and illuminated in a palette and foliate border style reminiscent of London work of the period. Unilluminated copies of important works of Scottish literature also survive, notably John Barbour's 'Bruce' (an early Scots verse account of the deeds of Robert the Bruce and the Scottish Wars of Independence, composed around 1375 and transcribed by Perth scribe John Ramsay in 1489) and Blind Hary's 'Wallace', a poetic account of the life of William Wallace composed around 1477 and transcribed by Ramsay eleven years later, written in English but sung by blind Henry the Minstrel before King James IV of Scotland to the accompaniment of two Gaelic harpers. Adv. MS 72.1.1 in the National Library of Scotland preserves a fifteenth-century anthology of material from the Gaelic bardic tradition, including genealogies of the clans.

The situation in Wales is similar, with imports from England, France and the Netherlands and some notable Welsh works. Some 250 manuscripts are estimated to have survived from medieval Wales, around 160 of them in Welsh, including several major collections of poetry, legends, chronicles and laws (such as the Book of Taliesin, the Book of Aneirin, the Red Book of Hergest, the White Book of Rhydderch, Geoffrey of Monmouth's *History of the Kings of Britain* translated into Welsh as *Brut y Brenhinedd*, the Hendregadredd Manuscript containing works of the Gogynfeirdd, the Welsh court poets active from the twelfth to fourteenth centuries, the Book of Llandaff and the Latin and Welsh copies of the Laws of Hywel Dda which contain crude but charming illustrations in the manner of Gerald of Wales's works). The Llanbeblig Book of Hours (National Library of Wales, MS 17520A), made circa 1390–1400, is a fully illuminated Welsh manuscript, connected to Caernarfon by its Calendar, where the obit of its original owner, Isabella Godynogh (d. 1413), is also entered. Its early sixteenth-century binding bears the arms of King Henry VIII (whose Tudor dynasty sprang from Wales) and Katherine of Aragon.

Returning to England, Edward IV spent extravagantly on Eltham Palace, including the magnificent Great Hall, which survives still as part of the remodelled art deco house, where he held a lavish feast for 2,000 people in December 1482, shortly before his death in April. He also began a major upgrade of St George's Chapel, Windsor, where he was buried in 1483.

Anthony Woodville was charged with bringing his young nephew, Edward V, and his brother Richard to join their mother, but they were apprehended by the princes' uncle Richard. Rivers was executed and the boys went missing (presumed assassinated) sometime between July and September 1483. Woodville soon joined them. Edward IV had added a codicil to his will at the end of his life, naming his brother, Richard, Duke of Gloucester, as next in line to the throne. Uncle Richard duly became King Richard III. Few monarchs have evoked such partisan feeling among their latter-day supporters or detractors as he. The discovery of his body beneath a car park in Leicester in 2012 and his subsequent interment in the cathedral there – during which Richard's prayerbook was used in the service – has piqued public imagination still further. The portentous poignancy of the relationships underlying the formal depiction of a family Christmas in our book is compelling.

Richard also owned several manuscripts, including the Hours of Richard III, his most personal book. This is now Lambeth Palace Library, MS 474, and was made in London around 1420, with prayers having been added specifically for him about 1483–5. It was probably made in Paternoster Row, beside St Paul's Cathedral, in the circle of fashionable illuminator Hermann Scheerre, who was from Cologne. The decoration is modest, with only three full vignettes including historiated initials for the Hours of the Virgin (Annunciation f. 15r), the Penitential Psalms (Christ in Judgement, now missing, f. 55r) and the Vigil of the Dead (Service for the Dead, f. 72r). As his personal prayerbook, this would likely have been in Richard's tent at the Battle of Bosworth in 1485.

It seems that the book was never used until selected to be his closest companion by Richard when he became king, perhaps to replace a previous prayerbook that reminded him too much of his dead wife and son. He entered his birth date in its prefatory calendar in his own hand: 'Hac die nat[us] erat Ricardus Rex Anglie iijus apud Foderingay anno domini Mcc[cclij]' ('This is the birthday of Richard, King of England, at Fotheringay in 1452'). Several devotions were added on blank pages (ff. 1, 181–4) by a professional clerk for Richard 'his personal use', with the king's name inserted where appropriate (some of which have been excised). These included a collect of St Ninian, patron saint of the Western March, where Richard had ruled as Duke of Gloucester, and a mutilated text that may have been a crusader litany.

A leaf was cut away between ff. 180v–181 containing a prayer to St Julian the Hospitaller and the opening of a prayer to St Augustine. Julian was said to have mistakenly killed his parents, for which he begged forgiveness of God, and it has been speculated that the prayer was included specifically for use by Richard III. St Augustine's prayer is intended to bring

Opposite: *The Hours of Richard III (Lambeth Palace Library, MS 474, f. 15r), the Annunciation. This personal devotional book would have accompanied Richard to the Battle of Bosworth in 1485, at which he died. It was used in his reinterment in Leicester Cathedral in 2015, following the discovery of his body under a car park nearby.* Below: *The Hours of Richard III (MS 474, ff. 7v–8r), calendar page with the day of Richard's birth, 2 October 1452, marked (towards the top of the left-hand page, lines 3–5), perhaps in his own hand.*

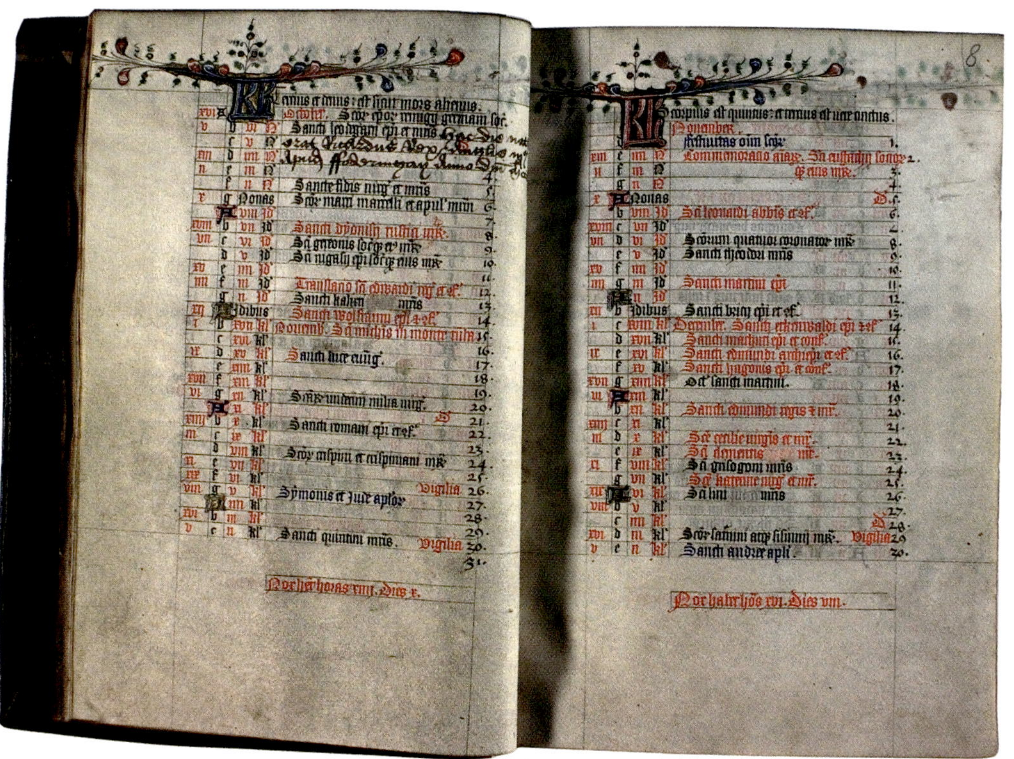

consolation by emphasizing God's goodness and relating how He supported Old and New Testament figures during affliction. It may have early roots, but this version was possibly composed in Franciscan circles in the fourteenth century. The word *dolor* (grief) in Richard's copy appears to be a unique inclusion and is linked to his own name in the text. In the 1540s or '50s the book was heavily cropped and rebound in the workshop of the anonymous King Edward and Queen Mary Binder, indicating that it was still valued by these Tudor monarchs despite the regime change it represented – or perhaps because of it.

The book passed, after Richard's death, to Lady Margaret Beaufort, the mother of Henry VII, who gave it to an unknown person who was asked to pray for her 'in the honour of God and Sainte Edmonde'. She also owned a little, equally modest, book of hours (the Lady Margaret Beaufort Hours, Westminster Abbey, MS 39) from the time of her marriage to her fourth husband, Sir Thomas Stanley (d. 1504). Margaret was devout, but even so she needed to have some of the texts or their rubrics/titles translated into English. The manuscript was probably painted by a Flemish illuminator working in London associated with the Masters of

Above: *Lady Margaret Beaufort Hours (Westminster Abbey,* MS *39), the Annunciation, with initial featuring the Beaufort emblem, the portcullis, adopted by Parliament, and border featuring the red roses of the house of Lancaster. Margaret was devout, and the depiction of Mary reading her prayerbook would have inspired her to do likewise and served as a reminder that she too had conceived a king.* Opposite, left: *The Annunciation, in the Beaufort/Beauchamp Hours (*BL*, Royal* MS 2 A XVIII*, f. 23v). It is likely that the kneeling patrons are John Beaufort, Earl of Somerset (d. 1410), and Margaret Holland (d. 1439), the great-grandparents of Henry* VII*, and that the miniatures were reused from an earlier family book of hours in this one, which was owned successively by Henry* VII*'s grandmother and mother, Lady Margaret Beauchamp and Lady Margaret Beaufort.* Opposite, right: *Calendar page for August, in the Beaufort/Beauchamp Hours, carrying added marginal notes of the landing of Henry Tudor at Milford Haven and the death of Richard* III *at the Battle of Bosworth (*BL*, Royal* MS 2 A XVIII*, f. 31v).*

the Dark Eyes (a group of artists from Ghent-Bruges who popularized a style characterized by the use of darkened eye sockets). The Beaufort family emblem, the portcullis, features in many of the borders and initials (which also feature marguerites as a play on Margaret's name, little strawberries symbolizing purity and the red roses of the house of Lancaster) and went on to become the emblem of the Houses of Parliament. Women played a key role in the dynastic power plays, as was often the case, but this was a century when they were also prominent as the patrons and makers of books.

Lady Margaret's first marriage, which she disregarded, was at the age of one. At twelve she was married to Edmund Tudor and bore his child when she was thirteen, after he had died of pestilence in captivity during warfare. Giving birth so young, she was never able to bear another child in her subsequent marriages. Having politicked to ensure their Tudor son came to the throne as Henry VII, Lady Margaret wielded a considerable political influence and enjoyed greater personal freedom than usual in her day. She became a major cultural patron and benefactor, leading the way for the Tudor dynasty's record for royal patronage, and founded two Cambridge colleges,

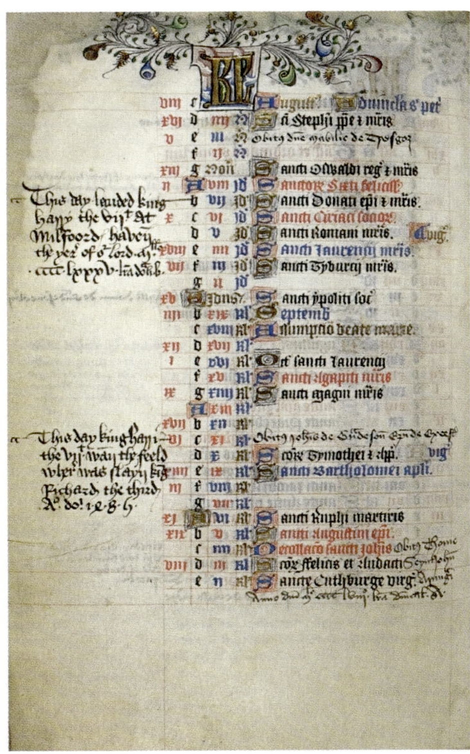

Christ's College and St John's College. Lady Margaret Hall, Oxford, founded and named for her in the nineteenth century, was the first Oxford college to admit women.

Lady Margaret also possessed a grander book of hours later in her life, the Beaufort/Beauchamp Hours, painted in the fashionable International Gothic style. Its calendar page for August carries added marginal notes of the landing of Henry Tudor at Milford Haven and the death of Richard III at the Battle of Bosworth (British Library, Royal MS 2 A X VIII, f. 31V).

Edward IV and his wife Elizabeth's daughter, Elizabeth of York (d. 1503), later owned the most opulent book of hours to have survived from fifteenth-century England, the Hours of Elizabeth the Queen (British Library, Add. MS 50001), which she appears to have signed on f. 22, beneath the depiction of the Crucifixion. This was made in London in the 1420s, with one of its several artists thought also to have worked on the Bedford Psalter-Hours (British Library, Add. MS 42131) It contains a series of splendid miniatures in International Gothic style, no less than 423 fine historiated and decorated initials and lavishly decorated borders. It had been made a little earlier for the Neville family, from which her paternal grandmother Cecily came and which had rebelled against her father (tellingly, her uncle Richard married Anne Neville). A prayer for Cecily occurs on f. 152 and it is possible that the book was previously owned by her and/or her father, Richard Neville, 5th Earl of Salisbury (Henry IV's nephew). As was often the case, such devotional manuscripts were passed down on the female line. Elizabeth's mother, Elizabeth Woodville, was so distraught at the death of her two young sons that she conspired with Margaret Beaufort to bring her son to the throne. The young Elizabeth of York became the wife of that son, Henry VII, the last Lancastrian claimant to the throne during the Wars of the Roses and the founder of the Tudor dynasty, which brought them to an end.

The Crucifixion in the Hours of Elizabeth the Queen, daughter of Edward IV and Elizabeth Woodville, wife of Henry VII, London, 1420–30 (BL, Add. MS 50001, f. 22r), with an inscription, perhaps by Elizabeth herself, at the foot reading 'Elisabeth the quene'. This is one of the most opulent books of hours from 15th-century England, and had probably passed to Elizabeth from her father's family, the Nevilles.

12

THE SIXTEENTH CENTURY: MUSICIAN, MONARCH, WOMANIZER

THE PSALTER OF KING HENRY VIII (BRITISH LIBRARY, ROYAL MS 2 A XVI)

King Henry VII (r. 1485–1509), founder of the Tudor dynasty, had his hands too full with the affairs of state and the socio-economic aftermath of the Wars of the Roses to spend much time or money on books. One associated with him that survives, however, is a large tome covered by an elegant burgundy velvet chemise binding (the medieval equivalent of a dust jacket, to keep the book clean), set with fine metalwork enamelled bosses and clasps and a gold and burgundy thread tassel (British Library, Harley MS 1498). It is listed in the inventory of Henry VIII's books as 'Item: A booke of Kynge Henry the viith his foundacion of his chappell at Westminster' and was kept in the little study next to the king's old bedchamber in Westminster Palace. It was of personal sentimental value to the monarch, for it contains agreements made in 1504 between Henry VII and the abbot and monks of Westminster Abbey relating to the splendid royal mausoleum that he was to build at its east end, the Henry VII Chapel. This was one of Henry VII's principal artistic commissions, a fine piece of architecture with impressive fan vaulting and glazing, its wall adorned with sculpted saints in the height of Flemish fashion. At its centre rest the peaceful effigies of the king and his queen, Elizabeth of York, modelled in bronze by a leading Italian artist, Pietro Torrigiano (who is said to have broken Michelangelo's nose). The manuscript contains an illuminated initial (f. 1r) depicting the enthroned and crowned king (recalling his coronation in the abbey) handing the very book, in its splendid binding, to the kneeling abbot and community.

The son of Henry VII and Elizabeth of York, King Henry VIII (b. 1491; *r.* 1509–47), later owned his own luxury devotional book, the Psalter of Henry VIII, which is our next book, made in 1540 when Henry was ailing and ageing. This will be discussed shortly, but now to happier times.

Henry's parents kept a large retinue of musicians at their court and Henry began experimenting with music as a child, his efforts being polished, from 1501, by his tutor Giles Duwes (d. 1535), who taught him languages as well as the lute. Henry also had a 'school master of pipes' named Guillam, who instructed him in the recorder and other woodwind instruments. Sebastian Giustinian, the Venetian ambassador from 1515 to 1519, also praised Henry's virtuosity as a musician, including his ability on the virginals.

Henry pursued other virginal trophies and the games of courtly love at his court fostered a taste for love songs and other pieces of secular music, a collection of which survives as the Henry VIII Songbook (British Library, Add. MS 31922), featuring work by popular composers, including a majority of 34 pieces by Henry himself, including 'Some Say Youthe Doth Rule Me' (or, colloquially, 'don't blame me, it's because I'm young!'). This is thought to have been written sometime between 1510 and 1520, when Henry was in his athletic prime.

One of the earliest manuscripts to be treasured by King Henry, however, was his Motet book (British Library, Royal MS II EXI). This is a collection of four- and five-part motets, in Flemish style, set out as a more conventional choir book. It was made in Antwerp under the guidance of Petrus de Opitiis, a Flemish-Italian merchant, in 1516 and was presented to King Henry by 1518. It contains eight separate pieces: two elegiac poems in honour of Henry VIII by a 'Magister Sampson' (Richard Sampson, Cardinal Wolsey's vicar-general and diplomat in the diocese of Tournai and later bishop of Chichester) and Johannes de Opitiis, and six motets by Sampson and Benedictus de Opitiis. Its seventeen large-format vellum folios are finely illuminated and written with calligraphic virtuosity, which in 1516 came together in the beautiful rose motet opening bearing a canon in honour of King Henry. Each of the two voices of this perpetual canon is written around

Below: *King Henry VIII's composition, 'Though sum saith that yough rulyth me', from the Henry VIII Songbook (BL, Add. MS 31922, ff. 71v–72r).* Opposite: *King Henry VIII's Motet Book, 1516 (BL, Royal MS II E XI, ff. 2r and 3r): frontispiece with elegiac poem to the king and an allegorical depiction of the Tudor genealogy and realm (left); a canon in honour of Henry (right).*

a painted red rose of the house of Lancaster, which would become hybridized with the white rose of York to form the Tudor rose (a bi-coloured bud can already be seen in the frontispiece), celebrating the peaceful conclusion of the Wars of the Roses with the accession of the Tudor dynasty. The bassus and contratenor parts, set at the musical interval of a fourth apart, are designed to be performed by two singers each, forming a double canon. This is the first musical component in a presentation volume to honour Henry VIII. Having honoured Henry, the rest of the music is in praise of the Virgin Mary, perhaps alluding to Henry and Katherine of Aragon's daughter, born that very year, Mary Tudor (who would later become queen of England and Spain, following the death of her brother, Edward VI).

The beautiful and intriguing title page of the work features an elegiac poem with illumination celebrating the union between the houses of York and Lancaster and the early Tudor line. Between the columns of the text grows a rose bush (a symbol of purity and the Virgin Mary), planted firmly in the soil of an island surrounded by a fortified, crenelated wall with four towers. Its gateway, inscribed 'Salve felix Anglia' ('Greeting, happy England'), boasts a portcullis (emblem of the Beaufort family of Henry's mother) guarded by the royal lion of England and flanked by the Welsh red dragon of the Tudors and the Beaufort greyhound. A daisy and marigold also grow from it, representing King Henry's sisters, Margaret of Scotland and Mary of France, respectively, while the heraldry refers to Henry and his first wife, Katherine of Aragon, daughter of Ferdinand and Isabella of Spain. The pomegranate bush also refers to the Spanish ancestry (the pomegranate of Granada) and is a traditional symbol of eternal life The English fleet circles the island protectively, commanding the seas, little suspecting that this union with Spain would lead in the time of Henry's daughter Elizabeth I to its attack by the Spanish Armada. The image is a masterly allegory of a dynasty's origins and a prophetic vision of its future.

In 1526 Henry began pursuing Anne Boleyn, one of his wife Katherine's ladies in waiting, having previously bedded Anne's sister, Mary. A poignant reminder of the first flush of their love is an exquisite little girdle book (British Library, Stowe MS 956), designed to be worn from the belt, with a metalwork binding. It contains the psalms and was both a symbol of piety and a fashion-statement jewel. It is thought that this may have belonged to Anne (or perhaps Henry gave such gifts out more widely as royal favours, as he did his intimate attentions). The text is prefaced (f. IV) by a miniature of Henry's bust, smugly grinning out at his beloved in a full-frontal pose, clad in velvet and ermine, jewelled chains around his neck and a rakish feathered cap upon his head. The great lover is already quite portly and flushed. By 1536 his beloved had literally lost her head – on the executioner's block.

Henry and Anne's reckless and inexorable quest for a divorce and the conception of a male heir to secure the line would expedite the implementation of the Reformation in England and the Dissolution of the Monasteries in 1536–40. This would lead to the destruction of the majority of the libraries accumulated by religious establishments across the centuries and would be lamented by John Leland, who travelled the realm surveying the wreckage and complained to Henry of their treasures being subject to the ravages of tailors and small boys, who made their leaves into the equivalent of dress patterns and paper aeroplanes (at that period perhaps vellum boats would have been the analogous pastime).

Henry had begun his reign as the golden boy, a Renaissance prince in the making, handsome, gifted and capable of learning. These attributes faded as time went by and in 1537 Cranmer noted that he did not read much himself, perhaps due to lack to time, patience or energy, and preferred to be read to. His early alacrity in filling the shelves of his royal libraries also faded and the books salvaged from the monastic wreckage for their usefulness in obtaining his divorce and countering the claims of Rome soon waned and innumerable bibliographical treasures were passed up.

Some of his wives scored better in their literary interests and skills. Katherine of Aragon was known for her humanistic learning and consulted the works of authors as diverse as St Jerome, Petrarch and Erasmus as consolation and ammunition in her distress. Her rival, Anne Boleyn, engaged in evangelical reading and she and her brother George, with whom she was later accused of incest to dispense with her, shared theological books that suggest an interest in the early stages of Protestantism on the Continent. Lust for Henry and/or the Crown may therefore not have been Anne's only motivation in wishing to change the nature of the Church in England, which resulted in the Church of England.

The youthful Catherine Howard had a taste for more decorative books, some of them jewelled girdle books, which could be worn at the waist as a fashion accoutrement and devotional symbol. By contrast, the more mature and serious Catherine Parr was herself an author and shared her humanist literary interests with her royal stepchildren, especially Elizabeth. Both women earned respect for their considerable intellectual abilities.

An aspect of Katherine of Aragon and Anne Boleyn's books repays examination. Henry and Anne married in 1533. In January 1536 Katherine died at Kimbolton Castle, where she had confined herself to one room, having been banished from court. Soon after, on 19 May 1536 Anne Boleyn was beheaded, on Henry's command, on charges of adultery and incest corroborated by evidence obtained through torture.

Both women were highly educated. Katherine, a Franciscan tertiary, was extremely devout and was herself lauded as defender of the Catholic faith. Her patronage of books included the controversial *De institutione feminae Christianae* (The Education of a Christian Woman) by Juan Luis Vives, advocating the right of women to have an education and intended for her daughter, Mary, and which she had commissioned and which was dedicated to her. It remained popular in both Catholic and Protestant circles into the seventeenth century, having been translated into English from Latin.

Anne, like other members of the Boleyn family, had an interest in the Protestantism sweeping through parts of northern Europe, which is evidenced by some of the books owned by them. Nonetheless, it was recently found that both women owned a copy of the same printed edition of a book of hours (both with hand-coloured images), printed on vellum in Paris by renowned French printer Germain Hardouyn around 1528, while the two women were still close as queen and lady in waiting.

Anne's copy (now preserved at her birthplace, Hever Castle) bears a poignant inscription in the margin of one page, which is in Anne's own hand and reads 'remember me when you do pray that hope doth lead from day to day. Anne Boleyn.' This is the book that she is thought to have taken to her execution, as her solace. Her inscription stands, movingly, beneath the place in the text of the Little Office of the Blessed Virgin Mary that focuses the reader's devotions upon the Crucifixion and the sorrow of Christ's mother in witnessing it. Opposite is a miniature depicting the presentation of Christ in the Temple, in which his mother performs the ritual that completes her giving birth to the Saviour, who is publicly acknowledged, unlike Anne,

Below: *Two copies of the same book of hours, printed on vellum by Germain Hardouyn in Paris,* c. *1528, owned by Katherine of Aragon (left) and Anne Boleyn (right), exhibited together at Anne's family home, Hever Castle in Kent, in 2021.* Opposite: *Anne Boleyn's own note, which reads 'remember me when you do pray that hope doth lead from day to day. Anne Boleyn', in the margin of one of her books of hours (now at Hever Castle, Kent), printed in Paris,* c. *1528, which she may have taken with her to her execution in 1536. The text is written beneath part of the Little Office of the Blessed Virgin Mary and focuses the reader's devotions upon the Crucifixion and the sorrow of Christ's mother in witnessing it.*

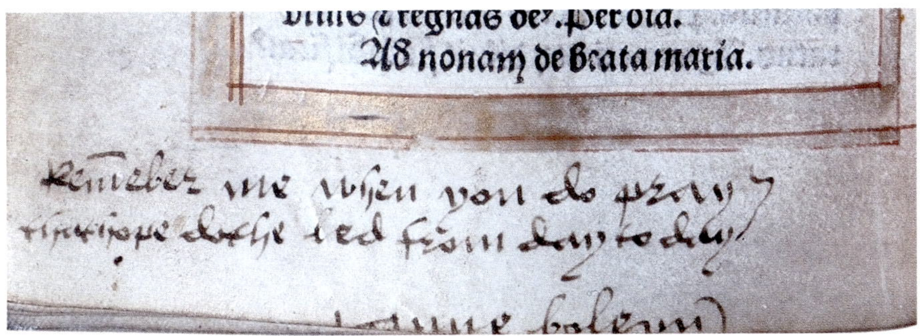

whose own longed-for son was stillborn, which lost her the throne and her life. It was her daughter, the future Elizabeth I, who would later prove England's salvation in its hour of need.

The commissioners of the inventory of Henry VIII's moveable goods, compiled after his death in 1547 (British Library, Harley MS 1419/1 and 2), included lists of the books and manuscripts in his palaces, many of which were transferred to the Old Royal Library and were presented to the nation by King George II (r. 1727–60) in 1757, becoming part of the British Museum and subsequently the British Library's collections.

One of the manuscripts identifiable from the inventory is 'a description of the holy lande and a boke covered with vellat enbrawdred with the kings armes declaring the same, in a case of blacke leather with his graces Armes', namely the *Tresample description de toute la Terre Saincte*, written by Martin de Brion of Paris (British Library, Royal MS 20 A IV). It retains its fine crimson velvet binding, embroidered with the royal badge, Tudor roses and Henry's initial, a personal style of binding that his daughter Elizabeth I would perpetuate, even embroidering some herself.

Overleaf, left: *The Psalter of Henry VIII (BL, Royal MS 2 A XVI, f. 30r), miniature with a young Henry depicted as David defeating Goliath. The camp in the background may have reminded Henry of his triumph, as a young man, at the Field of Cloth of Gold, a summit meeting between the young king and King Francis I of France from 7 to 24 June 1520 in the English Pale of Calais. This was a very expensive display of wealth by both kings to determine superiority – which Henry concluded was his victory. Within two years war was declared between England and France. The image has also been interpreted as Henry taking on the papacy – and winning.* Overleaf, right: *The Psalter of Henry VIII (BL, Royal MS 2 A XVI, f. 3r): King Henry in his bedchamber, reading a book, perhaps this very one, his personal devotional aid. He has noted in the margin in Latin, next to the opening of Psalm I (which begins 'Blessed is the man who hath not walked in the counsel of the ungodly . . . his will is in the law of the Lord'): 'Note who is blessed.' Made around 1540, Henry had by this time presided over the Dissolution of the Monasteries, been divorced and had three subsequent short-lived marriages. His bed here is temporarily empty. Henry annotated the volume, giving an insight into his meditations. Henry's notation perhaps implies that he considered himself ill-advised and ill-served at times to date.*

38

Dominus illuminatio mea & salus mea: quem timebo?
Dominus protector vitæ meæ a quo

Christi plena in Deum fiducia

BEATVS vir qui non abiit
in consilio impiorum, & in via
peccatorum non stetit, & in cathedra pe=
stilentiæ non sedit.

Henry VIII's most intimate devotional companion was a fine illuminated manuscript psalter written in humanistic script upon vellum, although printing with moveable type had been known in the West since the 1450s and the Gutenberg Bible and was popularized in England from the time of Caxton and Wynkyn de Worde. Vellum was also used, rather than the cheaper paper, for some early luxury printed books and early typefaces and page layout were deeply indebted to earlier manuscript practices. Images and decoration were also to be found adorning early printed books (known as incunables, from 'in the cradle', as printing was in its formative stages), but the colour drained out of the pages, with only two-colour red and black printing possible at that stage, or hand-coloured woodblock printing of images, and in many printed works the illumination was added by hand. For the ultimate luxury, hand-made manuscripts were still sometimes favoured by wealthy patrons throughout Europe, including Henry.

In 1540, with the messiness of the Dissolution of the Monasteries, his divorce and three subsequent short-lived marriages behind him, Henry commissioned for himself not a liturgically based book of hours, with its pre-Reformation associations, but the other devotional mainstay, a Psalter (British Library, Royal MS 2 A XVI), clad in a rich red velvet binding, reflecting Henry's own robe. This he annotated himself in the margins, in Latin written in an English version of a French secretary hand, commenting on points in the individual psalms and their application, giving us an insight into his most personal devotions. Its humanistic script and illumination by French artist Jean Mallard (who had previously worked for Henry's rival, King François I of France) befits the taste of a modern, educated Renaissance prince. Henry (who prided himself on his musical abilities and as, successively, 'Defender of the Faith' and then head of the Church of England, after his Dissolution of the Monasteries) had himself depicted in the book four times, including as the Psalmist, King David (a monarch with whom Henry evidently identified, while presumably not acknowledging the charges of adultery levelled at them both), kneeling before the Lord, as a penitent, slaying Goliath, sitting reading in his bedchamber (before an, unusually, empty bed, set in an imagined Italian cum northern Renaissance interior and exterior glimpsed through the door) and composing the psalms upon a harp, while his court jester, Will Somers (the only person from whom he would brook criticism), stands by. The psalm (no. 14) thus illustrated begins, ironically enough, 'The fool says in his heart, there is no God.' The Middle Ages were at an end.

Another of the book's images (f. 98v) depicts a group of musicians playing a harp, trumpet, pipe and tabor and a well-observed dulcimer, as befitted Henry's interests. They wear odd garbs, mixing imagined 'ye olde' biblical style and contemporary items and play around a remarkably heavy table, draped and partially surrounded by a crimson curtain, affording them some privacy in their outdoor setting. God hovers benignly at a suitable distance, blessing both them and the landscape they inhabit.

The decorated initials throughout feature the familiar symbols of medieval plant and animal-lore: butterflies and moths (for mortality), beetles and ladybirds, a dormouse eating grain, roses (for purity), forget-me-nots, grapes and cherries (and even a rather suggestive pair of marrows), a bird

The Psalter of Henry VIII (BL, Royal MS 2 A XVI, f. 63v): Henry VIII as King David composing the Psalms, with his court jester William Somers. This comes at the opening of Psalm 14, 'The fool says in his heart, there is no God.' No signs of gout yet in the king's comely legs.

Se selon mon affection la suvenance sera
en voz prieres ne seray gueres oblie
car bien suis [illegible]

with a breast as red as Robert Bruyning's robin and our old friend the snail (for humility). The text is written in a humanist hand that seeks to emulate the Roman typeface of Italian printed books (a font that, along with the italic typeface, had been inspired by humanist manuscript hands). Henry may have prided himself upon playing the Renaissance prince, but in many ways that facade was as artificial as this artificial script in his psalter.

The difference can be seen in the real thing, a splendid copy of the *Apologues* of Lucian (British Library, Royal MS 12 C VIII) commissioned in Italy by Henry Chambers, one of Henry's ambassadors, as a gift for his king, featuring the royal arms in the opening border, along with the Tudor rose. The refined yet opulent illumination was the work of Attavante degli Attavanti, a Florentine artist who worked for the Medici and King Matthias Corvinus of Hungary. The superb calligraphic script is that of Ludovico Arrighi, a leading scribe in the papal chancery who was instrumental in developing its most impressive humanist cursive script, known as *cancellaresca*. It was probably made in Rome and would have given Henry something to aspire to, both stylistically and intellectually. The Dialogues of the Gods had been composed in Antiquity in Greek, mocking the Homeric conception of the Greek gods, and this was one of two recent translations into Latin by Pandulfo Collennuccio, which was published in 1526, so this manuscript must be later. Arrighi's script became a model for fine European handwriting after he published the first of the printed writing masters' handbooks, *La Operina*, printed in Rome in 1522.

Henry's own handwriting can be seen in the annotations he made in the margins of his psalter and in a little love letter that he wrote in Anne Boleyn's book of hours (British Library, King's MS 9, f. 231v), in the lower margin beneath an image of Christ as the Man of Sorrows. Christ kneels before his tomb, surrounded by the instruments of the Passion, his body covered with bleeding wounds from his scourging and his brow pierced by the crown of thorns. Henry may have meant to compare this, implicitly, with his own sufferings of the pangs of love, which is as incongruous as the illusionistic Flemish-style strew-border that surrounds the miniature, with flowers strewn on a gold ground. The English rubrics in the text suggest that

*The Man of Sorrows (Christ after his scourging, with the instruments of the Passion) in Anne Boleyn's devotional Book of Hours (*BL*, King's* MS *9, f. 231v). In the lower margin King Henry* VIII *wrote, while they were still in love, 'If you remember my love in your prayers as strongly as I adore you, I shall hardly be forgotten, for I am yours, King Henry, forever' ('Si silon mon affection la sufvenance sera en voz prieres ne seray gers oblie car vostre suis Henry r(ex) a jammays').*

this Flemish artist may have been working in the Tudor court around 1500, when he illuminated this book. Henry wrote:

> *Si silon mon affection la sufvenance sera en voz prieres ne seray gers oblie car vostre suis Henry R(ex) a jammays*
> (If you remember my love in your prayers as strongly as I adore you, I shall hardly be forgotten, for I am yours, King Henry, forever)

Alas, his love did not bloom for as long as these painted flowers.

His signature is enlarged and penned in the florid manner of royal signatures and the rest of the script, also in his hand, is a secretary script of ultimately French origin, which was one of the options available in late medieval and early modern Britain for informal and documentary use and in non-sacred texts. It is the same hand that Henry used to annotate the margins of his own Psalter.

Some leading illuminators worked on well into the sixteenth century. One of the most famous was Simon Bening, a Flemish illuminator who was probably trained by his father, Alexander/Sanders Bening, in the family workshop in Ghent and who joined the Guild of St John and St Luke in Bruges as an illuminator in 1508. The family was also related to some of the leading panel painters of the day – his mother, Kathelijn van der Goes, was a relative of Hugo van der Goes, and his sister married Goswijn van der Weyden. Simon's exquisite and detailed work often recalls larger paintings in miniature, with influences moving across the media and the illuminator's art serving to inspire those riding the new wave of panel painting and 'art for art's sake'. Simon moved to Bruges around 1510, where he remained and served as a dean of the calligraphers, booksellers, illuminators and bookbinders in the Bruges guild in 1524, 1536 and 1546. He had six daughters, one of whom, Levina Teerlinc, became a miniature painter, specializing in portrait miniatures and moving to England where she painted an exquisite miniature portrait of the young Queen Elizabeth I (*c.* 1565, Royal Collection). Another of his daughters, Alexandrine Claeiszuene, became a successful art dealer, for illuminators were becoming 'artists' in their own right. One such was Gerard David, who illuminated manuscripts such as part of the sumptuous Rothschild Prayerbook (Perth, Kerry Stokes Collection) and who also created panel paintings and altarpieces, in one of which he left us a self-portrait. Simon Bening also left an illuminated self-portrait on a single purple vellum leaf (Victoria and Albert Museum, P. 159-1910) which is inscribed in Latin 'SIMO BINNIK ALEXANDRI FILIUS / SEIPSU PIGEBAT ANO ÆTATIS 75 / 1558 ('Simon Bennik, the son of Alexander, painted this himself at the age of 75 in 1558'). His brow is furrowed and his strained eyes take a well-deserved rest, as his hand holds the pince-nez glasses he has just taken off, but this master-illuminator announces proudly, in the form of a Renaissance framed portrait painted on the page in the *trompe l'œil* technique in which he excelled, that he is still working and pushing forward the parameters of his art on the threshold of the modern world – a century after the advent of moveable type and printed engravings in the West.

Hand-painted manuscripts lingered on occasionally until the eighteenth century and printed books might also feature paintings by hand or hand-coloured prints, until the advent of colour printing. Illuminated manuscripts would reappear in the nineteenth and early twentieth centuries as part of the Arts and Crafts movement and the revival of calligraphy in the early twentieth century by Edward Johnston and the master-gilder William Graily Hewitt and their students, many of whom were women. These female illuminators, who perpetuated the legacy of so many centuries of women's art in books, included Edith Bertha Crapper (1892–1979), who illuminated books and painted exquisite miniatures in the style of Levina Teerlinc (Simon Bening's daughter) of her mother and father (who invented an early flushing toilet).

Florence Kate Kingsford (1871–1949) worked with William Morris and the archaeologist Flinders Petrie and undertook an art expedition to Egypt. She was married to Sir Sydney Carlyle Cockerell, who staged the first exhibition of illuminated manuscripts, held at the Burlington Fine Arts Club in London in 1908, and was director of the Fitzwilliam Museum in Cambridge. William Morris collected medieval illuminated manuscripts and his *Rubaiyat of Omar Khayyam* (British Library, Add. MS 37832) was handwritten and illuminated by him (with collaboration from Edward Burne-Jones and Charles Fairfax Murray) as a gift for Georgiana Burne-Jones in 1872. Their designs went on to influence books printed at the Kelmscott Press, such as the *Kelmscott Chaucer,* widely thought to be one of the most beautiful books ever printed, which was so deeply indebted to the traditions of medieval book design and illumination that had evolved across a thousand years. They still inspire contemporary calligraphers, typographers and artists, including those working in the digital environment and, with the interest and knowledge of manuscripts among pioneering IT and communication specialists such as Willy Hall and David Levy, have helped to shape modern tablet technology.

BIBLIOGRAPHY

The Medieval Book

Brown, M. P., 'The Triumph of the Codex: The Manuscript Book before 1100', in *The Blackwell Companion to the History of the Book*, ed. S. Eliot and J. Rose [2007] (Oxford, 2019), pp. 179–93

—, *Understanding Illuminated Manuscripts: A Guide to Technical Terms*, revd edn (Los Angeles, CA, 2020)

—, ed., *In the Beginning: Bibles before the Year 1000*, exh. cat., Freer and Sackler Museum, Smithsonian Institution (Washington, DC, 2006)

Clemens, R., and T. Graham, *Introduction to Manuscript Studies* (Ithaca, NY, 2007)

De Hamel, C., *The Book: A History of the Bible* (London, 2001)

—, *Meetings with Remarkable Manuscripts* (London, 2016)

Gameson, R., ed., *The Cambridge History of the Book in Britain*, vol. I (Cambridge, 2011)

Griffiths, J., and D. Pearsall, eds, *Book Production and Publishing in Britain, 1375–1475* (Cambridge, 1989)

Hellinga, L., and J. B. Trapp, eds, *The Cambridge History of the Book in Britain*, vol. III: *1400–1557* (Cambridge, 1999)

Ker, N. R., *Books, Collectors and Libraries: Studies in the Medieval Heritage*, ed. A. G. Watson (London and Ronceverte, WV, 1985)

Leedham-Green, E., and T. Webber, eds, *The Cambridge History of Libraries in Britain*, vol. I (Cambridge, 2015)

Morgan, N. J., and R. Thompson, eds, *The Cambridge History of the Book in Britain*, vol. II (Cambridge, 2008)

Parkes, M. B., *Scribes, Scripts and Readers: Studies in the Communication, Presentation and Dissemination of Medieval Texts* (London and Rio Grande, OH, 1991)

—, and A. G. Watson, eds, *Medieval Scribes, Manuscripts and Libraries: Essays Presented to N. R. Ker* (London, 1978)

Taylor, J. H., and L. Smith, eds, *Women and the Book: Assessing the Visual Evidence* (London, 1997)

Making Medieval Manuscripts

Alexander, J. J. G., *Medieval Illuminators and Their Methods of Work* (New Haven, CT, 1992)

Avrin, L., *Scribes, Script and Books* (London and Chicago, IL, 1991)

Brown, M. P., *The British Library Guide to Writing and Scripts* (London and Toronto, 1998)

De Hamel, C., *Scribes and Illuminators* (London, 1992)

Marks, P., *The British Library Guide to Bookbinding* (London and Toronto, 1998)

Needham, P., *Twelve Centuries of Bookbinding, 400–1600* (New York and Oxford, 1979)

Literacy and Learning

Carruthers, M., *The Book of Memory: A Study of Memory in Medieval Culture* (Cambridge, 1990)

Cavallo, G., and R. Chartier, eds, *A History of Reading in the West* (Oxford, 1999)

Clanchy, M. T., *From Memory to Written Record: England, 1066–1307*, 2nd edn (Oxford, 1993)

Leclercq, J., *The Love of Learning and the Desire for God: A Study of Monastic Culture*, trans. C. Misrahi (London, 1978)

McKitterick, R., *The Uses of Literacy in Early Medieval Europe* (Cambridge, 1990)

Reynolds, L. D., and N. G. Wilson, *Scribes and Scholars: A Guide to the Transmission of Greek and Latin Literature*, 3rd edn (Oxford, 1991)

Illumination

Alexander, J.J.G., *The Decorated Letter* (London, 1978)

—, and P. Binski, eds, *Age of Chivalry: Art in Plantagenet England, 1200–1400*, exh. cat., Royal Academy (London, 1987)

—, et al., eds, *Survey of Manuscripts Illuminated in the British Isles*, 6 vols in 9 (London, 1976–96) [individual vols by J.J.G. Alexander, E. Temple, C. M. Kauffmann, N. J. Morgan, L. F. Sandler and K. L. Scott]

Avril, F., *Manuscript Painting at the Court of France: The Fourteenth Century, 1310–1380* (London, 1978)

—, *Les fastes du Gothiques: Le siècle de Charles* V, exh. cat., Galeries nationales du Grand Palais (Paris, 1981)

—, *Dix siècles d'enluminure italienne (*VI–XVI *siècles)*, exh. cat., Bibliothèque nationale de France (Paris, 1984)

—, *L'Art au temps des rois maudits: Philippe le Bel et ses fils, 1285–1328*, exh. cat., Galeries nationales du Grand Palais (Paris, 1998)

—, and N. Reynaud, eds, *Les manuscrits à peinture en France, 1440–1520*, exh. cat., Bibliothèque nationale de France (Paris, 1993)

Backhouse, J. M., *Books of Hours* (London, 1985)

—, *The Illuminated Page* (London, 1997)

Brown, M. P., *The Luttrell Psalter: A Facsimile* (London, 2006)

—, *The Lion Companion to Christian Art* (Oxford, 2008)

Camille, M., *Image on the Edge: The Margins of Medieval Art* (London, 1992)

De Hamel, C., *A History of Illuminated Manuscripts* (London, 1986)

Duffy, E., *The Stripping of the Altars: Traditional Religion in England, c. 1440–c. 1580* (New Haven, CT, 1992)

—, *Marking the Hours: English People and Their Prayers, 1240–1570* (New Haven, CT, 2011)
Kren, T., ed., *Renaissance Painting in Manuscripts: Treasures from the British Library* (New York, 1983)
—, and S. McKendrick, *Illuminating the Renaissance. The Triumph of Flemish Painting in Europe*, exh. cat., J. Paul Getty Museum, Los Angeles, CA, and Royal Academy, London (Los Angeles, CA, 2003)
Marks, R., and P. Williamson, eds, *Gothic: Art for England, 1400–1547*, exh. cat., Victoria and Albert Museum (London, 2003)
Marrow, J., et al., eds, *Golden Age of Dutch Manuscript Painting* (Stuttgart, 1989)
Meiss, M., *French Painting in the Time of Jean de Berry: The Limbourgs and Their Contemporaries*, 2 vols (London, 1974)
Morison, E., and L. Grollemond, *Book of Beasts: The Bestiary in the Medieval World* (Los Angeles, CA, 2019); for a full online facsimile of the Aberdeen bestiary, see the Internet Archive, https://archive.org, and for a site exploring the manuscript in detail, see www.abdn.ac.uk/bestiary, both accessed 28 May 2024
Pächt, O., *Book Illumination in the Middle Ages: An Introduction* (London, 1986)
Plummer, J., *The Last Flowering: French Painting in Manuscripts, 1420–1530* (New York, 1982)
Smeyers, M., and J. Van der Stock, *Flemish Illuminated Manuscripts, 1475–1550* (Ghent, 1997)
Watson, R., *Illuminated Manuscripts and Their Makers* (London, 2003)
Wieck, R. S., *Painted Prayers: The Book of Hours in Medieval and Renaissance Art* (New York, 1997)

Script

Bately, J., M. P. Brown and J. Roberts, eds, *A Palaeographer's View: Selected Papers of Julian Brown* (London, 1993)
Bischoff, B., *Latin Palaeography: Antiquity and the Middle Ages*, trans. D. Ó Cróinín and D. Ganz (Cambridge, 1990)
Brown, M. P., *A Guide to Western Historical Scripts from Antiquity to 1600*, revd edn (London, 1993)
Lowe, E. A., *Handwriting: Our Medieval Legacy* (Rome, 1969)
Parkes, M. B., *Pause and Effect: An Introduction to the History of Punctuation in the West* (Aldershot, 1992)
Roberts, J., *Guide to Scripts Used in English Writing up to 1500* (London and Toronto, 2005)

The Book Before 1200

Alexander, J. J. G., *Norman Illumination at Mont St Michel, 966–1100* (Oxford, 1970)
Badawry, A., *Coptic Art and Archaeology* (Cambridge, MA, 1978)

Brown, M. P., *The Lindisfarne Gospels: Society, Spirituality and the Scribe* (Lucerne, London and Toronto, 2003)
—, ed., *In the Beginning: Bibles before the Year 1000* (Washington, DC, 2006)
—, *Manuscripts from the Anglo-Saxon Age* (London and Toronto, 2008)
—, *The Book and the Transformation of Britain, c. 550–1050: A Study in Written and Visual Literacy and Orality*, The Sandars Lectures in Bibliography, 2009 (London and Chicago, IL, 2011)
—, *Art of the Islands: Celtic, Pictish, Anglo-Saxon and Viking Visual Culture, c. 450–1050* (Oxford, 2016)
Déroche, F., and F. Richard, *Scribes et manuscrits du Moyen-Orient* (Paris, 1997)
Diebold, W., *Word and Image: A History of Early Medieval Art* (Boulder, CO, 2000)
Gameson, R. G., *The Manuscripts of Early Norman England, c. 1066–1130* (Oxford, 1999)
Ganz, D., *Corbie in the Carolingian Renaissance* (Sigmaringen, 1990)
Henderson, G. H., *From Durrow to Kells: The Insular Gospel-Books, 650–800* (London, 1987)
Henry, F., *The Book of Kells* (London, 1974)
Ker, N. R., *English Manuscripts in the Century after the Norman Conquest* (Oxford, 1960)
Kessler, H., *The Illustrated Bibles from Tours* (Princeton, NJ, 1977)
Lapidge, M., and H. Gneuss, eds, *Learning and Literature in Anglo-Saxon England: Studies Presented to Peter Clemoes* (Cambridge, 1985)
Lowden, J., Early Christian and *Byzantine Art* (London, 1997)
McKitterick, R., *The Carolingians and the Written Word* (Cambridge, 1989)
Mayr-Harting, H., *Ottonian Book Illumination: An Historical Study*, 2 vols (London, 1991)
Nersessian, V., *Treasures from the Ark: 1700 Years of Armenian Christian Art* (London, 2001)
Nordenfalk, C., *Early Medieval Book Illumination* (New York, 1988)
Palazzo, E., *A History of Liturgical Books: From the Beginning to the Thirteenth Century*, trans. M. Beaumont (Collegeville, MN, 1998)
Safran, L., ed., *Heaven on Earth: Art and the Church in Byzantium* (University Park, PA, 1998)
Turner, D. H., J. M. Backhouse and L. Webster, eds, *The Golden Age of Anglo-Saxon Art, 966–1066*, exh. cat., British Museum (London, 1984)
Van der Horst, K., W. Noel and W.C.M. Wüstefeld, eds, *The Utrecht Psalter in Medieval Art: Picturing the Psalms of David* ('t Goy and London, 1996)
Walker, R., *Views of Transition: Liturgy and Illumination in Medieval Spain* (London and Toronto, 1998)
Webster, L., and J. M. Backhouse, eds, *The Making of England: Anglo-Saxon Art and Culture, AD 600–800*,

exh. cat., British Museum (London, 1991)
Weitzmann, K., *Late Antique and Early Christian Book Illumination* (London, 1977)
Zarnecki, G., J. Holt and T. Holland, eds, *English Romanesque Art, 1066–1200*, exh. cat., Hayward Gallery (London, 1984)

Urban Book Production

Bataillon, L. J., et al., eds, *La production du livre universitaire au moyen âge* (Paris, 1988)
Christianson, C. P., *A Directory of London Stationers and Book Artisans, 1300–1500* (New York, 1990)
—, *Memorials of the Book Trade in Medieval London* (Woodbridge, 1987)
L'Engle, S., and R. Gibbs, eds, *Illuminating the Law: Illuminated Legal Manuscripts in Cambridge Collections* (London, 2001)
Parkes, M. B., 'The Provision of Books', in *The History of the University of Oxford*, vol. II: *Late Medieval Oxford*, ed. J. I. Catto and T.A.R. Evans (Oxford, 1992), pp. 407–83
Piltz, A., *The World of Medieval Learning*, revd edn, trans. D. Jones (Oxford, 1981)
Raven, J., *The Business of Books: Booksellers and the English Book Trade, 1450–1850* (London and New Haven, CT, 2007)
Rothwell, W., 'The Trilingual England of Geoffrey Chaucer', *Studies in the Age of Chaucer*, XVI (1994), pp. 45–67
Rouse, R., and M. Cartolai, *Illuminators and Printers in Fifteenth Century Italy* (Los Angeles, CA, 1988)
—, *Manuscripts and Their Makers: Commercial Book Producers in Medieval Paris, 1200–1500*, 2 vols (Turnhout, 1999)

Specific Bibliographies by Chapter

1 The Eighth Century

Alexander, J.J.G., *A Survey of Manuscripts Illuminated in the British Isles*, vol. I: *Insular Manuscripts, 6th to the 9th Century* (London, 1978)
Breay, C., and B. Meehan, *The St Cuthbert Gospel: Studies on the Insular Manuscript of the Gospel of John* (London, 2015)
Breay, C., and J. Story, eds, *Anglo-Saxon Kingdoms, Art, Word, War*, exh. cat., British Library (London, 2018)
Brown, M. P., *The Lindisfarne Gospels: Society, Spirituality and the Scribe* (London, Lucerne and Toronto, 2003), issued as a commentary volume accompanying the facsimile (*The Lindisfarne Gospels, a Facsimile*, Lucerne and London, 2003)
—, *Painted Labyrinth: The World of the Lindisfarne Gospels* (London, 2003)
—, *How Christianity Came to Britain and Ireland* (Oxford, 2006)
—, *Manuscripts from the Anglo-Saxon Age* (London and Toronto, 2008)
—, *The Book and the Transformation of Britain, c. 550–1050: A Study in Written

and Visual Literacy and Orality, The Sandars Lectures in Bibliography, 2009 (London and Chicago, IL, 2011)
—, *The Lindisfarne Gospels and the Early Medieval World* (London, 2011)
—, *Art of the Islands: Celtic, Pictish, Anglo-Saxon and Viking Visual Culture, c. 450–1050* (Oxford, 2016)
—, 'Imagining, Imaging and Experiencing the East in Insular and Anglo-Saxon Cultures: New Evidence for Contact', in *Anglo-Saxon England and the Visual Imagination, ISAS 6, Proceedings of the ISAS Conference, Madison, 2012*, ed. J. D. Niles, S. Klein and J. Wilcox (Tempe, AZ, 2016), pp. 49–84
—, *Bede and the Theory of Everything* (London, 2023)
—, **I. Garipzanov and B. C. Tilghman**, eds, *Graphic Devices and the Early Decorated Book* (Woodbridge, 2018)
Dark, K. R., *Civitas to Kingdom: British Political Continuity, 300–800*, Studies in the Early History of Britain (Leicester, 1994)
Dodwell, C. R., *Anglo-Saxon Art: A New Perspective* (Ithaca, NY, 1982)
Farr, C. A., *The Book of Kells, Its Function and Audience* (London and Toronto, 1997)
Gameson, R., *The Codex Aureus: An Eighth-Century Gospel Book* (Copenhagen, 2001)
—, ed., *From Holy Island to Durham: The Contexts and Meanings of the Lindisfarne Gospels* (London, 2013)
Ganz, D., and B. Schellewald, eds, *Clothing Sacred Scripture* (Berlin, 2019)
Hawkes, J., and S. Mills, eds, *Northumbria's Golden Age* (Stroud, 1999)
Henderson, G. H., *From Durrow to Kells: The Insular Gospel-Books, 650–800* (London, 1987)
—, *Vision and Image in Early Christian England* (Cambridge, 1999)
—, **and I. Henderson**, *The Art of the Picts: Sculpture and Metalwork in Early Medieval Scotland* (London, 2004)
Henig, M., 'High Culture in Roman Britain: Epics of Troy and of Carthage', *Antiqvvs*, IV/2 (Spring 2022), pp. 27–32
—, 'Illuminated Christian Manuscripts in Roman Britain and Beyond', *Antiqvvs*, IV/4 (Autumn 2022), pp. 11–15
Henry, F., *The Book of Kells: Reproductions from the Manuscript in Trinity College, Dublin* (London, 1988)
Higham, N. J., *Rome, Britain, and the Anglo-Saxons* (London, 1992)
Kendrick, T. D., et al., eds, *Evangeliorum quattuor Codex Lindisfarnensis*, 2 vols (Olten and Lausanne, 1956–60)
MacGabhann, D., *The Book of Kells, a Masterwork Revealed: Creators, Collaboration, and Campaigns* (Leiden, 2022)
Meehan, B., *The Book of Durrow* (Dublin, 1996)
—, *The Book of Kells* (London, 2012)

Moss, R., ed., *Art and Architecture of Ireland*, vol. I: *Medieval, c. 400–c. 1600* (London, 2014)
Netzer, N., *Cultural Interplay in the Eighth Century: The 'Trier Gospels' and the Making of a Scriptorium at Echternach* (Cambridge, 1994)
Neuman de Vegvar, C. L., *The Northumbrian Renaissance: A Study in the Transmission of Style* (Selinsgrove, PA, 1987)
Pulliam, H., *Word and Image in the Book of Kells* (Dublin, 2006)
Stafford, P., ed., *A Companion to the Early Middle Ages: Britain and Ireland, c. 500–1100* (Chichester, UK, and Malden, MA, 2009)
Verey, C. D., T. J. Brown and E. Coatsworth, eds, *The Durham Gospels: Together with Fragments of a Gospel Book in Unical, Durham, Cathedral Library, MS A.II.17* (Copenhagen, 1980)
Webster, L., *Anglo-Saxon Art: A New History* (Ithaca, NY, 2012)
—, and J. M. Backhouse, eds, *The Making of England: Anglo-Saxon Art and Culture, AD 600–900*, exh. cat., British Museum (London and Toronto, 1991)
—, and M. P. Brown, eds, *The Transformation of the Roman World*, exh. cat., British Museum (London, 1997)
Wilson, D. M., *Anglo-Saxon Art from the Seventh Century to the Norman Conquest* (London, 1984)
Wright, D. H., *The Vespasian Psalter* (Copenhagen, 1967)

Sources

Bede, *Ecclesiastical History of the English People*, ed. L. Sherley-Price, revised by R. Latham and D. H. Farmer (Harmondsworth, 1990)
Farmer, D. H., ed., *The Age of Bede*, revd edn (Harmondsworth, 1983)
Wilcock, P., trans., *Bede's Lives of the Abbots of Wearmouth and Jarrow* (Newcastle upon Tyne, 1973)
Two Lives of Saint Cuthbert, ed. and trans. B. Colgrave (Cambridge, 1985)
For an online translation of Bede's Prose Life of St Cuthbert, see https://sourcebooks.fordham.edu/basis/bede-cuthbert.asp

The Lindisfarne Gospels reside in the British Library, London, where they are often on display, but check before visiting. A complete digital facsimile, together with a description and bibliography, can be viewed at www.bl.uk

The Book of Kells is on display in Trinity College Dublin, as is the Book of Durrow.

2 The Ninth Century

Brown, M. P., *The Book of Cerne: Prayer, Patronage and Power in Ninth-Century England* (London and Toronto, 1996)
—, 'Female Book-Ownership and Production in Anglo-Saxon England: The Evidence of the

Ninth-Century Prayerbooks', in *Lexis and Texts in Early English: Papers in Honour of Jane Roberts*, ed. C. Kay and L. Sylvester (Amsterdam, 2001), pp. 45–68
—, 'The Barberini Gospels: Context and Intertextuality', in *Text, Image, Interpretation: Studies in Anglo-Saxon Literature and its Insular Context in Honour of Eamonn Ó Carragáin*, ed. A. Minnis and J. Roberts (Turnhout, 2007), pp. 89–116
—, 'Mercian Manuscripts: The Implications of the Staffordshire Hoard, Other Recent Discoveries, and the "New Materiality"', in *Writing in Context: Insular Manuscript Culture, 500–1200*, ed. E. Kwakkel (Leiden, 2013), pp. 23–66 [Inaugural Lecture to the Chair of Medieval Manuscript Studies, School of Advanced Study, University of London, 22 June 2010]
—, *Art of the Islands: Celtic, Pictish, Anglo-Saxon and Viking Visual Culture, c. 450–1050* (Oxford, 2016)
—, and C. A. Farr, eds, *Mercia: An Anglo-Saxon Kingdom in Europe* (London, 2001)
—, and P. Furniss, 'The Hereford Gospels Reappraised', in *Art and Worship in the Insular World: Papers in Honour of Elizabeth Coatsworth*, ed. G. R. Owen-Crocker and M. Clegg Hyer (Leiden, 2021), pp. 317–41
Dodwell, C. R., *Anglo-Saxon Art: A New Perspective* (Ithaca, NY, 1982)
Dumville, D. N., 'Liturgical Drama and Panegyric Responsory from the Eighth Century? A Re-Examination of the Origin and Contents of the Ninth-Century Section of the Book of Cerne', *Journal of Theological Studies*, new series, XXIII (October 1972), pp. 374–400
Gameson, R., *The Role of Art in the Late Anglo-Saxon Church* (Oxford, 1995)
Kuypers, A.B., ed., *The Prayer Book of Aedeluald the Bishop, Commonly Called the Book of Cerne* (Cambridge, 1902)
McKitterick, R., *The Carolingians and the Written Word* (Cambridge, 1989)
Sims-Williams, P., 'Cuthswith, Seventh-Century Abbess of Inkberrow, near Worcester, and the Würzburg Manuscript of Jerome on Ecclesiastes', *Anglo-Saxon England*, V (1976), pp. 1–21
Smyth, A. P., *King Alfred the Great* (Oxford, 1995)
Thomas, R., 'The Vita Alcuini, Asser and Scholarly Service at the Court of Alfred the Great', *English Historical Review*, CXXXIV/566 (2019), pp. 1–24
Walker, I. W., *Mercia and the Making of England* (Stroud, 2000)
Webster, L., *Anglo-Saxon Art: A New History* (Ithaca, NY, 2012)
—, and J. M. Backhouse, eds, *The Making of England: Anglo-Saxon Art and Culture, AD 600–900*, exh. cat., British Museum (London and Toronto, 1991)

Sources

Dumville, D. N., and S. Keynes, eds, *The Anglo-Saxon Chronicle: A Collaborative Edition* (Cambridge, 1983)

Keynes, S., and M. Lapidge, eds, *Alfred the Great: Asser's Life of King Alfred and Other Contemporary Sources* (Harmondsworth, 1983)

3 The Tenth Century

Backhouse, J. M., D. H. Turner and L. Webster, eds, *The Golden Age of Anglo-Saxon Art, 966–1066*, exh. cat., British Museum (London, 1984)

Brown, M. P., *Manuscripts of the Anglo-Saxon Age* (London, 2007)

—, *Art of the Islands: Celtic, Pictish, Anglo-Saxon and Viking Visual Culture, c. 450–1050* (Oxford, 2016)

Davies, W., *Wales in the Early Middle Ages* (Leicester, 1989)

Deshman, R., *The Benedictional of Æthelwold*, Studies in Manuscript Illumination, 9 (Princeton, NJ, 1995)

—, 'The Galba Psalter: Pictures, Texts and Context in an Early Medieval Prayerbook', *Anglo-Saxon England*, XXVI (1997), pp. 109–38

Foote, S., *Athelstan: The First King of England* (New Haven, CT, 2012)

Karkov, C. E., *The Ruler Portraits of Anglo-Saxon England* (Woodbridge, 2004)

—, *The Art of Anglo-Saxon England* (Woodbridge, 2011)

Keynes, S., 'King Athelstan's Books', in *Learning and Literature in Anglo-Saxon England*, ed. M. Lapidge and H. Gneuss (Cambridge, 1985), pp. 143–201

Temple, E., *A Survey of Manuscripts Illuminated in the British Isles*, vol. II: *Anglo-Saxon Manuscripts, 900–1066* (Oxford, 1976)

Wood, M., *In Search of England: Journeys into the English Past* (Berkeley, CA, 2001)

Sources

Whitelock, D., *English Historical Documents*, vol. I: *500–1042* (Oxford, 1979)

4 The Eleventh Century

Barlow, F., *Edward the Confessor* (Los Angeles, CA, 1984)

Bartlett, W. B., *King Cnut and the Viking Conquest of England, 1016* (Stroud, 2016)

Bolton, T., 'Ælfgifu of Northampton: Cnut the Great's Other Woman', *Nottingham Medieval Studies*, LI (2007), pp. 247–68

—, *Cnut the Great* (New Haven, CT, 2017)

Brown, M. P., *Manuscripts of the Anglo-Saxon Age* (London, 2007)

—, *Art of the Islands: Celtic, Pictish, Anglo-Saxon and Viking Visual Culture, c. 450–1050* (Oxford, 2016)

Campbell, M. W., 'Queen Emma and Ælfgifu of Northampton, Canute the Great's Women', *Medieval Scandinavia*, IV (1971), pp. 60–79

Crick, J. C., and E.M.C. van Houts, eds, *A Social History of England, 900–1200* (Cambridge, 2011)

Darby, H. C., *Domesday England* (Cambridge, 1977)

Davies, W., ed., *From the Vikings to the Normans* (Oxford, 2003)

Duggan, A., *Queens and Queenship in Medieval Europe: Proceedings of a Conference Held at King's College London, April 1995* (Woodbridge, 2002)

Hallam, E. M., *Domesday Book through Nine Centuries* (London, 1986)

Higham, N. J., *The Norman Conquest* (Stroud, 1998)

Karkov, C. E., *The Ruler Portraits of Anglo-Saxon England* (Woodbridge, 2004)

Lifshitz, F., 'The Encomium Emmae Reginae: A "Political Pamphlet" of the Eleventh Century?', *Haskins Society Journal*, 1 (1989), pp. 39–50

McGurk, P., *An Eleventh-Century Anglo-Saxon Illustrated Miscellany* (Copenhagen, 1983)

Neveux, F., and C. Ruelle, *A Brief History of the Normans: The Conquests that Changed the Face of Europe* (London, 2008)

O'Brien, H., *Queen Emma and the Vikings: The Woman who Shaped the Events of 1066* (London, 2006)

Roesdahl, E., and D. M. Wilson, eds, *From Viking to Crusader: The Scandinavians and Europe, 800–1200* (New York, 1992)

Rushforth, R., *St Margaret's Gospel-Book* (Oxford, 2007)

Sawyer, P. H., *The Oxford Illustrated History of the Vikings* (Oxford, 1997)

Stafford, P., *Queen Emma and Queen Edith: Queenship and Women's Power in Eleventh-Century England* (New York, 2001)

—, 'Ælfgifu [Ælfgifu of Northampton] (*fl.* 1006–1036)', *Oxford Dictionary of National Biography* (Oxford, 2004)

Stenton, F., *Anglo-Saxon England* (Oxford, 1971)

Strachan, L., *Emma, the Twice-Crowned Queen: England in the Viking Age* (London, 2004)

Ward, Sr B., *The Prayers and Meditations of St Anselm* (London, 1973)

Sources

'The Battle of Maldon', trans. Jonathan Glenn, 2003–23, available at www.lightspill.com, accessed 3 June 2024

Campbell, A., and S. Keynes, *Encomium Emmae Reginae* (Cambridge, 1998)

Dumville, D. N., and S. Keynes, eds, *The Anglo-Saxon Chronicle: A Collaborative Edition* (Cambridge, 1983)

Martin, G., *Domesday Book: A Complete Translation* (London, 2003)

Mynors, R.A.B., R. M. Thomson and M. Winterbottom, eds and trans., *William of Malmesbury. Gesta Regum Anglorum. The History of the English Kings*, 2 vols (Oxford, 1998), vol. 1

Snorri Sturluson, *Heimskringla, or The Lives of the Norse Kings*, trans. Erling Monsen and A. H. Smith (Mineola, NY, 1990)
Swanton, M. J., *The Anglo-Saxon Chronicles*, 2nd edn (London, 2000)
Online edition of Domesday Book, The National Archives, www.nationalarchives.gov.uk [downloads are charged]
Searchable index of landholders in 1066 and 1087, Prosopography of Anglo-Saxon England (PASE) project, https://domesday.pase.ac.uk/domesday
For a full listing of Anglo-Saxon names, their meanings and sources, see https://pase.ac.uk
For the Exon Domesday, the earliest extant manuscript of William's Domesday surveys (now in Exeter Cathedral Library), covering southwest England and Cornwall, see www.exondomesday.ac.uk

5 The Twelfth Century I

Bates, D., and A. Curry, eds, *England and Normandy in the Middle Ages* (London, 1994)
Collins, K., P. Kidd and N. K. Turner, *The St. Albans Psalter: Painting and Prayer in Medieval England* (Los Angeles, CA, 2013)
Evans, M. R., *Inventing Eleanor: The Medieval and Post-Medieval Image of Eleanor of Aquitaine* (London, 2014)
Gallistl, B., 'The Christina of Markyate Psalter. A Modern Legend: On the Purpose of the St. Albans Psalter', *Concilium medii aevi*, XVII (2014), pp. 21–55
Geddes, J., *The St Albans Psalter: A Book for Christina of Markyate* (London, 2005)
Guyer, F. E., *Chrétien de Troyes: Inventor of the Modern Novel* (London, 1960)
Kauffmann, C. M., *A Survey of Manuscripts Illuminated in the British Isles*, vol. III: *Romanesque Manuscripts, 1066–1190* (London, 1975)
Marie de France, *The Lais of Marie de France: A Verse Translation*, trans. Judith P. Shoaf, 1992, available at https://people.clas.ufl.edu, accessed 4 June 2024
Morgan, N. J., and R. Thomson, *The Cambridge History of the Book in Britain*, vol. II (Cambridge, 2008)
Somner, H. O., *The Vulgate Version of the Arthurian Romances* (Washington, DC, 1909)
Swabey, F., *Eleanor of Aquitaine: Courtly Love and the Troubadours* (Santa Barbara, CA, 2004)
Stirnemann, P., 'The St Albans Psalter: One Man's Spiritual Journey', in *Der Albani Psalter: Stand und Perspektiven der Forschung/ The St Albans Psalter: Current research and perspectives*, ed. J. Bepler and C. Heitzmann (Hildesheim, 2013), pp. 96–128
Talbot, C. H., *The Life of Christina of Markyate: A Twelfth Century Recluse* [Oxford, 1959] (Toronto, 1998)

Thomson, R., *Books and Learning in Twelfth-Century England: The Ending of Alter Orbis,* The Lyell Lectures for 2000 (Walkern, Herts., 2007)
Weir, A., *Eleanor of Aquitaine: By the Wrath of God, Queen of England* (New York, 1999)
The Dover Bible may be viewed online at Parker Library on the Web, https://parker.stanford.edu, along with other of the Corpus Christi College, Cambridge, manuscripts
The St Albans Psalter is available online, as part of a full study of the manuscript hosted by the University of Aberdeen in partnership with the Dombibliothek Hildesheim, at www.albani-psalter.de. It is also available in facsimile, with commentary, by J. Bepler, J. Geddes and P. Kidd, *The St Albans Psalter* (Simbach am Inn, 2008)

6 The Twelfth Century II

Bartlett, R., *Gerald of Wales, 1146–1223* (Oxford, 1982)
Brown, M. P., 'Gerald of Wales and the "Marvels of the East": The Role of the Author in the Development of Marginal Illustration', in *Decoration and Illustration in Medieval English Manuscripts*, ed. A.S.G. Edwards, English Manuscript Studies, 10 (London, 2002), pp. 34–59
Butler, H. E., trans., *The Autobiography of Giraldus Cambrensis* (London, 1937)
Martin, F. X., 'Gerald of Wales, Norman Reporter on Ireland', *Studies*, LVIII/231 (1969), pp. 279–92
Richter, M., *Giraldus Cambrensis* (Aberystwyth, 1972)
—, 'Gerald of Wales: A Reassessment on the 750th Anniversary of His Death', *Traditio*, XXIV (1973), pp. 379–90
Walker, D., 'Gerald of Wales: A Review of Recent Work', *Journal of the Historical Society of the Church in Wales*, XXIV (1974), pp. 13–26

Sources

For the texts of Giraldus's writings, including his topographical works (the *Topographia Hibernica,* the *Expugnatio Hibernica*, the *Itinerarium Kambriae* and the *Descriptio Kambriae*), see J. S. Brewer, J. F. Dimock and G. F. Warner, *Giraldi Cambrensis Opera*, Rolls Series, 8 vols (London, 1861–91), where the *Topography of Ireland* is printed in vol. v (1867)
O'Meara, J. J., trans., *Gerald of Wales: The History and Topography of Ireland* [1951] (New York and Harmondsworth, 1982)
Richter, M., ed., *Symbolum Electorum*, trans. B. Dawson (Cardiff, 1974)
—, ed., *Speculum Duorum* (Cardiff, 1974)
Thorpe, L., trans., *Gerald of Wales: The Journey Through Wales/The Description of Wales* (Harmondsworth, 1978)

For Giraldus's autobiography, *De Rebus a se Gestis*, see Brewer, Dimock and Warner, *Giraldi Cambrensis Opera*, I (London, 1861)

7 The Thirteenth Century

Alexander, J. J. G., and P. Binski, eds, *Age of Chivalry: Art in Plantagenet England, 1200–1400*, exh. cat., Victoria and Albert Museum (London, 1987)
Backhouse, J. M., and C. de Hamel, *The Becket Leaves* (London, 1988)
Bataillon, J., ed., *La production du livre universitaire au Moyen Age: Exemplar et pecia* (Paris, 1988)
Christianson, C. P., *Memorials of the Book Trade in Medieval London* (Woodbridge, 1987)
—, *A Directory of London Stationers and Book Artisans, 1300–1500* (New York, 1990)
Destrez, J., *La Pecia* (Paris, 1935)
Donovan, C., *The de Brailes Hours: Shaping the Book of Hours in Thirteenth-Century Oxford* (London and Toronto, 1991)
Lewis, S., *The Art of Matthew Paris in the Chronica Majora* (Berkeley, CA, and Aldershot, 1987)
—, *Reading Images: Narrative Discourse and Reception in the Thirteenth-Century Illuminated Apocalypse* (Cambridge, 1995)
Lowden, J., *The Making of the 'Bibles Moralisées'* (Philadelphia, PA, 2000)
Marks, R., and N. J. Morgan, *The Golden Age of English Manuscript Painting, 1200–1500* (London, 1981)
Morgan, N. J., *A Survey of Manuscripts Illuminated in the British Isles*, vol. IV/2: *Early Gothic Manuscripts, 1250–1285*, 2 vols (London, 1985–8)
—**, and M. P. Brown,** *The Lambeth Apocalypse, Manuscript 209 in Lambeth Palace Library* (London, 1990)
—**, and R. M. Thomson,** eds, *The Cambridge History of the Book in Britain, 1100–1400*, vol. II (Cambridge, 2008)
Rouse, R., and M. Rouse, *Manuscripts and Their Makers: Commercial Book Producers in Medieval Paris, 1200–1500*, 2 vols (London, 2000)
Vaughan, R., *Matthew Paris* (Cambridge, 1958)
Weiler, B., 'Matthew Paris on the Writing of History', *Journal of Medieval History*, XXXV/3 (2012), pp. 254–78

8 The Fourteenth Century I

Brown, M. P., *The Holkham Bible Picture-Book* (London, 2008) [facsimile with accompanying commentary, transcription and translation]
Browne, C., G. Davies and M. A. Michael, eds, *Medieval English Embroidery: Opus Anglicanun*, exh. cat., Victoria and Albert

Museum, London (New Haven, CT, 2016)
Christianson, C. P., *Memorials of the Book Trade in Medieval London* (Woodbridge, 1987)
—, *A Directory of London Stationers and Book Artisans, 1300–1500* (New York, 1990)
Hassall, W. O., *The Holkham Bible Picture Book* (London, 1954)
Rouse, R., and M. Rouse, *Manuscripts and Their Makers: Commercial Book Producers in Medieval Paris, 1200–1500*, 2 vols (London, 2000)
Sandler, L. F., *A Survey of Manuscripts Illuminated in the British Isles*, vol. V: *Gothic Manuscripts, 1285–1385*, 2 vols (London, 1986)
—, *Omne Bonum: A Fourteenth-Century Encyclopedia of Universal Knowledge: British Library* MSS *Royal 6* E VI–*6* E VII, 2 vols (London, 1996)

Sources

For entries relating to John Fifhide in documents of the period, see the following, all of which, except for that in the National Archives, are available at www.british-history.ac.uk, accessed 29 May 2024:

1370–71: John Fyfhide lends £100 to the king; 'Folios CCLXI–CCLXX: Dec 1370–', in *Calendar of Letter-Books of the City of London: G, 1352–1374* (London, 1905), pp. 272–82

1373–4: John Fifhide elected as Sheriff of London; 'Folios CCCI–CCCX: May 1373–', in *Calendar of Letter-Books of the City of London: G, 1352–1374* (London, 1905), pp. 307–17; and John Noorthouck, 'Addenda: The Mayors and Sheriffs of London', in *A New History of London Including Westminster and Southwark* (London, 1773), pp. 889–93

1374: John Fyfhide is listed as Aldorman of Bassishaw Ward; Alfred P. Beaven, 'Aldermen of the City of London: Bassishaw Ward', in *The Aldermen of the City of London Temp. Henry* III – *1912* (London, 1908), pp. 16–21

1375: As an aldorman of the City of London, Fifhide enforces a settlement of a dispute about access; 'Misc. Roll. FF: 12 May 1374–7 May 1378 (nos 600–619)', in *London Assize of Nuisance, 1301–1431: A Calendar*, London Record Society 10 (London, 1973), pp. 154–63

1377: Again as an aldorman, Fifhide helps to resolve a similar dispute about stone walls; ibid., pp. 154–63

1379?: As sheriff Fifhide is involved in a dispute about the restitution of wine; National Archives, SC 8 – Special Collections: Ancient Petitions, SC 8/96/4752

1384–93: A mercer named John Fyfhyde is recorded as having a claim upon rents in Fenchurch Street; 'Parishes: St Dionis Backchurch', in *The Cartulary of Holy Trinity, Aldgate,*

London Record Society, 7 (London, 1971), pp. 22–3

9 The Fourteenth Century II

Backhouse, J. M., *The Luttrell Psalter* (London, 1998)
Brown, M. P., *The Luttrell Psalter* (London, 2006) [facsimile with accompanying commentary]
—, *The World of the Luttrell Psalter* (London, 2006)
—, 'Sidelong Glances and Silent Screams: The Emotional World of the Luttrell Psalter', in *Quand la peinture était dans les manuscrits: Mélanges François Avril*, ed. M. Hofmann and C. Zöhl (Paris, 2007), pp. 45–56
Camille, M., *The Gothic Idol: Ideology and Image-Making in Medieval Art* (New York, 1989)
—, *Image on the Edge* (Cambridge, MA, 1992)
—, *Mirror in Parchment: The Luttrell Psalter and the Making of Medieval England* (Chicago, IL, 1998)
Coleman, J., M. Cruse and K. A. Smith, eds, *Manuscripts, Images, and Communities in the Late Middle Ages* (Turnhout, 2013)
Dennison, L., 'The Technical Mastery of the Macclesfield Psalter: A Preliminary Stylistic Appraisal of the Illuminators and Their Suggested Origin', *Transactions of the Cambridge Bibliographical Society*, XIII/3 (2006), pp. 253–88
Law-Turner, F.C.E., *The Ormesby Psalter: Patrons and Artists in Medieval East Anglia* (Oxford and Chicago, IL, 2005)
Nishimura, M., *The Gorleston Psalter: A Study of the Marginal in the Visual Culture of Fourteenth-Century England* (New York, 1999)
Sandler, L. F., *The Peterborough Psalter in Brussels and Other Fenland Manuscripts* (London, 1974)
—, *Gothic Manuscripts, 1285–1385* (London, 1986)
Smith, K. A., *Art, Identity, and Devotion in Fourteenth-Century England: Three Women and Their Books of Hours* (London, 2003)
—, *The Taymouth Hours: Stories and the Construction of the Self in Late Medieval England* (London, 2012)
Stanton, A. R., *The Queen Mary Psalter: A Study of Affect and Audience* (Philadelphia, PA, 2001)

10 The Fifteenth Century I

Backhouse, J. M., *The Sherborne Missal* (London, 1999)
Brown, M. P., *The Sherborne Missal*, Turning the Pages CD-Rom (London, 2002)
—, 'The Sherborne Missal and "Roddoke Robertus": The Anatomy of a Major Manuscript Commission', in *The Medieval Book: Glosses from Friends and Colleagues of Christopher de Hamel*, ed. R. A. Linenthal, J. H. Marrow and W. G. Noel (Houten, 2010), pp. 84–97

De Hamel, C., *A History of Illuminated Manuscripts* (London, 1986)
Scott, K. L., *A Survey of Manuscripts Illuminated in the British Isles*, vol. VI: *Later Gothic Manuscripts, 1390–1490*, 2 vols (London, 1996)
For an online facsimile of the **Sherborne Missal**, see www.bl.uk.

11 The Fifteenth Century II

Backhouse, J. M., 'Founders of the Royal Library: Edward IV and Henry VII as Collectors of Illuminated Manuscripts', in *England in the Fifteenth Century: Proceedings of the 1986 Harlaxton Symposium*, ed. D. Williams (Woodbridge, 1987), pp. 23–41
Bale, A., *Margery Kempe: A Mixed Life* (London, 2021)
Bühler, C. F., 'The Verses in Lambeth Manuscript 265', *Modern Language Notes*, LXXII/1 (1957), pp. 4–6
Gillingham, J., *The Wars of the Roses*, revd edn (London, 2001)
Grosvenor, B., and D. Starkey, eds, *Lost Faces: Identity and Discovery in Tudor Royal Portraiture*, exh. cat. (London, 2007)
Hellinga, L., *Caxton in Focus: The Beginning of Printing in England* (London, 1982)
Higgitt, J., *The Murthly Hours: Devotion, Literacy, and Luxury in Paris, England, and the Gaelic West* (Toronto, 2000)
McKendrick, S., 'A European Heritage: Books of Continental Origin Collected by the English Royal Family from Edward III to Henry VIII', in *Royal Manuscripts: The Genius of Illumination*, ed. S. McKendrick, J. Lowden and K. Doyle, exh. cat., British Library (London, 2011), pp. 43–65
Palmer, R., and M. P. Brown, eds, *Lambeth Palace Library: Treasures from the Library of the Archbishops of Canterbury* (London, 2010)
Penn, T., *The Brothers York* (London, 2019)
Raven, J., *The Business of Books: Booksellers and the English Book Trade, 1450–1850* (London and New Haven, CT, 2007)
Scott, K. L., *A Survey of Manuscripts Illuminated in the British Isles*, vol. VI: *Later Gothic Manuscripts, 1390–1490*, 2 vols (London, 1996)
Stratford, J., ed., *The Bedford Inventories: The Worldly Goods of John, Duke of Bedford, Regent of France, 1389–1435* (London, 1993)
Sutton, A. F., and L. Visser-Fuchs, *The Hours of Richard III* (London, 1996)
The Hours of Richard III can be seen online at https://leicestercathedral.org.

12 The Sixteenth Century

Alamire, 'Henry's Music-Motets from a Royal Choirbook Songs by Henry VIII', dir. David Skinner, recorded 2009, CD 705, Obsidian Records

Bell, N., and D. Skinner, *Music for King Henry, Facsimile of British Library Royal* MS *11* E XI (London, 2009).

Bernstein, J., 'Phil Van Wilder and the Netherlandish Chanson in England', *Musica Disciplina*, XXXIII (1979), p. 59

Camille, M., 'Before the Gaze: The Internal Senses and Late Medieval Practices of Seeing', in *Visuality Before and Beyond the Renaissance: Seeing as Others Saw*, ed. R. S. Nelson (Cambridge and New York, 2000), pp. 197–223

Carley, J. P., *The Books of King Henry* VIII *and His Wives* (London, 2004)

Duffy, E., *The Stripping of the Altars: Traditional Religion in England, c. 1440–c.* 1580 (New Haven, CT, 1992)

Penn, T., *Winter King: Henry* VII *and the Dawn of Tudor England* (London, 2011)

Starkey, D., *The Inventory of Henry* VIII. *Society of Antiquaries* MS *129 and British Library* MS *Harley 1419: The Transcript* (London, 1998)

—, *Henry – Virtuous Prince: The Prince Who Would Turn Tyrant* (London, 2008)

Stevens, J., 'Carols and Court Songs of the Early Tudor Period', *Proceedings of the Royal Music Association*, LXXVII (1950–51), pp. 59–60

Weir, A., *Henry* VIII (New York, 2001)

—, *Henry* VIII: *King and Court* (London, 2002)

ACKNOWLEDGEMENTS

I should like to take this opportunity to thank some of the many from whose wisdom and learning I have benefited in these areas across the years: My teachers and mentors, especially Julian Brown, Malcolm Parkes, Linda Brownrigg, Henry Loyn, Brenda Bolton, Michael Clanchy, Nigel Morgan and Janet Backhouse, my peers and students . . . and, of course, my husband Cecil and our many dear friends.

I should also like to thank Michael Leaman and the staff of Reaktion, for making beautiful, enlightening books.

PHOTO ACKNOWLEDGEMENTS

The author and publishers wish to express their thanks to the sources listed below for illustrative material and/or permission to reproduce it. Some locations of works are also given below, in the interest of brevity:

Ashmolean Museum/Heritage Image Partnership Ltd/Alamy Stock Photo: p. 67; Biblioteca Medicea Laurenziana, Florence (MS Amiatino 1), photos World Digital Library: pp. 26 (f. 5r), 27 (f. 67v); Bodleian Library, University of Oxford (MS Hatton 20, f. 1r): p. 66; British Library, London: pp. 16 (Add. MS 89000, f. 1r), 60–61 (Cotton MS Vespasian A I, ff. 30v–31r), 62 (Royal MS 2 A XX, f. 17r), 63 (Harley MS 2965, f. 40v), 81 *left* (Add. MS 9381, f. 13r), 81 *right* (Royal MS I B VII, f. 15v), 84 (Cotton MS Tiberius A II, f. 74v), 85 (MS Cotton Galba A XVIII, f. 21r), 89 (Cotton MS Vespasian A VIII, f. 2v), 90 (Cotton MS Tiberius A III, f. 2v), 92 *left* (Add. MS 49598, f. 51v), 92 *right* (Add. MS 49598, f. 118v), 100 (Stowe MS 944, f. 6r), 103 (Arundel MS 155, f. 133r), 105 (Cotton MS Tiberius B V/1, f. 56v), 107 (Add. MS 33241, f. 1v), 120 (Cotton MS Claudius B II, f. 341r), 164 (Royal MS 14 C VII, f. 136r), 166 (Royal MS 14 C VII, f. 6r, photo Bridgeman Images), 167 (Harley Roll Y 6, roundel 8), 169 (Cotton MS Claudius D VI/1), 174 (Sloane MS 1975, f. 93r, photo Bridgeman Images), 182 (Add. MS 49999, f. 43r), 207 (Cotton MS Nero A X/2, fol. 94v), 209 (Royal MS 6 E VI, f. 503v), 214 (Royal MS 2 B VII, f. 256v, photo Bridgeman Images), 241 (Harley MS 7026/1, f. 4v), 256 (Add. MS 61823, f. 71v), 267 (Royal MS 16 F II, f. 73r), 273 *left* (Royal MS 2 A XVIII, f. 23v), 273 *right* (Royal MS 2 A XVIII, f. 31v), 274 (Add. MS 50001, f. 22r, photo Bridgeman Images), 278 (Add. MS 31922, ff. 71v–72r), 279 *left* and *right* (Royal MS 11 E XI, ff. 2r and 3r), 284 (Royal MS 2 A XVI, f. 30r), 285 (Royal MS 2 A XVI, f. 3r), 287 (Royal MS 2 A XVI, f. 63v), 288 (King's MS 9, f. 231v, photo Bridgeman Images); British Library, London (Add. MS 42130): pp. 216 (f. 202v), 217 (f. 170r), 218 (f. 158r), 222–3 (ff. 159v–160r, photos Bridgeman Images), 226 (f. 63r), 227 (f. 208r); British Library, London (Add. MS 47682): pp. 194 (f. 1r), 196 (f. 21v), 199 (f. 8r), 200 (f. 18v); British Library, London (Add. MS 74236): pp. 236 (p. 380), 239 (p. 81), 240 (p. 382), 244 (p. 276, photo Bridgeman Images), 245 (p. 489); British Library, London (Cotton MS Nero D IV): pp. 31 (f. 94r), 34 *above* (ff. 26v–27r), 34 *below* (ff. 94v–95r), 35 *above* (ff. 138v–139r), 35 *below* (ff. 210v–211r), 36 (f. 259r), 38 (f. 25v), 39 (f. 93v), 40 (f. 137v), 41 (f. 209v); British Library, London (Royal MS 13 B VIII): pp. 149

(f. 22r), 152 (f. 20r), 157 *above* (f. 28v), 157 *below* (f. 19r); The British Museum, London (1884,0606.6): p. 193; Cambridge University Library: p. 69 (MS Ii.6.32, f. 29v); Cambridge University Library (MS Ll.1.10): pp. 49 (f. 43r), 53 *above left* (f. 2v), 53 *above right* (f. 12v), 53 *below left* (f. 21v), 53 *below right* (f. 31v); Corpus Christi College, Cambridge: pp. 79 (MS 183, f. 1v), 134 *below* (MS 4, vol. II, f. 242v), 173 (MS 161, f. iir); Corpus Christi College, Oxford (MS 122, f. 5v): p. 83; photo © Ollie Dixon, Hever Castle: p. 282; Dombibliothek Hildesheim (MS St. God. 1), property of the Basilica of St Godehard, Hildesheim: pp. 128 (p. 36), 129 (p. 51), 131 (p. 350), 134 *above* (p. 285); Hereford Cathedral Library: pp. 70 (MS P.I. 2, ff. 35v–36r), 170; Hever Castle Library: p. 283; The Huntington Library, Art Museum, and Botanical Gardens, San Marino, CA (MS EL 26 C 9, f. 153v): p. 204; Lambeth Palace Library, London: pp. 252 and 265 (MS 265, ff. viv–1r), 270 (MS 474, f. 15r), 271 (MS 474, ff. 7v–8r); Lichfield Cathedral Library: pp. 56, 57 (MS 1, p. 218); The Morgan Library and Museum, New York (MS M.619): p. 125; Musée de la Tapisserie de Bayeux: p. 110; Museo Civico Medievale, Bologna: p. 191; National Library of Ireland, Dublin (MS 700, f. 48r): p. 148; Royal Irish Academy, Dublin: p. 18 (MS 12 R 33, f. 19r); Trinity College Dublin: pp. 68 (MS 50, fol. 35r), 175 (MS 177, fol. 59v); Westminster Abbey Library, London (MS 39): p. 272.

INDEX

Page numbers in *italics* refer to illustrations